Also by Katie Hafner

CYBERPUNK: OUTLAWS AND HACKERS

ON THE COMPUTER FRONTIER

(WITH JOHN MARKOFF)

KATIE HAFNER

SCRIBNER

New York Toronto London Sydney Tokyo Singapore

THE HOUSE AT THE BRIDGE

A Story

of Modern

Germany

SCRIBNER
ROCKEFELLER CENTER
1230 AVENUE OF THE AMERICAS
NEW YORK, NY 10020

DESIGNED BY KAROLINA HARRIS
MANUFACTURED IN THE UNITED STATES OF AMERICA

10 9 8 7 6 5 4 3 2 1

LIBRARY OF CONGRESS CATALOGING-IN-PUBLICATION DATA
HAFNER, KATIE.
   THE HOUSE AT THE BRIDGE : A STORY OF MODERN GERMANY /
KATIE HAFNER.
      P.   CM.
INCLUDES BIBLIOGRAPHICAL REFERENCES AND INDEX.
   1. BERLIN (GERMANY)—BIOGRAPHY. 2. BERLIN
(GERMANY)—POLITICS AND GOVERNMENT 1945-1990. 3. BERLIN
(GERMANY)—ETHNIC RELATIONS. 4. JEWS—GERMANY—BERLIN—
HISTORY—PERSECUTIONS. 5. BERLIN WALL, BERLIN, GERMANY,
1961-1989. 6. GERMANY—HISTORY—20TH CENTURY.
I. TITLE.
DD857.A2H34   1995
920.043157—DC20
[B]   94-33580   CIP
ISBN 0-684-19400-7

ACKNOWLEDGMENTS

This book is based on a story I wrote for the *New York Times Magazine* in 1991. I am grateful to Katherine Bouton and Warren Hoge at the magazine for the interest they took in the subject of property claims in the former East Germany. Barbara Grossman, my editor at Scribner, is everything anyone could want in an editor. She encouraged me to turn the magazine piece into a book, she visited me in Berlin, she waited patiently for the final product, and she never stopped saying nice things. Bob Bender, my once and future editor at Simon & Schuster, happily took the book under his wing after Barbara left Scribner. Working with him is a privilege and a joy. And the same goes for his assistant, Johanna Li.

Paula Butturini, Barbara Howard, Jonathan Kaufman, John Tagliabue, Tom Gjelten, Debra Immergut, John Marks, Adele Riepe and Ed Serotta provided me with a home away from home. Victor Homola, John Tagliabue and Stephen Kinzer in the *New York Times* Berlin bureau generously allowed me to use the office.

Dick Lyon, wordsmith, logician and humanities professor par excellence, came to know the book as well as I did, gamely reading each new version I presented to him. Daphne Berdahl applied her considerable knowledge of the former East Germany to a careful reading of an early draft. The manuscript was also read in its various stages of completion by Molly Dougherty, John Kelley, Denny Lyon, Ann Walther and Sarah Woelk. Denny Lyon saved the day by taking care of her granddaughter Zoë.

Hedda von Heynitz, a distant Wallich cousin, was a supportive ally from the day I met her. Various other members of the Wallich family went out of their way to answer my questions and provide me with archival material. Karl-Viktor von Schöning, a descendant of the house's original owner, was generous to a fault, offering his time and insights and Berlin connections whenever he could. Jutta Kahlcke, a true friend, helped in dozens of ways both large and small.

Professors David Crew and Peter Jelavich of the history department at the University of Texas at Austin were generous with their time and knowledge, helping me with dozens of historical questions. David Hendler flew all over the map when he really didn't have the time. Peter and Peggy Preuss provided a quiet place to think and write during a particularly rough stretch. Tony Bianco went to the movies for me. Richard Hicks spent a sweltering Sunday in my office helping me read through old letters. Fred Kempe, then Berlin bureau chief for the *Wall Street Journal,* was an enthusiastic cheerleader and loyal friend during the brief time we overlapped in Berlin.

Not only did Matthew Lyon offer invaluable comments as I plodded along, but he loved me even during my most distracted moments. Zoë Lyon brightened every day with her marvelous sense of humor. She and her father have my thanks and my love.

Thanks, too, to my agents, John Brockman and Katinka Matson, who urged me to write about Germany after a trip they took to Berlin in 1990.

Finally, I have accrued a mighty debt to Regine Wosnitza. I was constantly astounded by her willingness to check the most niggling of facts, to trek to Potsdam on some quest or other for me, and to conduct follow-up interviews after I had left Berlin. She possesses a rare ability to think up a creative way to root out anything, be it a statistic, a photograph or a telephone number. Without her help and skill and friendship, I would have been lost.

To Dick and Denny

CONTENTS

CONTENTS

INTRODUCTION

*I*n early 1991, six months after German reunification, I went to Berlin to write about the wrenching effects of the government's decision to restore ownership to those whose property had been seized decades earlier by the Nazi and Communist regimes. I became interested in one house in particular, a once elegant, now dilapidated nineteenth-century villa in Potsdam that was the object of a claim by the twelve grandchildren of the house's former owner, Paul Wallich, the son of a prominent Jewish banker.

As far as Paul Wallich's descendants were concerned, in the fifty years that the house was inaccessible to them, first during the Nazi period, then in Communist East Germany, it had stood in a state of abeyance. Although Wallich family pictures showed its grandeur frozen in time, the house had in fact taken a new identity. The Communists had turned it into a *Kinderwochenheim,* or weekly Kindergarten, a uniquely socialist child-care arrangement that crosses a boarding school or orphanage with a day-care center. By the time I arrived, the Kindergarten had occupied the house for more than four decades.

In the two years I spent researching this book, I watched tensions between western Germans ("Wessies") and eastern Germans ("Ossies") grow. The jubilation following the November 1989 fall of the Wall had long since disappeared and each side now regarded the other with undisguised contempt.

By the time I was leaving Berlin in the fall of 1992, friction between east and west was higher than ever. Eastern Germans were increasingly bitter about the system that had been thrust on them by the west. They resented the high prices for consumer goods and food that unification had brought. They resented the soaring unemployment in eastern Germany. They resented the disappearance of social services, subsidized child care and crime-free streets. Eastern Germans especially resented those aspects of the unification process that resembled a corporate takeover more than a political melding. West German laws subsumed East German laws, East German university faculties were dismantled as Marxist professors were fired and replaced by West German scholars. East Germany's state-run factories and businesses were put on the block in one gargantuan closeout sale.

Before the Wall fell, West Germans had felt more affinity with France and Holland than with East Germany. Few West Germans outside of Berlin ever visited East Germany. Why bother? There was nothing to see. The roads were bad. The country stank of brown coal. And the food was a bland, greasy version of standard German fare from decades past that West Germans had spent the postwar years diversifying, their palates growing accustomed to more exotic cuisine.

After reunification, westerners were furious to see in every paycheck a deduction for a reunification tax. By the end of 1992, the gap between eastern and western salaries was closing, placing a further strain on the German economy. Germany was headed into economic recession as westerners laid the blame for dragging them down on their backward cousins. Billions were being spent to modernize eastern Germany and westerners were sick of footing the bill. A majority of those in the west accused easterners of wanting to live like them but of wanting to work at the same lazy pace they had enjoyed before 1989.

Nothing revealed the change in relations between Wessies and

Ossies better than the reaction to the Trabant, or Trabi, the People's Car of East Germany. With no catalytic converter, Trabis are an environmental menace. Made of fiberglass and pressed cotton, Trabis are also known to be rolling coffins. Getting into an accident in subzero weather means that if you aren't killed by the impact of the crash then you're in grave danger of being impaled by Trabi shards—a frozen Trabi doesn't crumple, it shatters. And yet, for nearly forty years, East Germans strove to own a Trabant, essentially the only game in town.

The night the Wall fell, the Trabi was the star attraction, as hundreds of them rolled through various checkpoints to the cheers of West German bystanders. It wasn't unusual, in the days following the opening of the Wall, for an East German to return to his or her Trabi parked in West Germany and find a West German mark note tucked under a windshield wiper. But it wasn't long before driving a Trabi on the streets of Berlin became an invitation to be abused. Germans tend to be aggressively self-confident drivers as it is, and they do not tolerate tentativeness from others. Unfortunately, the Trabi's two-stroke engine has hesitation built into it. Where BMWs and VW Golfs zip and zoom, the Trabi lurches and sputters and smokes. Western drivers shake their heads at Trabis, curse from behind their closed windows and honk at the slightest excuse. "People here saved for half a lifetime for a spluttering Trabant," remarked Hans Joachim Maaz, an eastern German psychotherapist. "Then along comes the smooth Mercedes society and makes our whole existence, our dreams and our identity, laughable."

While I lived in Berlin, I drove a Trabi. I bought it because, at $600, it was cheap, and practical for making the daily twenty-minute drive from my apartment in Berlin to the house in Potsdam. But the novelty wore off for me rather suddenly when, one morning in 1992, I came down and saw an aluminum foil–wrapped package on the windshield. Inside the foil was dog feces.

While I was in Germany, neo-Nazis and skinheads began to emerge. Violence against foreigners was in the news regularly. With nearly as much regularity, determined to show that the skinheads were a minority not to be tolerated, tens of thousands of Germans joined mass demonstrations opposing the violence. In the four years after the Wall fell, Germany was not so much unified as it was frayed by the process of unification.

The house at the center of this book bore silent witness to these events. But the house was not merely a bystander. By 1991, part of a discarded social system, the Kinderwochenheim's existence was threatened. The teachers who worked there resented the social upheaval and feared for their jobs. They lamented that there was no place for them in a reunified Germany. Descendants of the former owner, meanwhile, were returning from overseas to claim what they regarded as their heritage. The fact of their claim engendered still more uncertainty. Would their ownership be restored? If it was, would the family want to live there? Even if they owned the house, could they ever be Germans? Were they ever Germans in the first place? Here, as elsewhere in Germany, Germans were examining the past, as if the experience of reunification had not settled but only raised anew the question: to whom does Germany belong?

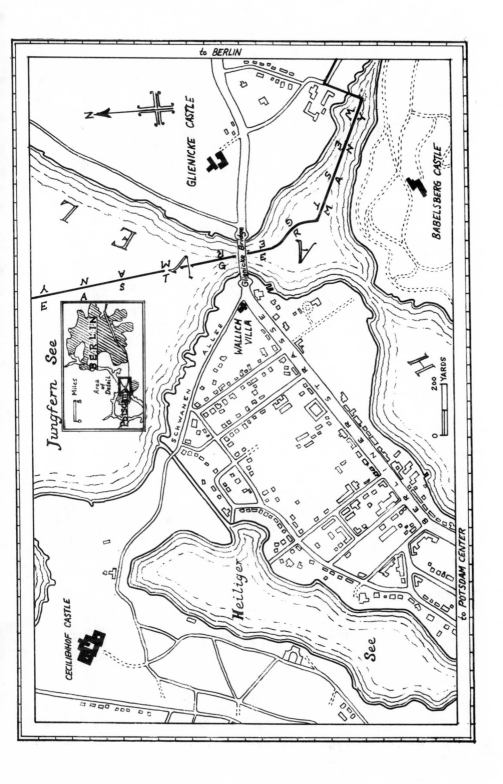

to BERLIN

N

GLIENICKE CASTLE

GERMANY

BABELSBERG CASTLE

HAVEL

Glienicke Bridge

WEST

Jungfern See

BERLIN

Miles
0   5

Area
of
Detail

Potsdam

SCHWANEN ALLEE

WALLICH VILLA

0   200
YARDS

H

Heiliger

See

CECILIENHOF CASTLE

to POTSDAM CENTER

1 : THE PARTY

July 1991

In central Berlin, rain was pounding down in a midsummer's fury. But a few miles south the sky was clear. The patch of blue over this square mile of Berlin's outer reaches was a stroke of good fortune for the three dozen people gathered for a small celebration on the elegant grounds of the Glienicke Castle, its lawns and gardens sloping down to the western edge of the Havel River. The guests strolled the lawns, sipping champagne and nibbling from plates piled with salads, meats and cheeses. They were members of Berlin's privileged set, professors, landscape architects, city planners, architectural historians and landmark preservationists. The purpose of the gathering was to welcome into the cherished constellation of castles and mansions along the shore a freshly rediscovered structure: a simple but elegant Italianate villa across the river, in perfect view from where they stood.

In particular, they were there to toast the garden behind the villa and the student, Dirk Heydemann, who had lately proved through his research that the garden was the creation of one of Prussia's most celebrated landscape architects, a treasure obscured by forty years of Communism. They listened to speeches from the student's advisor, then the student himself. They passed around copies of the student's thesis, a luxuriously bound and illustrated history of the house and its garden and the famous Glienicke Bridge nearby. They learned of the princely courtier who once lived in the house, and the family of Jewish bankers, the Wallichs, who succeeded him. Now the Wallich family was reclaiming the riparian villa.

For the afternoon, the gathered party trained a slightly out-of-focus lens on this corner of Berlin. Squint a little and you were back to the days of the reign of the Hohenzollerns, when the princely estates and rolling gardens were of a piece, when residences were built of imported materials and furnished with restrained refinement—an Italian marble statue here, a bit of chinoiserie there. Squint some more and across the water stood a nineteenth-century villa, a small sparkling jewel of elegant Potsdam, home to Prussian nobility.

That was the effect from their romantic remove of two hundred yards. Had they held their celebration on the opposite bank, just a few feet from the villa itself, they would have seen a very different picture, the marks that recent history had left on the house, the neglect of the past fifty years. They'd have seen that the stucco facade was crumbling to expose the original red brick, that the garden was not royal in any sense. Yes, there were the magnificent 150-year-old trees, but only a few remained and a rather dusty unkempt collection of rusted playground equipment stood now in the backyard. In front of the house, they'd have walked across an overgrown, muddy bank—the women in their high heels and the men in their shiny tasseled shoes—clambering over large pieces of concrete that resembled highway dividers but were really vestiges of the Berlin Wall, which had once divided the two shores and now lay in bits and pieces near the water at the foot of the famous Glienicke Bridge, which was, like the pieces of the Wall, an avatar of the Cold War.

But they did not see what was really there. They remained safely on the other side of the river, seeing what they wanted to see. At the party itself, perhaps they did see two women—one young and dark and striking, the other middle-aged, with a crimped, uncomfortable face—standing on the perimeter of the festivities. Perhaps they noticed that these two women did not quite fit into the picture. They were dressed differently, in plain, untailored clothing. They held themselves differently. They had no champagne glasses in their hands, and no small plates piled with delicacies.

In his speech, the student, a smiling young man with a pale complexion accented by ruddy cheeks, made a passing reference to these women. He thanked them for having given him access to the garden during his many months of research. But he did not refer to them by name. Instead, they were "the teachers at the Kinderwochenheim." No one paid much attention to his acknowledgment. They assumed from what he said that during the forty years of Communism in the eastern part of Germany, whose border ended precisely in the middle of the Havel River, the villa had been a child-care facility of some sort. Perhaps it still was. But they also assumed that this chapter in the life of the house—a misstep, to be sure—would soon pass into history.

Dirk Heydemann was recommending to the city of Potsdam that the house be turned into a museum. Pictures in his thesis depicted the house and garden as they appeared unblemished in nineteenth-century Prussia and as they would look once again after renovation. His great hope, he told the audience, was that Hermann Wallich's descendants would help him bring the house full circle and support him in his efforts to see the villa restored to its former grandeur.

2: THE WALLICHS

Hermann and Anna

Hermann Wallich's ambitious streak was a mystery. The son of a Jewish merchant in Bonn who took comfort and refuge in his piety, Hermann seemed destined for a similar life. It was his mother who quietly laid the foundation for assimilation into German society by encouraging her son to look beyond the family's narrow sphere. The impression she made on her son would echo through the Wallich family for generations to come. The devotion his father had to religion was equaled by Hermann's commitment to business. The young Hermann displayed a knack for finance, and in 1854, at age twenty-one, he moved to Paris and embarked on a career in banking.

Two decades later, in the midst of a flourishing career in international banking, Hermann moved to Berlin to help run the newly founded Deutsche Bank. He was called in by Georg von Siemens, who was impressed with Hermann's credentials, and together the two men built the foundation for what would become one of the world's most powerful banks. When Hermann Wallich came to the profession, banking in Europe was already a sophisticated service industry, not unlike banks of the late twentieth century. Deutsche Bank was the capstone in German banking development that started in the late eighteenth and early nineteenth centuries with the Rothschilds and the Warburgs. It engaged in basic deposit taking, lending, underwriting of securities and currency exchange. Hermann's greatest contribution to the bank was his skill in international finance, which was instrumental in helping the bank establish its global reach over the next hundred years.

At the start of their partnership, Wallich and von Siemens complemented each other. Von Siemens was a forceful, strong-willed man, bent on risky ventures. Hermann acted as a sobering influence. While von Siemens was more like a Morgan or Rothschild in his pioneering knack for entrepreneurship, Hermann was a technician who earned the bread and butter for Deutsche Bank by building up a regular banking business, along the lines of British banks.

When Hermann arrived in Berlin, he was over forty, and it was time to acquire a wife. At a dinner party shortly after his arrival in Berlin, he took to a young woman nearly twenty years his junior, Anna Jacoby. Hermann was a short man, just over five feet. Luckily, Anna was just as small. She lived with her father, Moritz Jacoby, in a house about ten miles southwest of central Berlin in Potsdam at the foot of the Glienicke Bridge. The house, she informed Hermann with some pride, was an Italianate villa built for a courtier to Prussian Prince Carl. It stood directly across the water from both the Glienicke Castle, Prince Carl's residence, and the Babelsberg Castle, where Carl's brother Wilhelm lived. Tending to the garden behind the house was her father's passion. His roses, she told Hermann, were famous throughout Potsdam.

After a brief courtship, Hermann and Anna married in 1875. Three years later, Moritz Jacoby died. Although Hermann had already accrued a tidy fortune of his own, the inheritance from his father-in-law improved the couple's financial standing considerably. Among Herr Jacoby's legacies was the house at the Glienicke Bridge. But for all its aesthetic appeal the house had remained largely unimproved since its construction thirty years earlier, and Anna found it drafty and primitive. The couple decided to spend their winters in

Berlin; the villa in Potsdam would be a summer place.

Their first child was a daughter, Ilse, born in 1880. Two years later came a long-awaited son. He was named Paul. With the birth of their children, Hermann and Anna struggled with the question of how to raise them—as Christians or as Jews. Like his mother, Hermann had long been in favor of Jewish assimilation. Keenly aware and fearful of German anti-Semitism, he had already considered leaving Germany during the anti-Semitic uprisings of the 1870s. But Anna, born and raised in Berlin, wished to stay. She considered herself more German than Jewish, and had even adopted the Christian faith. Although Hermann could never quite bring himself to convert as well, he told his wife that if they were going to stay in Germany the children should be baptized and raised as Lutherans. By having his children baptized, he argued, he was making it easier for them to become useful members of society. He considered it folly to martyr oneself to a religion and to ideas that one didn't necessarily believe in. "Instead of bad Jews, I wanted to make good Christians out of my children," he later wrote. So shortly after Paul's birth, Paul and his sister were both christened in the Protestant faith.

Above all, Hermann Wallich would instill in his children a sense of the importance of assimilating. His fear of anti-Semitism pervaded his thinking. Hermann told his children they might one day have to flee Germany. In the late nineteenth century Hermann predicted that "Jewish arrogance," which he saw spreading everywhere, creating an illusion of security in an anti-Semitic land, would someldday bring terrible consequences.

Hermann's thinking was hardly out of the ordinary for the period. So common was the practice of baptizing children of Jewish heritage that Gentile Germans jokingly renamed the Kaufhaus des Westens (Department Store of the West), Berlin's large Jewish-owned department store, the Taufhaus (Baptism house) des Westens.

By 1911, with a declared fortune of 31 million reichsmarks, Hermann was the wealthiest man in the province of Brandenburg, in which Potsdam was located. Though his financial standing brought him acceptance into Berlin's moneyed circles, he would never fit in entirely, as Berlin was a city with an entrenched aristocracy, Prussian Junkers who did not take kindly to the new breed of bumptious capitalists, particularly the Jews among them.

Hermann warned Paul and Ilse that although they would someday have plenty of inherited wealth, they should not rely on it, as it might not remain entirely safe. Moreover, he was firm in his belief that money brought neither happiness nor security, and that one must learn a profession.

Paul had neither the need nor the desire to increase the family fortune. He decided to study philosophy. He went to Freiburg in 1901, when his own anti-Semitism was at its peak. His social milieu, he decided, should consist entirely of non-Jews. But the Gentile circles at the university didn't let in the sons of Jewish bankers. Paul ended up with no social life at all. Frustrated, he left Freiburg after two terms and in 1902, at age twenty, began his military service, eventually becoming a reserve officer.

At the start of his studies in Freiburg, Paul's hope was to become a university professor. For years he wrote poetry as well. (As a middle-aged man, he sealed a sheaf of papers in an envelope, to be destroyed in the event of his death. The envelope survived, however, and when many years later it was opened by a member of the family, it was found to contain scores of poems with a risqué theme.) But when Paul returned to Berlin in 1903 he decided to pursue a career in banking, a decision born both of resignation and entitlement. He went to Munich to begin the new course, and as in Freiburg, he encountered two circles. He described one as being composed of "Jewish intelligence" and the other of "blonde crème." Once again he was torn between two worlds. Paul's own attitude toward his Jewishness would always remain deeply ambivalent. He harbored a craving for blondness, but remained drawn to Jewish intellectuals, in whose company he felt most at home.

When Paul settled in Berlin to begin his banking career, his preference was to work at Deutsche Bank, but he was disappointed with the positions the bank offered him and went to a much smaller bank, J. Dreyfus & Co. He steered clear of the stock market because, as he described it, he lacked the *Fingerspitzengefühl* (literally, it means the feeling at the tips of one's fingers; it is a way to describe fine instinct) that dealing in stocks required. Instead, he chose to work in the bank's credit department.

In 1910, at the age of twenty-eight, Paul embarked on what was to become a protracted, frustrating and occasionally humiliating search for a wife. He dismissed as ineligible all young women of Jewish origin. But being Gentile wasn't enough: his bride must also belong to a family of social status and wealth comparable to that of the Wallichs. She must be, in short, a member of Berlin's haute bourgeoisie.

Though not quite as diminutive as his father, Paul was small in stature, his face somewhat homely. As far as Paul was concerned, however, his only blemish as a potential catch was his Jewish background. He learned in short order that prosperous Gentiles would make no marriages with Jews regardless of their means.

His first humbling experience came when he went to Cologne to visit his friend Julius vom Rath, the son of a well-to-do sugar manufacturer. During his two-day stay, Paul fell in love with vom Rath's sister, "a well developed 19-year-old blonde." So infatuated was the shy young Paul that he implored his friend to propose to his sister on Paul's behalf. The next time Paul visited Cologne he was made to feel thoroughly unwelcomed by the mother. "I never entered that household again," he wrote in his memoirs. A flirtation with another young woman ended abruptly when the eligible young woman's father died and left no estate. After several more months of chasing mirages, Paul resorted to consulting a marriage broker. That failed, too.

By 1912, Paul was nearing thirty. At last, after resigning himself to the necessity of descending a rung or two on the social ladder, he found his wife.

Hildegard Rehrmann came from a middle-class Berlin family. Her father was the civilian head of a Prussian military training institute. Paul and Hildegard met one day at a Christmastime tea given by a mutual acquaintance. Hildegard had no idea who Paul Wallich was and she did little to find out. But when she got up to leave, she found herself flanked by two young men who offered to walk with her. One of them soon went his own way, but the other, Paul Wallich, stayed fixed at her side. Paul insisted on accompanying her to her next appointment. She told him that she planned to take a tram to a piano recital, but Paul dissuaded her. She wrote in her own memoir many years later, "[Paul] had already decided he wanted to marry me and suggested that we walk a bit, then he would take me the rest of the way by taxi, since he had to travel in that direction, which was a complete invention of course."

Hildegard may not have been precisely what Paul had set out to find, but she was, above all, not Jewish. Though not terribly wealthy, Hildegard was cultivated. She spoke fluent French and English; she had studied in Paris and she played the piano. For her part, at age twenty-five Hildegard was no longer in her first youth, and Paul seemed like a reasonably good catch. Any disadvantage she saw in his Jewish background was apparently outweighed by his other attributes.

During their first walk together they established a few things they had in common. Hildegard said that while at the Sorbonne she had attended the lectures of the novelist Romain Rolland. Paul was an admirer of Rolland, particularly of his *Jean Christophe*. Hildegard had never read it, as she couldn't afford the novel's ten volumes and the library didn't carry it. Paul then courted her with a clever scheme. He began sending her the Rolland volumes, one at a time, each accompanied by a letter. She was to let him know when she was finished with each installment and he would send the next one.

Thus ended Paul's search for a non-Jewish wife. Two months after their first meeting, in February 1913, they were officially engaged. So certain was Paul of Hildegard's acceptance that even before the engagement he had two sets of stationery engraved: H.R. for his future wife's notes before the wedding, and H.W. for those written after. A month after their engagement, the two were first married in a civil ceremony, then exchanged vows in the Kaiser Wilhelm Memorial Church on Kurfürstendamm in the center of Berlin. Paul's marriage to Hildegard was to mark the high point of his drive to assimilate.

Hildegard's strong will first emerged during their honeymoon in Italy, when she refused to pack and unpack her husband's suitcase, a chore he was accustomed to having done for him by his mother, sister or household servants. Packing bags, as well as carrying them, was not a job he was prepared to undertake. Hildegard, however, was adamant that this was a task she would not accept either. She finally capitulated, but her initial stubbornness kept the newlyweds in Genoa for several days more than planned.

In the first months of her marriage, Hildegard was a bit overwhelmed by the Wallichs' luxurious lifestyle. "It was another world, that I didn't know and had to learn to understand," she wrote. Hers was a family of accomplished budgeters. Where the Wallichs took taxis everywhere, the Rehrmanns traveled on the tram. Wallichs slept on pure linen while Hildegard's family was content with cotton. When the Rehrmanns wanted to read a book, they often took it out of the library, a practice that was regarded as beneath any member of the Wallich household. Hildegard's sojourn to study in Paris had been at considerable expense to her family. Paul had already traveled much of the world and had made no discernible dent in his father's fortune.

And then there was the Wallich family property: a large and luxurious apartment in Berlin, and a large country estate thirty miles west of Berlin in the village of Jerchel (the estate and its grounds comprised most of the small village), with crops and animals and a full vegetable garden. And there was Paul's mother's old home, the villa in Potsdam at the foot of the Glienicke Bridge.

A Princely Estate Finds an Heir

Moritz Jacoby's Potsdam residence, a tribute to nineteenth-century Prussian nobility, was an integral piece to an architectural puzzle that had its origins two centuries earlier.

Although Potsdam first received mention as a locality as early as 993, it was not until the seventeenth century that it acquired its identity as an important political and cultural center in Prussia. In 1640, the Grand Elector Friedrich Wilhelm abandoned his residence on the lower Rhine to pursue his governing duties closer to Berlin. As a result, all the properties in Potsdam and the surrounding areas fell into the hands of the Prussian aristocracy, whose intent it was to enhance the area's natural landscape by constructing a picturesque arrangement of palaces and park grounds.

Greatly influenced by Italian and Dutch buildings, the Grand Elector imported architects from Holland and Italy to enlarge and beautify the city palace. The renovations aimed to provide Friedrich Wilhelm a panoramic view of the Havel River landscape, using the existing city palace as the centerpoint for an axis system affording views in all directions. The newly constructed electoral palaces, park grounds, the "Pleasuregrounds" (the landscapers for the Prussian nobility used some English to describe their ornate gardens) and the Elector's nearby hunting lodge were connected by avenues and *Blickachsen* (view axes) pointing toward the Havel and Klein-Glienicke. A tree nursery in the Grand Elector's day, the several acres known as Klein-Glienicke on the western edge of the Havel, in 1824 came into the possession of Prussia's Prince Carl.

Friedrich Wilhelm's successors continued the development of the Potsdam landscape. Potsdam's proximity to the growing industrial and shipping city of Berlin, as well as its role as the seat of the militaristic government of Prussia, meant that the city on the Havel represented more than a nature retreat for the nobility. The urbanization of Berlin profoundly affected the idyllic Havel landscape. Although the notion of maintaining Blickachsen pervaded the rhetoric of Potsdam's developers, the Prussian aristocracy's financial interest in industrial modernization clashed with their goal of preserving the Havel landscape for their own aesthetic enjoyment.

An exception to the preoccupation with vistas was Friedrich Wilhelm I, who was known as the Soldier King. Under his reign, Potsdam established itself as a military city, expanding its residential capacity fivefold. Construction was aimed, however, not at developing culture and the arts, but rather at solving the more mundane problem of where to house the expanding army. The hundreds of barrack constructions built under his reign did little to enhance the beauty of the expanding city.

The Soldier King was also responsible for increased industry in the area. In the 1720s he asked manufacturers and craftsmen to come to Potsdam. One, a Jewish wool merchant named David Hirsch, settled there and captured the corner on the velvet market. Craftsmen from Hamburg, Holland and Denmark then followed Hirsch to Potsdam.

Friedrich Wilhelm's son, and next in line to the throne, was Frederick the Great, who dedicated himself throughout his forty-six-year reign to advancing Berlin's role as the capital city and center for Prussian culture and politics. By decreasing the size of his father's army, Frederick was able to invest in the architectural development of Potsdam. Following in the footsteps of his seventeenth-century predecessors, Frederick imported architects who expanded Potsdam's Dutch Quarter and constructed the magnificent rococo Sanssouci Palace in 1745. His successor, Friedrich Wilhelm II, combined Frederick's interest in architecture and his father's investment in the expansion of Potsdam's political powers by extending the Berlin–Potsdam Avenue, which substantially shortened the route between Potsdam and Berlin.

Friedrich Wilhelm II's grandson Friedrich Wilhelm IV ascended the throne as King of Prussia in 1840. He, too, invested great sums of money in Potsdam's aesthetic surround. At the urging of his brother, Prince Carl of Prussia, the new king hired the architect Ludwig Persius, a protégé of the court architect Karl Friedrich Schinkel's, to perfect the Potsdam landscape. Schinkel's designs—by and large studies in elegant simplicity and exacting lines—borrowed heavily from the famed Italian architect of the High Renaissance, Andrea Palladio. Like Schinkel, Prince Carl had traveled extensively in

Italy; he was so taken with the architecture there that he decided to import it to his homeland.

Both the king and the prince were beset with worry over the unappealing effects that urbanization and industrialization had visited on Berlin. They feared that the opening of the Berlin–Potsdam railway would cause the visual blight to spill over into their beloved Potsdam. They resolved to protect the picturesque Havel landscape for their viewing pleasure. If it was necessary to build a factory, then it should be disguised as a villa whose tower would be used as a smokestack.

An important part of the beautification project was a small plot of land next to the Glienicke Bridge. It didn't look like much, but the patch of property was a vital element in the royal family's collection of Blickachsen. From Prince Carl's own Glienicke Castle and Pleasureground the property was in direct view across the bridge. But what he saw at the other end was a disgrace: a squat, stark two-story home that had been built by a shipbuilder and was now owned by a carpenter. Prince Carl's close friend and courtier Kurd Wolfgang von Schöning coveted the property but lacked the money with which to build on it. The prince's solution was a discreet one. He presented von Schöning with an elegantly bound copy of the Old Testament, and between its pages he laid gold coins. The funds enabled the courtier to buy the land, tear down the house and hire the architect Persius to build a new one. As the story goes, the money ran out before the house was completed. Von Schöning then told the prince that he had studied the Old Testament the prince had given him and hinted very delicately that he would enjoy studying the New Testament as well. Soon thereafter, the prince presented him with a copy of the New Testament with equally generous insertions.

Together with Persius, the prince and his attendant transformed the house and grounds into a simple yet decorous riparian villa. The idea was to build a structure that would complement the Pleasureground across the way. The finished product to emerge in 1845 was a complex of buildings that the architect referred to as a "painterly ensemble," a series of three compartments, each a carefully proportioned, precisely symmetrical mass that stood beautifully both by itself and with the other sections. In a clever imitation of the Greek method of building with large stone blocks, Persius used ordinary bricks but plastered them heavily, then sculpted large squares out of the plaster.

Each of the wings had slightly different dimensions, resulting in an asymmetrical whole, a layering of perspectives. A steep narrow tower at the top, a departure from the Italian influence, was Persius's own signature. To enhance the effect of proximity to water, Persius placed the villa as close to the Havel as possible, surrounding it with poplar trees. The effect, however, was to leave no room for a majestic approach to the house. The front of the house fairly abutted the road, which gave the house a welcoming air.

From all its sides, the Villa Schöningen, as it came to be called, served an aesthetic purpose. The most interesting was the east side, facing Prince Carl's Glienicke Castle across the way. This side of the house contained the only concession to privacy—the entry, which withdrew from the front of the house like a receding hairline. The niche was decorated by a statue garden. Directly over that, on the second story, was an open-air loggia, a breezeway connecting the two wings of the house.

Von Schöning died in 1859, and he passed the villa on to his children, who in turn sold it to the prince. Prince Carl resold it in 1864 to a court counsel, stipulating that the new owners refrain from building a factory or any other business that could produce foul-smelling fumes in his proximity. Moritz Jacoby bought the villa in 1871, and passed it on to Anna and Hermann when he died six years later.

During their first summers at the villa, Anna was displeased by what she saw happening to the Havel landscape. In 1880, noisy horse-drawn street carts had invaded the peaceful neighborhood. Industrialization was taking its toll on the area. Hermann tried to buy the property across the street in order to ensure that nothing would be built there to obstruct the view of Babelsberg Castle from the villa. He did not succeed, and before long a row of buildings went up across the way. Anna was particularly unhappy about the presence of an unattractive restaurant at the foot of the bridge directly across the street. In a gesture of self-protection, Hermann bought two plots of land next to the house and expanded the garden.

For all its opulent history, the house in Potsdam became the problem child among the Wallich properties. Twelve miles south of their Berlin apartment, it was too far from the banking district to be a residence, and it wasn't particularly well suited to lodging a family. Its quirky floor plan and limited number of bedrooms didn't allow for much privacy. The vast farm at Jerchel became the family's preferred summer residence, and by 1890 the family had stopped using the Potsdam house for anything at all. They let it stand empty for nearly two decades while an elderly couple lived there to look after it, tend the garden and harvest the fruit trees.

Finally, in 1910, Hermann decided to sell it. But he knew his son, Paul, had developed a special attachment to the house—the place where he had been born. Paul was in the United States at the time, continuing his banking apprenticeship. Hermann wrote his son asking for his opinion of a possible sale. Paul responded immediately, objecting vehemently. He'd like to live in it someday, he told his father.

Paul was not long in having his wish. When he returned to Berlin he moved into the house for a summer. After he arrived, he had an elaborate invitation printed and sent one to all his Berlin friends. It included a drawing of the villa and announced that Paul Wallich, restaurateur, was opening his new establishment every evening, with the promise of "fine wines and quality beer. Milk available throughout the day." The invitation was at once a lighthearted gesture on the part of the twenty-eight-year-old Paul, and a clear display of pride in his family's home.

Hildegard's first visit to the Potsdam house came in May of 1913, shortly after she and Paul returned from their honeymoon.

The house was visually elegant but primitive for its inhabitants. It had no central heating, and the only toilet in the house—with no sink—was downstairs. The two giant lime trees and the two-branched chestnuts were beautiful, but they blocked out most of the light and the house remained dark throughout the day. Hildegard wasn't struck so much by the view across to the princely castles, or by the regal garden in the back, as she was by the damp chill inside the house, even in late spring, as if it suffered from a chronic flu. There was no running water on the second floor. As the Wallichs were averse to the hard Potsdam water, the servants collected rainwater and carried it upstairs to the bedrooms for the family's daily ablutions.

Still, the house exerted a certain charm over everyone who saw it. For all the house's disadvantages, Hildegard in spite of herself became enchanted by it, by its history, and its setting. The house faced Schwanenallee, a cul-de-sac that ran past the Imperial Yacht Club and ended at Cecilienhof, the plush residence of the Crown Prince. At the end of Schwanenallee was the New Garden, one of the Hohenzollern residences. Scores of nightingales made their nests in the trees there and in the gardens along the Schwanenallee. They shied away from the Wallich garden, Hildegard surmised in her memoir, because of the noise coming from the cars and carriages traveling across the bridge.

Hildegard was particularly taken with the prestige of the Berliner Vorstadt, the pie-shaped wedge of Potsdam that led to the Glienicke Bridge, home to so many prominent people. Bankers, merchants, military officers and Prussian aristocracy had permanent or weekend residences there. A soldier stood posted at the bridge to guard the safety of the royal family.

Despite their infrequent visits to the house, Hermann and Anna had appointed each room carefully. Furnished in dark Victorian mahogany with red wallpaper, the dining room was the most social of rooms in the house. It had a view to the Schwanenallee directly below and across the water, as well as one into the garden in back.

The large second-floor dining room with the marble fireplace eventually became, by virtue of its size, Paul's library. Hermann's passion had been wine—his vast wine cellar was known throughout Berlin—and Paul's was his extensive book collection. He was constantly on the lookout for books to add to his collection. His was no idle hobby. He knew by heart the dates of most first editions. Whenever he traveled he made a point of scouting out the local antiquarian; so keen was his eye that he could often gauge a book's value with more accuracy than could the bookshop's proprietor. Paul disliked spending a great deal of money on his books, or on anything, for that matter. It was Hildegard who occasionally prodded him into buying more expensive works. Still, Paul's library was unique in its completeness—nearly thirty thousand volumes in all. His collection contained first editions of Martin Luther, the philosopher Immanuel Kant and the nineteenth-century writer Heinrich von Kleist. He had a large collection of Prussian history volumes, as well as dozens of volumes of Judaica. His larger investments were in eight volumes of the writer Theodor Fontane's handwritten diaries, which he bought at auction in 1933, and in a set of Fredericiana, the writings of Frederick the Great. And unlike many libraries of the wealthy, this one was employed for its purpose. Paul read nearly every book he acquired.

When Paul and Hildegard moved into the house for a summer

shortly after they were married, it rained without interruption, which did little to endear Hildegard to the house. After an early morning ride, her husband left the house for work at 7:45 and didn't return until 7:30 in the evening. She was saved from complete isolation by her brother, Walter, a military officer whose first passion was painting. Hildegard adored her brother. A tall, striking man with a square jaw and bushy dark mustache, Walter dwarfed his brother-in-law. He was a prolific artist, and when he wasn't painting buildings and landscapes he was busy producing likenesses of family members. His sister, as beloved to him as he to her, was one of his favorite subjects. Walter came for lengthy stays in Potsdam and sister and brother would sit for hours in the dining room, overlooking the Havel, as Walter painted his sister's portrait. When he was killed in 1914 during the First World War, Hildegard was overwhelmed with grief.

The marriage between Paul and Hildegard was one born of pragmatic considerations and it would remain that way through their twenty-five years together. Paul had achieved his goal of finding a non-Jewish wife, and Hildegard had married into considerable wealth. While their emotional bond was less than insoluble, they collaborated well on the acquisition of things, purchases made in the course of travels through Europe: paintings and household furnishings as well as scores of bibelots that caught their whimsy. Paul enjoyed buying all manner of knickknacks, as long as they were pretty and, by his standard, cheap. As the years passed, Hildegard came to treasure her things more and more, but she was as much encumbered by them as she was comforted.

Paul was given to occasional bouts of depression. He coped by steeping himself in his work. As his preoccupation with his job at Dreyfus increased (he was now part owner), he turned into a largely absentee husband. His days consisted of solid routine. He arose every morning at 6:30, arrived in his office well before his employees, and stayed until 7 or 8 P.M. He could go on little sleep, and often did. But he also had a remarkable ability to catch brief naps anywhere. And he could carry on conversations simultaneously with Hildegard or, later, his children while reading and writing down his thoughts.

Paul's weekends, too, were defined by routine. He played tennis on Saturday at midday and on Sunday at 7 A.M., in order to spend the rest of the day sailing on the Havel.

Henry, named for Hermann, was the first child born to Paul and Hildegard, in the summer of 1914. Hildegard had been determined to give birth in the Potsdam house rather than Berlin, as she considered Potsdam a more prestigious place to be born. But when complications during childbirth set in, she was transported to Berlin for the remainder of the labor. Henry's middle name, Christopher, was in honor of Romain Rolland's hero Jean Christophe. After Henry came Christel, and sixteen months later, in 1918, Walter was born. There was no doubt that the children were to be raised in the Protestant faith. All three were baptized, and Christmas was celebrated each year with a great deal of fanfare.

Of the two sons, Henry was considered the most well rounded. Where Walter was a small, sickly child who had difficulty digesting his food, Henry was robust and naturally athletic. Like Henry's, Christel's hair was light brown. Walter had the Wallich family's darker complexion and dark hair, and he suffered taunting from other children for his Semitic looks. Henry, by contrast, had inherited Hildegard's fairer complexion, and features considered to be "Aryan." Henry was the insouciant son; Walter inherited his father's inclination to brood.

As in all upper-class households, the three Wallich children were placed for the most part in the hands of a nanny. In an unfinished memoir, Walter described his childhood. "We were accustomed to regarding our parents' . . . living and entertaining rooms as places which we visited, rather than lived in," he wrote. "Our own living quarters were the children's playrooms, where we could do more or less as we pleased." Walter in particular developed a far greater attachment to the nanny than to his parents. He found his own mother to be something of a tyrant. He was so delicate in constitution that he often could not eat his food. If he left a full plate, Hildegard would have it saved and warmed up for the next meal. Occasionally she force-fed him. And when he began to feel nauseated, Hildegard would order him to lie flat on his back and sternly wag her finger at him, ordering him to refrain from vomiting. "Often it worked," he wrote. "Fear of my mother's wrath overcame the sickness."

Hildegard kept Christel on a short tether as well. She maintained total control over her daughter's wardrobe until the day Christel was engaged. Christel was not allowed to use makeup of any kind, Walter wrote in his memoir, "and on one memorable occasion, when, at a big festivity . . . she ignored this injunction, egged on by a worldly friend, and rather inexpertly put on a little lipstick and powder, my mother firmly wiped it off her face with a handkerchief *coram publico*. Poor Christel, totally discountenanced, fled the room and ran home."

For the first several years of their marriage, Paul and Hildegard and the children spent winters in Berlin, and in summers they moved the entire family to Potsdam. Though both residences were independently furnished, each year the move was an ambitious undertaking, complete with moving vans and considerable upheaval. Eventually, to avoid these semiannual migrations, they decided to move the household to Potsdam permanently. So in the late 1920s they installed central heating and hired an architect to extend the house. Living there year-round, Hildegard had decided, would require attaching a new wing to the house.

Hildegard's mother-in-law, an aesthetic purist, was infuriated by the news that the villa was to be altered. If Hildegard went through with her plans, she threatened, she would never visit the Potsdam house again. As Anna Wallich saw it, perhaps, Hildegard's impulse to add on to the house derived not from a real need for space as much as it did from an imagined need. Hildegard went about the task with a parvenu's tendency to overdo. As Anna had feared, the result was something of an eyesore. The architect tried to render it in an antique style but failed, and his product was a bulky, blocklike protrusion at the back of the house that undid entirely the original effect of asymmetrical elegance that the royal architect Persius had achieved. Hildegard and Paul also rebuilt the loggia and the front entrance, pulling both out toward the front and further distorting Persius's original plan. On the grounds next to the house Paul had a tennis court built, and at the water's edge he installed a dock. For her part, Anna Wallich remained true to her word and never set foot on the Potsdam grounds again.

Hildegard was glad to move closer to nature. Berlin was too noisy and confining for her. But there were some physical hardships she encountered as well. The linen sheets that Anna had insisted on buying for the newlyweds may have been dear, but in the cold Potsdam house they made Hildegard long for her more modest cotton bedding because she believed the linen ones brought on her spells of rheumatism.

Potsdam at the time remained the Prussian military city it had been in the days of Frederick the Great. Its landscape was dotted with palaces, military barracks and large parade grounds. "[The Crown Prince] had the reputation of being something of a rake," Walter wrote, "and the roar of his compressor-powered Mercedes could often be heard late at night as he returned from Berlin and accelerated past our house down the lane." As a young boy, Walter had occasional encounters with the royal family. "On my bicycle, I would occasionally see at a distance, the imperial party—the Crown Princess with her ladies-in-waiting, taking the air along the same path. It was then my duty to keep an eye on the ladies-in-waiting as I approached the party. If one of them gave me the nod, I had to get off my bike, drop it unceremoniously where it was, approach the party and kiss the imperial hand, at the same time clicking my heels and making a deep bow. Of course, you didn't actually kiss the hand—that would have been an unpardonable solecism: you kissed your own thumb. Her imperial highness would address a few kind words to me, enquiring about the health of my family or how I was getting on at school, and then I could get back to my bicycle and go on my way. On other occasions, when the Crown Princess did not feel in the mood, I would get no signal from the ladies-in-waiting. In that case, it was a matter of 'eyes front' and carry on bicycling past the group at speed, as if they had not been there."

The house in Potsdam had twelve rooms before the addition was built, and seventeen afterward. By the standards of the era, even after the expansion it was not ostentatiously huge. But in the children's eyes it was immense. When Walter described it many years later, he estimated that it contained thirty rooms, a testament not only to how much larger things can seem to small children, but to the general effect the house conveyed.

The children's favorite feature was the garden. The immense trees on the grounds provided so much shade that the grass beneath was in a continuous struggle for life. On one side of the garden stood a wooden garden house furnished with a table and benches, a huge chestnut tree arching overhead. Beyond an ornamental hedge of hazelnuts and hawthorns was the children's playground, complete with sandbox, swings and parallel bars. Next to that was the fruit orchard, with apple, pear, plum and cherry trees, and next to that a fruit and vegetable garden, with everything from strawberries to red currants. The adults occupied themselves more with the flowers,

which were of little interest to the three children. Walter, in particular, spent countless hours in the garden, often by himself, playing
with characters of his own conjuring.

At Hildegard's urging, the family purchased a sailboat and all became proficient sailors. They named the boat the *Lahn,* after the
river north of Frankfurt near Hildegard's birthplace in northern Germany, and in summers spent nearly every weekend out on the wa-
ters of the Havel.

The family always had dogs. One, a schnauzer named Strolly, was
particularly clever. He was also known for his literacy. In the library,
where the family spent many evenings particularly when guests
came, was a long row of red leather-bound books on a bottom
bookshelf, a twelve-volume edition of the works of Frederick the
Great. Strolly had a habit of lying against the books, which worried
Paul, who thought this might eventually discolor them. Next to
those books were the works of Martin Luther, these bound in
pigskin, which Paul regarded as a hardier material. When Strolly settled down in front of Frederick the Great, Paul ordered him to "go
to Luther," and he dutifully moved.

An Education for the Wallichs

As the eldest son, Henry Wallich was accorded certain privileges
and came of age under the burden of certain expectations. When he
began attending an elite high school in Berlin in the 1920s, Henry
accompanied Paul every day from Potsdam to Berlin, and during the
hour's drive, Paul would hold forth to his eldest son about such
principles as the gold standard and arbitrage. A bit ashamed of his
family's wealth, Henry had the chauffeur leave him off around the
corner from his school and he walked the rest of the way. His
schooling was mostly in classical languages, though he later wrote
that he would probably have benefited from a more scientific education. "I hated every classroom hour but remained indebted to my
teachers for leaving me with a general sense of the values of culture
and civilization, even though I acquired little enough of either.
However, somehow I graduated at the head of the class."

There seemed little doubt that Henry, too, would pursue a career
in banking. In fact, it was taken for granted that Henry would join
Dreyfus, the small bank where his father was a partner. To prepare
for such employment, Henry was sent off to Munich University for a

law degree, which was then considered the most useful training for an aspiring banker. But he spent most of his time on the tennis court. After one term in Munich ("I won some minor tennis tournaments but never discovered the university library"), in 1932 he went off to Oriel College at Oxford for a year, where he polished his tennis strokes and acquainted himself with sherry.

For her schooling, Christel was sent to a girls' high school in Potsdam. This was the school that served as the model for a 1931 film called *Mädchen in Uniform,* which became famous for its depiction of the overly strict and regimented way in which girls were still being taught in such schools. The school was packed with Potsdam's minor nobility, and when Christel—a girl of Jewish origin—enrolled, the mistress apparently thought it remarkable enough to announce to her pupils that a girl who had a Jewish father would be arriving. Still, in part because of her "Aryan" looks and in part because of her sunny disposition, Christel suffered no stigma at school.

Walter, attending a different school, had a more unfortunate experience. His dark features invited no end of derision from his schoolmates. "From the start I was made very much aware that I was an outsider, not fully accepted, and my Jewish origins and appearance were the subject of a good deal of taunting comment," he wrote. "Nevertheless I made a number of friends who were happy to visit me at our house and enjoy the amenities of the garden and the swimming and sailing facilities. I was not really aware of the fact that they rarely, if ever, reciprocated my hospitality. . . . Nor did I greatly mind that, when in a crowd, most of them were quite ready to join in the taunting and teasing, and not one of them ever defended me against my enemies. I understood their problems in this matter, and was grateful that there were, at any rate, some who were prepared to accept my hospitality in private."

Hildegard, however, was of a different mind in tolerating such treatment of her youngest child. "Although I did not talk much about my school problems at home, knowing that they were insoluble and would only have worried my parents, I must have let slip enough about them to give my mother a fair idea of what was going on," Walter wrote. "One afternoon when one of these friends, Eckehard Scholz, the son of a judge, came to visit me she took him aside for a long walk around the garden. What exactly she said to him I never found out, but when she finally left him to return to me he was in tears, refused so much as to look at me or shake my hand in farewell, but jumped on his bike and rode off furiously." Whether his mother did this because she objected to the schoolboy's anti-Semitism, or because she insisted that her children were not Jewish, Walter did not say.

Hermann Wallich died in 1928. Sadly, he lived to see some of his predictions materialize. In 1923, Adolf Hitler led his National Socialist German Workers' Party into the ill-fated Munich beer hall putsch. At his trial, Hitler railed against Jewish financiers who were conspiring to take over the world. The same year, a pogrom against Jews took place in the streets of Berlin. Hitler served less than nine months of a five-year prison term. While in prison, he began to write *Mein Kampf.* Germany's greatest enemies, he declared, were world Jewry, international Communism, effete liberalism and decadent capitalism.

At first, the rise of the Nazis and Hitler's seizure of power in 1933 had but indirect effects on the Wallich family. As the children were growing into young adults, an atmosphere of right-wing and nationalist youth groups flourished in Germany. Christel joined an organization that was eventually subsumed by the Bund deutscher Mädel, the girls' equivalent of the Hitler Youth. Walter, too, joined a group for young Christians, but when all the youth groups were combined to form the Hitler Youth, Walter was forbidden from joining. Curiously, he later wrote, the fact that "the Nazis were inherently a vicious, bloody-minded and thoroughly dangerous lot who ought to be opposed at every turn, hardly occurred to me at the time. Indeed, when, prior to the amalgamation of all the youth clubs in the Hitler Youth there took place a huge demonstration . . . to glorify the new-born German Reich, I took part and, at the climactic moment, knelt down to swear allegiance to this monstrosity . . . feeling elated rather than depressed by the proceedings."

Walter ascribed his behavior to the fact that his parents never discussed politics in front of the children. He was apparently oblivious to some of the obvious portents of Nazi oppression, such as the boycott of Jewish shops and businesses, and the burning of books in early 1933. He claims to have gotten his first sign of the coming trouble in 1935, when he overheard his father and his uncle listening intently to the proclamation on the radio of the Nuremberg Laws, which deprived Jews of all civil rights and forbade intermarriage and sexual relations between Jews and non-Jews. After the broadcast the two men began to discuss what they had heard, but when they noticed Walter standing in the doorway they stopped and told him to leave.

In the early 1930s, just as the spread of Nazism was prompting many Jews to leave the country, Paul and Hildegard remained firmly planted in Potsdam. As their sailing ambitions grew, they bought a second, much larger boat, which they christened the *Lahn II*. This vessel was an eight-meter international racing yacht, and only a handful of ships in its class in northern Germany could compete with it. In 1934, Paul and Hildegard entered the *Lahn II* in the Kiel Week, a regatta of such high profile that the industrialist Krupp family had a boat custom-built for the occasion. The *Lahn II* was far and away the superior vessel in all categories, and was awarded the Joseph Goebbels prize for outstanding boat of the regatta. But when Hitler's propaganda minister heard he was to present the prize to Paul Wallich, he refused to appear at the ceremony, thus sparing himself the embarrassment of handing a prize bearing his name to a man he regarded as a Jew. Goebbels gave orders that in the future, such people were not to be allowed to enter the race. From then on, the family confined its sailing to weekends on the Havel.

At around the same time, Paul Wallich's brother-in-law, a non-Jew named Oskar Mulert married to Paul's sister, Ilse, was dismissed by the Nazis from his position as president of his municipality. To achieve their goal, the Nazis had accused him of a shady financing deal involving Paul's bank. Oskar fought the charges vigorously, and for several days the incident was on the front page of the Berlin papers, with Oskar's and Paul's names in large print, and Paul described as "the Jewish banker."

According to the categories the Nazis created with their Nuremberg Laws, the Wallich children were considered *Mischlinge ersten Grades,* or half-Jews. While Henry was at Oxford, the exchange control, which prohibited Jews from exporting money, cut off his source of funds, forcing him to leave Oxford. The eighteen-year-old Henry had been planning to return to Germany in 1933 to join his father's firm. Instead, however, he went to Argentina to pursue his training as a banker. In his later years, Henry occasionally wrote about the path his career had taken. But when it came to explaining why he didn't return to Germany after his stay in Oxford, Henry was uncharacteristically inexact. "Rather than go back to Berlin, it was arranged that I would work for a Buenos Aires exporting firm, which already had done business with my grandfather." For the rest of his life, Henry Wallich avoided the subject of his Jewish origins, not only with professional colleagues but with his own children as well. Henry remained in Argentina for two years. In 1935 he set sail for the United States and a new job as a bond analyst with Chemical Bank in New York.

In 1936 Henry left Chemical Bank, took a job as a securities analyst for a small New York brokerage firm, and enrolled in night classes at New York University's Wall Street Division. The following year, Henry made what he described as an abortive attempt to return to Germany. He stayed there and in Holland for six months but "found the outlook too depressing" and returned to New York.

Paul and Hildegard worried next about what to do with Walter. Their first aim was to get him out of his high school, where a systematic campaign to evict Jewish pupils was under way. They looked into sending him to Paul's old school in Pforta, Saxony, a Christian-aristocratic boarding school known for allowing no racial bias. But the school had lost its independence and was set to convert to a school for privileged children of Nazi Party members. So in 1933, helped by British friends, Paul and Hildegard sent Walter to a boarding school in England. Later lodged in family lore was the story that these same friends paid for Walter's tuition, and Paul and Hildegard repaid them in fine German wines. In 1936, Walter then entered Cambridge University. He continued to return to Potsdam for holidays until the Christmas of 1937, when his passport was confiscated at the border. He was told he would get it back only if he assured the authorities that he would never return to Germany. He complied and returned to England. (In 1939, in a strange lapse on the part of the Third Reich's bureaucracy, Walter received a draft notice from the German army. From the safe keep of England, he wrote back a letter reminding them that according to their definitions he was partly Jewish and therefore not exactly draftee material.)

Christel, in the meantime, had fallen in love with Adel Körte, a farmer, but under the Nuremberg Laws the two were not allowed to marry. Undeterred, they emigrated to Argentina in 1937 and married secretly in Buenos Aires. For years afterward Hildegard worried about her son-in-law's unsuitability for her daughter, and his inability to find a job in Argentina. Adel did find work as a sheep farm administrator. Though seven thousand miles from their home, Christel and Adel continued to speak German with their four children.

It was Paul's good fortune to belong to a moneyed elite that could buy its way out of Nazi Germany. But he refused to acknowledge his country's rejection of him. In the year after Hitler took control of the Parliament in January 1933, some 37,000 Jews fled Germany. Nonetheless, even as friends around Paul were leaving and urging him to do the same, even though he held a passport and his chances of finding refuge elsewhere were far better than those of most of Germany's 500,000 Jews, Paul eschewed thoughts of emigration. He considered himself a Christian. And he stood to lose a great deal of his wealth if he did leave. In the process of "Aryanizing" Jewish property, the Nazis were forcing Jews to sell their homes and businesses for sums far below their market value, then imposing a high punitive tax on them for abandoning it. Moreover, Jews were prohibited from taking all but a small percentage of their liquid assets out of the country.

Hildegard was not disposed to the idea of leaving. She had too much invested in Germany, and both she and Paul believed that to leave would be too significant a disruption. So they put up with the changes imposed on their lives, changes they believed would be temporary, just as they believed Nazism to be a fleeting menace. Paul had already transferred title of the Potsdam house to Hildegard in 1932, so there was no need to register it as Jewish property. Moreover, Paul continued to believe, at least outwardly, that his considerable efforts at assimilation would shelter him from the worst that might come.

Many years later, in an interview for the oral archives of England's Imperial War Museum, Walter attempted to explain his family's reluctance to emigrate. "My family might have arranged things better had they thought in terms of emigration at all at the time. They thought that the Hitler period would be a short one, that their children were going abroad temporarily wherever it was most suitable for them to go and that they would all one day, when Hitler had finished his work, be returning to Germany and be reunited there. Had they thought initially in terms of emigration they might have arranged things so that we would all have been in the same country, but it did not at that time occur to them and by 1938, when it became perfectly clear that the Jews were going to have a very thin time of it indeed in Germany, it was too late."

Other friends and family members were considerably less charitable in their speculation as to why Hildegard and Paul didn't leave

Germany. Some rested blame on Hildegard and her attachment to the family's many valuable possessions. What she hadn't received from her husband in emotional commitment she had taken instead in material compensation. After a while, material possessions had supplanted any other source of comfort for her in her arid marriage.

When the world went into economic crisis in the early 1930s, Paul's bank, Dreyfus & Co., managed to survive. And when Hitler came to power, the bank continued business as usual. But with time, the Nazis would make survival difficult for all Jewish banks. By 1937, it was clear that Paul could not continue to hold the bank. Because of sharply reduced clientele, its assets had dwindled. Like his father, Paul excelled at international banking. But once the Nazis were installed, the bank lost much of its international business. By 1938 Paul had little alternative but to sell the bank. He found a purchaser in Merck, Finck & Co., a Munich-based bank, and signed a ten-year contract as a consultant, at an annual salary of 50,000 reichsmarks. In the event that the firm had to let him go for political reasons, he would receive a lump sum of 500,000 reichsmarks. Perhaps to keep the Nazis from discovering that Merck, Finck had a Jew on its payroll, the firm paid Paul in cash.

But the relationship with Merck, Finck did not go well. Not long after signing on with the bank, Paul's office was moved to a different floor. He began to arrive home from work increasingly preoccupied and low in spirits.

Paul's circle of friends, in the meantime, grew smaller. In the Wallichs' corner of Potsdam, it was as if the Nazi Party was slowly surrounding the villa. Jewish neighbors were leaving, some of them disappearing suddenly. Some of the neighboring houses were sold to the Nazis, or simply occupied by the National Socialists to serve as residences or as headquarters for various Nazi organizations. Jews were now required to register all their property and were excluded from all real estate and stock exchange trade. In October 1938 Goebbels ordered that Jewish money be used to finance Germany's arms buildup.

Finally, in late 1938 Paul acknowledged that it was growing late for him. He sailed to New York to see Henry.

While in New York, Paul conducted some business for Merck, Finck. But one of his reasons for making the long journey was to explore the possibility of emigrating to America. Apparently the visit did not go well. Tired and discouraged, he returned to Berlin to try to make the best of it in Germany. Years later family members would speculate about the reasons for his decision not to move to New York. Using Henry's Wall Street connections, Paul probably could have landed a new position with ease. But, comfortable and settled in the relatively staid Berlin banking milieu, Paul may have dreaded a new professional start at age fifty-six in the unfamiliar, dog-eat-dog world of Wall Street, which was still mired in the Depression. The Wall Street crash had thrown Central European banks into crisis as well, although Merck, Finck remained relatively unscathed. Some of Paul's grandchildren also speculated later that, for reasons that no one in succeeding generations understood, Henry had made his father feel less than welcome. Perhaps Paul remained driven by his desire to gain acceptance in the country he considered his home, even if it meant colluding with the Third Reich. In a memoir, Johannes Schultze, one of Paul's closest friends, remarked in passing that Paul had maintained professional ties to the Nazis, and that as late as 1938—perhaps during the visit to New York—he helped to arrange a U.S. loan to Hitler.

Shortly after Paul's return to Germany in the fall of 1938 the culmination of years of anti-Semitism and violence came with Kristallnacht, the night of shattered glass. One desperate act—the shooting of a German diplomat in Paris, Ernst vom Rath, by a young Jew whose family had just been deported from Germany—was seized upon by the Nazis, who called the attack part of a plot by "International Jewry." Vom Rath died from his wounds on November 9, and Hitler used the assassin as a convenient scapegoat. That night the massive pogrom swept Germany: 91 Jews were killed and thousands more arrested, 170 synagogues were burned to the ground and more than 7,000 shops were destroyed. Kristallnacht served as a qualitative sharpening of fear among German Jews. It was a renewed outburst that they had thought wouldn't happen again after the first days of violence following Hitler's seizure of power. Thousands of Jews fled Germany in the days following the pogrom.

On the day following Kristallnacht, the Gestapo set out to arrest more Jews. At about eleven o'clock on the morning of November 10, a car drew up in front of the Wallichs' Potsdam house and three men got out. Hildegard opened the door herself. The men asked where they could find Herr Wallich. Hildegard told them that he was in Berlin in his office. She asked if they were from the Gestapo and what they could possibly want with her husband—he had not been accused of anything. Yes, they said, they were with the Gestapo and would return the following morning at 8 A.M. Hildegard called Paul at work to warn him not to come home.

At the bank that morning Paul had already been planning a business trip. Throughout the day, he heard of arrests taking place all over Berlin. Heeding his wife's warning, he boarded a train and went straight to Cologne, where he checked into a hotel.

The Gestapo didn't wait until the next morning to return to Potsdam. Police officials in civilian dress rang the bell early that evening and asked once again for Herr Wallich. Advised he was not at home, they left. Three hours later, a Nazi in civilian dress accompanied by another in an SS uniform arrived at the house. Hildegard turned them away, saying her husband had not yet returned from work. When they came back the following evening a servant answered the door and said that Herr Wallich was away on business. A few hours later three uniformed Nazis returned and searched the entire house.

By Saturday, Hildegard had still heard nothing from Paul and was beside herself. At midday, the police returned. She told them she had had no sign from her husband for three days. On Monday afternoon, Paul's lawyer received a letter from Paul dated November 11, the previous Friday.

> Dear Dr. Günther, When you receive these lines, I will be drowned in the Rhine. Please take [the enclosed letter] to my wife personally. . . .
>
> I'd like to ask you to cable my sons and tell them not to come to Germany to comfort my wife. They won't be able to help, and will just be placing themselves in danger.

The typed letter went on to explain to the lawyer how he would like to have his personal financial affairs put in order. Then he returned to a personal note:

> I have a special favor to ask of you. I think it is possible that particular friends of mine . . . will blame my death on my wife and her deep attachment to Germany. You know these men well, and so I ask you to write them and tell them that I have decided to take my life because there is no place in Germany for me any longer and I am no longer interested in trying to start a new life elsewhere. Had I asked her to, my wife would have accompanied me in emigra-

tion. However, the solution I have chosen is not just in my own best interest, but in that of our children as well, for it aryanizes our worldly assets, and perhaps it will also open the way to assimilation for the children, which I, like my father before me, see as the goal of the civilized Jew.

As for my own person, nothing will surface for a long time, as I plan to jump from the Hohenzollern Bridge considerably weighed down around the middle.

When Franz Kafka wrote *The Trial* in 1914, his famous waking nightmare of a novel about Joseph K., an accused man in search of his crime, he made a change in the final sentence that was as intriguing as it was dark. Originally, he wrote that K.'s last feeling as he watched his two executioners thrust a knife into his chest was his own shame. Kafka then crossed that out and wrote, "It was as if the shame of it would outlive him."

Paul's final line in the note to his lawyer conveyed an eerily similar tone, and the message's obverse: the shame of his Jewishness would die with him. "It is my assumption," he wrote, "that a dead Jew is no longer a Jew." As Paul saw it, the biggest favor he could do for his children was to stop living. If he could not assimilate in the end, then jumping to his death from the Hohenzollern Bridge in the very center of Cologne should make it possible for them to do so.

Paul's letter to Hildegard was handwritten:

My Darling,

I wanted to do it tomorrow, but now I've decided to do it today as I don't want to run into any danger. Don't be angry with me. You know that I have never really hung much on life and now, when everything seems to be saying that nonexistence is better than existence, I can no longer deny it. I am so tired and know that I'll be doing you and the children no good if I act any differently. All the worries and excitement that would come with trying to start over—I don't even have the nerves to go over the border, with or without a passport. This morning, when I was calmer, I wrote several letters, which are here in the suitcase. Say hello to all our friends, and thank you for all the goodness that I've had from you. My greetings to the children. Give them something of mine. I've enjoyed much from life and so I am parting without anger.

You needn't resist placing the Nazi flag outside the old house at the Glienicke Bridge. The power that I've succumbed to is a world power. Do not be ashamed of my end, but do acknowledge the victor, as I myself am doing. I shall be thinking of you, my most beloved, in the last moment. All the best to you and the children.

Your husband.

Paul's letter to his wife exuded the aloofness that defined his marriage. Still more chilling was his open submission to the power of Hitler's Germany.

The "danger" Paul referred to was still pounding at the door in Potsdam. The Gestapo didn't let the appearance of suicide notes conclude the matter. His body had not been recovered. They searched the house again. They interrogated the staff, and scoured the carriage house next door, where the gardener lived with his family. The entire household was under suspicion of hiding the master. The police confiscated Paul's letter to Hildegard and six days after his disappearance, on Prayer and Repentance Day, a German national holiday, they confiscated her passport, too. The passport was returned a few days later.

A month later, Paul's body washed up on the shores of the Rhine. On January 10, 1939, a memorial service was held, presided over by a Potsdam pastor.

After Paul's death, Hildegard went into a long period of bereavement and depression. She sold the *Lahn II* to another sailing family in Potsdam, at a price far below what she and Paul had paid for it. The new owners later sank the boat as the Russians approached Berlin during the war, to prevent it from falling into Russian hands. Hildegard urged her children not to return to Germany, for fear they might not be allowed out again. Following Kristallnacht, measures against Jews had accelerated, and the number of suicides among Jews increased. All Jewish students who hadn't already been expelled from German schools were dismissed. Curfews were instituted. Jews lost their driver's licenses and were no longer allowed to own cars. And yet Hildegard continued to refuse to believe there would be a war and disregarded her sons' advice that she emigrate. Determined to get her out of Germany, Walter and Henry finally persuaded her to visit them in the summer of 1939. She took enough clothing, jewelry and money for a month or two abroad. The only possession aside from her personal effects that she took from the house was a small statue of a horse biting his back, intended as a gift for Christel in Argentina. She told Mamsell, the cook, to look after the house and the other servants, then she traveled to Cambridge to see Walter, who then put her on an ocean liner from Liverpool bound for New York.

While the ocean liner was on the high seas Hitler invaded Poland. By the time Hildegard arrived in the United States, she saw that she would not be able to return anytime soon. As things turned out, she would never return to Germany to live.

On Hildegard's arrival, Henry welcomed her at the New York dock. But she chose not to remain with her son. Instead, at the invitation of relatives there, she went to Los Angeles and settled into a modest hotel in Hollywood, her living costs paid by Henry. She was lonely in California, but distracted herself with courses in Spanish and French. To cope with her lingering depression she also took pottery courses. As a further salve, she wrote lengthy letters to her children, scattered now across three continents. So mindful was she of the cost of things that after being told she must add extra postage to a particularly hefty letter, she subsequently made certain she got her money's worth by writing as much as possible on the pages.

Hildegard reported to Walter that the books he and Henry had read as children—Carl May's novels set in the Wild West—had certainly failed to give the right impression about America. "I somehow kept the idea that most of the country here was still grazing ground for buffalos, or at least prairie without any dwellings," she wrote.

Walter's Return to Berlin

> "We have been rather unfortunate, I feel, in having the American zone of occupation ending just on the wrong side of the Glienicke Bridge."
>
> —WALTER WALLICH IN A LETTER TO HILDEGARD

With the end of the war in 1945, Hildegard's letters to Walter grew longer; she now wrote to him once or twice a week. As an enemy alien in England, in 1940 Walter had been detained and transported to an internment camp in Canada. On his release shortly afterward, he joined the Royal Artillery, returning to Berlin at the end of 1945 as a British officer. As a principal advisor to the controlling forces in the British sector occupying Berlin, Walter was assigned to aid in the dismantling of Goebbels's propaganda ministry and the rebuilding of a free press. His special area of responsibility was radio. Walter was now able to tell Hildegard of her homeland, of Berlin, of her friends, and of the house at Potsdam.

The Berlin Walter returned to six months after the German capitulation was nearly unrecognizable. One third of the city's buildings had been reduced to rubble or severely damaged. Tens of thousands of civilians had been killed and nearly half of the city's inhabitants were homeless. Although he had already seen the city several times from the air, Walter was shocked. He still recognized the place as being Berlin, but for two miles on either side of the Brandenburg Gate there was no building still habitable in its entirety. In some of the largest buildings certain sections among the ruins had been made habitable for the few families living in them. One of the city's two large department stores, though largely gutted, was now occupied by three families. The other was so completely destroyed it had been abandoned.

Walter walked through acre upon acre of ruins. The desolation was so great that he expected to hear wolves howling. The Landwehr Canal in the center of the city, once a promenade for Berlin high society, stank of rotting corpses. The block around the Matthais Church, near Potsdamer Platz, was a wilderness of rubble with a few gaunt chimneys left standing here and there. All that remained of the church was its facade. The Reichs Chancellery was being used as a public lavatory and the Reichstag was covered with graffiti. When he got closer, Walter saw that it was scrawled with the names of Allied soldiers.

"I have never had any trouble yet in finding my way about among the ruins," Walter wrote in a letter to Hildegard soon after his visit. "Perhaps this is because I was always accustomed to orienting myself by streets rather than by the surrounding buildings, of which I was inattentive. It is one of the many queer and surprising things about Berlin that, whereas everywhere there is destruction amid mountains of ruins and rubble, the streets are all clear, bomb-craters carefully mended, and the streets themselves kept as spotless and sanitary as ever they were during the propagandistic drive of the 1936 Olympic Games. The contrast is very startling and has been favorably commented on by many who have seen fewer ruins and dirtier streets in other European capitals.

"Food shops are few and far between; when they have anything to sell, there are queues in front of them. On the other hand, you will find advertisements stuck up on trees telling you that Lehmann's marriage brokerage is functioning again, you will see on the Kurfürstendamm, on a bombed-out shop, a notice to the effect that Rochlitz, the sports shop, will be opening here 'soon.' So will Rodenstock the photographer, a few houses further on. Amelang and Bother and Bock are already open but they have nothing to sell. The same applies to the numerous tobacconists who are establishing themselves in the hope that there will be cigars and cigarettes soon. Everybody is advertising for someone or something. The number of papers in Berlin . . . is limited. As a result you see every tree in every large street absolutely plastered with handwritten or typed advertisements. These range from the marriage agency mentioned above to requests for an exchange of a Leica camera against 200 cigarettes. These multicoloured cards give the streets a queerly rakish appearance, as if we were on the morning after carnival, with streamers and confetti not yet gone.

"The people have, all of them, shrunk. Their suits are several sizes too big for them, and there is no doubt at all that they get nothing like enough to eat. Many of them have an unhealthy grey colour, and it is truly terrible to ride in public vehicles and see the look of settled apathy and despair on their faces. . . . Yet in spite of this shortage of food, there are still some dogs to be seen about. There is one woman lurking somewhere off the Tauentzienstrasse who has three large and lovely borzois, which she dare not take out in the daytime since other Berliners would stone her, I should think. She cannot possibly be keeping herself and three dogs of that size alive on the ration she gets lawfully. So she takes them out at night, and that is the time when I have encountered her and the dogs. Something similar you will see at the zoo. There is an elephant, half a dozen dogs and foxes, a few birds and mountain goat, and that just about completes the list. However, you will still find people coming there with paper bags and actually feeding the animals. How they do it heaven only knows."

In the same letter, he described his return to Taubenstrasse 22, the offices of Merck, Finck, where he hoped to find someone who could tell him about the family's assets that had been left behind.

"I found number 22 completely gutted, quite obviously uninhabited and uninhabitable. The [building] next door, however, seemed to be in better repair, and I went inside to see whether anyone would know of the whereabouts of Merck, Finck or their staff. In the front building I drew a complete blank. Only the ground floor and first floor were at all habitable, and the human ghosts living there had nothing to do with the banking world, knew nothing and nobody and were terrified of seeing an allied soldier. A depressing spectacle. I descended once more and crossed a courtyard in ruins to the back building. The ground floor and basement here are a large cave full of rubble. There is, however, a sort of improvised fly-ing staircase built over the void by which you reach the second floor which also does not look habitable. I went up the stairs, along a narrow ledge which once must have been a passage, but now the outside wall has fallen away, and you hug the only remaining one rather precariously in order to avoid falling into the courtyard be-low. Suddenly you find yourself in a room, two walls of which are made of brick, the other two improvised wooden structures. The whole has a tarpaulin spread over the top of it, which turns it into as nice and dry a living room as most Berliners can boast these days. In this was sitting a grey-haired man who turned out to be Herr Schultz, late of Merck, Finck & Co, who apparently was pre-pared to vegetate on there until the firm started up again. When I gave him my name he started to become active, full of delight—I don't know whether feigned or real—and before I knew where I was I was surrounded by about half-a-dozen bank-clerks of both sexes all talking about the good old days of Dreyfus and treating me with a sort of hideous deference as 'Der Sohn des Chefs.' I cannot remember when I have been quite so deeply embarrassed. Their feelings, and the delight of their reminiscences may have been quite genuine, for all I know, but I seem to remember that Father was not always persona grata after 1933 with all the employees, and since I remembered none of those present, I was going to take the whole ovation with a grain of salt. After this had gone on for a while (and you may rest assured that you have, according to these representa-tives, their full loyalty and support should you, suitably armed with an American passport, wish to start up the firm of Dreyfus and Co again), we cut the cackle and came down to earth and the safes."

The bankers told Walter that shortly after the end of the war, Russian troops arrived, took the keys to all the safes, opened them, removed their contents, loaded them into trucks and drove off. Herr Schultz told the young Wallich that he informed the Russians that they were taking Jewish or American property, but they ignored him. Boxes containing the Wallich family silver, as well as a trunk of Paul's, were taken along with everything else.

"The same fate," Walter continued, "I understand from other people I have talked to, has befallen every safe anywhere in Berlin. Those to which they could not get the keys have been forced open with blow-lamps and flame throwers. I then asked Herr Schultz to let me have a signed statement on what he had seen, intending to get a signature to it. Herr Schultz, I thought, showed the most unaccountable reluctance to do anything of the kind, but I think I have persuaded him that no harm can come to him from so dangerous a commitment."

Soon after arriving in Berlin, Walter went to see the Potsdam house for the first time since he had left Germany as a child. Potsdam had been bombed during the final days of the war, and Walter had no idea what to expect. When he came to the Glienicke Bridge, he saw that the bridge had been destroyed, and a temporary wooden bridge erected alongside it. But he could see clearly that the house had survived. He saw that the big dining room window-pane was smashed, and so were one or two others. Apart from that, the house appeared quite undamaged. But as a British officer, Walter was to come no closer. Russian soldiers guarding the border area wouldn't let him approach the house, or even stay in the neighborhood for any length of time without a permit. In muted frustration, Walter wrote dryly to his mother, "We have been rather unfortunate, I feel, in having the American zone of occupation ending just on the wrong side of the Glienicke Bridge."

A few weeks later, he was able to meet with Mamsell, the cook who had remained in the house and was still living there. Because Walter could not set foot in Potsdam, she traveled to his apartment in Berlin. Mamsell had remained a loyal servant to the Wallichs throughout the family's wartime absence. She was so overcome with emotion upon seeing Walter after so many years that he had difficulty consoling her. From the start of the war she told Walter, she had been fighting all encroachments on the house, waiting for and dreaming of the day when the mistress of the house would return and find it as she had left it. The three family servants, Walter was to discover, had become rather lonely old women. During the war, they had turned into close friends, pulled together by memories of happy days shared in the Wallichs' employment.

It wasn't until Mamsell surfaced that Walter received word that the contents were still largely intact, save what the Russians had looted. It appeared that Mamsell had secreted and saved many things in the house that otherwise would have been stolen. She had in fact guarded the house with passion and perseverance.

Mamsell told Walter that during the war the house had periodically stood empty; at various times it served as a library for the Nazis and a military office of some kind. For a brief period toward the end the house had served as a hospital for wounded Russian soldiers.

Immediately after the war, Russians had occupied the house and ejected her for a short time. She was evicted again during the Potsdam Conference, the meeting among the victorious Allies to divide the occupied territory. Just before the meeting, which took place down the street from the Wallich house at Cecilienhof, residents in houses leading to the conference site were given a few hours to gather their things and leave. During the three-week conference, all the houses up and down Schwanenallee were shut down. Some residents never returned.

Mamsell's stories of the damaging and looting of the villa at the hands of the Russians were both humorous and horrifying. The occupying soldiers used an oversized bathtub on the second floor to slaughter pigs. They put their bayonets through the paintings. They guzzled precious wines that the family had left behind in the cavernous wine cellar.

This kind of behavior was widespread and was the start of a forty-year relationship of mutual resentment between the East Germans and their occupiers. As far as the fastidious Germans were concerned, Russians were filthy and coarse. One day, Mamsell told Walter, she found a Russian soldier pointing at the bust of Friedrich Wilhelm the IV over the stairs. The soldier yelled, "Kapitalist!" and drew his pistol to shoot the statue down. "No, not a capitalist," Mamsell protested. "A red poet. A very famous, red poet." Satisfied, the soldier put his pistol away.

Ruppi, the family's nasty little schnauzer prone to biting, was alive and well and as fierce as ever, Mamsell reported. But the Russians liked him and they fed him. Mamsell told Walter that she and Ruppi were still living on the ground floor in servants' quarters off the kitchen. On the second floor the Russians had moved into the library and Hildegard's and Paul's bedrooms. A German woman and her two children were living in Christel's bedroom and in an adjoining drawing room. Another German family of five had made themselves at home on the top floor, the only warm place in the house.

In his letters to his mother, Walter spoke of Mamsell's feat as an incredible one. By hiding many of the family's valuable possessions in various places around the house, she had succeeded in keeping many things out of the hands of pilferers. (One thing the Russians did seem intent on stealing was the family's collection of timepieces, all the portable watches and clocks they could find.) Walter promised Mamsell that he would keep her on as a caretaker, at her modest prewar salary. He also offered the use of the tennis court to the local youth organization of the occupying Russian forces but they declined on the grounds that it was an artifact of the bourgeoisie.

Walter and Mamsell established a routine of regular visits. Sometimes she traveled to Walter in Berlin, and occasionally they met at the Glienicke Bridge, the edge of the occupied zone and the farthest he was allowed to travel as a British officer.

The Glienicke Bridge was the only structure in the vicinity of the house to have been bombed. On April 24, in the final days of the war, in one last desperate attempt to keep the advancing Russians from crossing the Havel into Berlin, the Germans destroyed their own bridge. The middle of the bridge sagged into the water. It took more than four years for the bridge to be repaired. When it was eventually rebuilt in 1949, East Germany provided the labor and West Germany the materials.

When Mamsell walked across the temporary wooden span she pushed a pram that she had filled with items from the house: Hildegard's favorite dresses and both Hildegard's and Paul's fur coats; literary curios that Paul had procured through the years, such as checks and counterfoils of Heinrich Heine, a favorite poet of Paul's; and loose photographs torn from an album. Mamsell explained to Walter that when the Russians discovered the album they tore out the photos and kept the empty book. In return Walter gave Mamsell packets of chocolate, food, biscuits for Ruppi, cotton thread and other provisions that Hildegard had sent from America. Their meetings inevitably attracted the attention of passersby. Germans, Russians and Americans stopped to stare at what looked like a lucrative black market exchange in progress.

• • •

The Absentee Owner

From her remote California outpost, Hildegard received Walter's news of her homeland and of her house with avid interest. It was an anxious and busy watch. She sent parcels for Walter to distribute to relatives in Germany, who were without the most basic foods and supplies. She even encouraged Walter to engage in black market exchanges—coffee, for instance, was selling on the black market for as much as 600 marks—only to be sharply reprimanded by Walter about the illegality of black market trade.

Hildegard had no reason to believe that the family no longer owned the house, or that it would ever be seized from them. From the remove of another continent, she considered the Soviet occupation a temporary state of affairs, the result of a madcap postwar scramble for land. Germany had been divided into four zones, occupied by the victors: Britain, France, Russia and the United States. And Berlin, which as a consequence of the division now lay in the middle of the Russian zone in northeastern Germany, was divided into four sectors as well and put under quadripartite administration. In her letters she referred to Potsdam as if its inclusion in the restricted Russian zone were part of a bureaucratic mess-up that would all get straightened out in time. And there was nothing the occupying forces did to indicate otherwise. The Russians made it clear that the house remained the family's financial responsibility, and the accumulated bills overwhelmed Walter. Since he was not allowed on the premises, he was forced to conduct all business through an intermediary. And because Hildegard's assets in Germany were still frozen, Walter paid all the bills from his own pocket. To offset the expense he charged rent to the three parties living in the house and leased out the land by the shore, where a small house stood. He sought exemptions from certain property taxes and gave as the reason his family's victimization under the fascists.

In her letters, Hildegard conveyed the ambivalence that she had always felt toward the Potsdam house. "I don't think that I will ever come back to live in the house, apart from the fact that I would not like to, I certainly will not be able to afford it," she wrote in 1945. "It is a sad business . . . to see all the property, acquired by your grandfather and your father with the hard labor of their lives, to vanish into nothingness."

The prospect of tenants in the house made Hildegard extremely nervous. She wrote Walter that she would rather the house be put at the disposal of relatives. (Walter may not have been allowed into Potsdam, but Germans were.) The garden was a particular source of concern to Hildegard. She instructed Walter to prohibit the renters from cutting down any trees, which she feared the tenants would sell in order to pay their rent. She claimed she was amused, but was obviously a bit scandalized to hear that the former table tennis room on the ground floor had been rented out as a small makeshift pub. "I do not think it would add to the safety of the house if that would be allowed. . . . It would not be worth it. I would rather sell things instead." She was, however, pleased to hear that a stoker was living in her bedroom, as he could provide coal. And she did her best to make constructive suggestions: "Do people in Germany hold rabbits, which saved France from hunger?" she inquired of Walter. "All this could easily be done in the garden. Hens also, if people would take the trouble."

Hildegard urged Walter to find out what had become of relatives during the war, as well as neighbors in Potsdam. Her letters reflected a curious ignorance about what had become of the old neighborhood in Potsdam. She ticked off the names of old friends for Walter to contact as if they had remained suspended in the middle of whatever activity she had last seen them engaged in. None of the Jewish neighbors remained, of course. The next-door neighbors had long since left, their house transformed to a military district headquarters; down the street had been a Nazi Youth training center.

When Hildegard left Germany in 1939, she had done so in some haste, leaving behind about 1 million reichsmarks in cash and stocks. She had a good accounting of it in her head, but had neglected to take any bank statements with her. Curiously, the fate and accessibility of her fortune didn't seem to concern her much. "Money does not mean much more to me, since there is nobody who understands as well to spend it as father did, and I do not believe that capitalism is going to last very much longer," she wrote to Walter in early 1946. "My children will have to look out for themselves, which they are doing; if I can leave them something, so much the better. But of course we have to do everything to try keeping the fortune."

It was her son Henry who dealt with the question of Hildegard's remaining assets. Henry corresponded regularly with Herr Guenther, his father's lawyer, who was in the best position to save what was left of Hildegard's holdings. Henry reminded the lawyer of Merck, Finck's promise in 1938, that Paul would receive 500,000 reichsmarks should he be forced to leave the company for political reasons. The payment, of course, had not been made and now Henry and the lawyer were considering pressing a claim through the State Department. Moreover, Henry reported to the lawyer, shortly after Paul's death, following what Hildegard described as an "ultimatum" of sorts, Hildegard had written a letter stating that Merck, Finck had played no role in inciting her husband's suicide. Eventually, Merck, Finck did add 700,000 marks to Hildegard's holdings.

Though relatively unconcerned with bank accounts, Hildegard had an ongoing preoccupation with what had become of the house and everything in it. Before her departure, convinced that she would be returning, she had taken relatively few precautions with the valuables in the house. She had put the silver in a vault at Merck, Finck, and deposited Paul's cherished collection of Fredericiana with the family lawyer in Munich. She had also deposited the Fontane diaries, along with jewels and important documents, in a vault at the Deutsche Bank in Berlin. The small statue she had taken to give to Christel she later decided to keep, as it was now her sole memento from the house.

Just after the war, when a number of conflicting accounts of the villa's fate had filtered through to Walter, he had passed them on to his mother. At first they believed all the contents of the house were missing or destroyed. In her letters to Walter, she described in meticulous detail some of the pieces whose loss she especially mourned: a silver breadbasket; a silver tray with sugar and milk jars; a favorite tea cozy; a statue of Hercules; the horse hair mattresses. And she wanted to know what might have become of her brother Walter's many paintings.

Another topic of obsessive discussion in Hildegard's letters was Paul's extensive library, with its thirty thousand volumes, some of them priceless. In late 1945, Walter wrote to Hildegard that the library was safe, thanks to the efforts of an old friend of Paul's, who had heard that the Russians intended to remove the entire contents of the library and had preempted them by arriving one day with trucks and hauling most of the volumes into the safe custody of the Potsdam Museum. The Fontane diaries, however, appeared to be missing.

Hildegard's attitude toward the private library had always been ambivalent. "The collection, with exception of the historic part, was lovely to look at, but no use otherwise, as nobody wanted to touch them for fear to damage them, and the Gothic script was so hard to read that I always bought an [inexpensive paperback] edition of whatever I wanted to read in that line." Nonetheless, she welcomed the news that the library had been saved. From her command post in California Hildegard wrote Walter that the books taken to the museum must have *ex libris* labels affixed to them with "Paul Wallich" printed on them, and the labels were to appear exactly as the ones Paul had in many of his books. She also wanted the books locked up. She asked Walter to look into recovering the Fredericiana from Munich.

Walter continued to seek permission to visit the house, but each attempt failed. From what he could gather, the house was badly in need of repair. The roof needed replacing and the plumbing needed repairs, as did the central heating system. To pay for these repairs, with his mother's permission Walter sold one of the fur coats retrieved by Mamsell, one with a particularly valuable skunk lining. "It seems strange that repairing of the roof should be cheaper than a fur," Hildegard remarked in one letter.

Finally, in 1946, Walter was able to see the family villa at close quarters. He traveled on an officially sanctioned sightseeing tour to Potsdam. After crossing the Glienicke Bridge, the tour van drove slowly past the house. It looked well preserved except for missing windows, which had been replaced by boards. The center of Potsdam struck Walter as even more desolate than Berlin. It was a complete heap of rubble. Potsdam had gone through most of the war unscathed, and it wasn't until April 14, 1945, just weeks before German capitulation, that Potsdam suffered heavy bombing. While sparing the ornate grounds of Sanssouci, Frederick the Great's eighteenth-century rococo castle, bombers had drawn a bead on the inner city—the city palace, landmark churches, and the city hall were all badly damaged. Those buildings that sustained the least damage would later stand for years as partial ruins, then razed one by one to make way for buildings the Communists deemed more suitable for the period: a large and unattractive hotel, and a block of spartan buildings for shops and services. There had been no attempt to clear the debris, and the canal stank of corpses and putrefaction. The trip included a stop at Sanssouci. The building itself was undamaged and the only things removed, their tour guide told the group, were the library and the washing and shaving equipment of Voltaire.

The same year, Mamsell received notice that the entire house was to be requisitioned for the Russian army, and that she had forty-eight hours in which to make arrangements to remove what things she could. Mamsell informed Walter, and added that she planned to continue living in the house whatever happened. Walter found a relative with access to a truck to move what he considered the most important items. The payment: 1,600 cigarettes from America. A day later, four vanloads of furniture and pictures arrived at the British forces radio building. Much of the furniture was damaged and several of the pictures had bayonet cuts through them. It seemed only a fraction of the furniture Walter remembered: a Dutch cupboard from the downstairs hall, a chest of drawers from the salon, Paul's bed chair, and a favorite chair of Paul's with a carving of hammer-and-tongs on the back. The delivery included many minor things, such as plates that hung on the walls of the veranda, the compass from the *Lahn,* and countless odds and ends. The china, too, had survived the war unscathed, complete with salt cellars, mustard pots, sauce vessels and ragout shells.

Many of the family's belongings remained, in fact, in the house at Potsdam, including many of the things, as Walter would discover, most prized by his mother. In the meantime, he arranged to store in Berlin what had been retrieved.

Rather than simplifying matters, the saving of the household belongings became a tremendous onus. It was unclear just what the family should do with all the furniture. Everyone was either living in an apartment or, as in Walter's case, without permanent living quarters at all. Now fifty-nine years old, Hildegard was tired. "I cannot imagine myself to take a house or even a small apartment," she wrote Walter. "I lack energy and courage for that. . . . I hate furnished rooms, but they are better than all what has to be accomplished in a house of one's own, without any help. . . . There does not seem to be very much hope of continuing much of the family tradition as far as furniture etc. is concerned, though we were so concerned about it. . . . But we must wait and see, maybe Henry wants to get married some day."

In 1947, her fear of cockroaches and silverfish notwithstanding, Hildegard did decide to move to New York, in part to be close to Henry and in part to have a place to receive the household goods from Berlin. Not that she had relented and planned now to establish a new household. She told Walter that age was taking its toll; the relatively small task of wrapping parcels and taking them to the post office she found enervating. "What would happen if I had to attend to an apartment all alone with cooking, laundering and the rest of it?" she lamented.

That same year, Hildegard traveled to Argentina for an extended visit with Christel and her family. While there, with plenty of time on her hands, she apparently began to brood over the Potsdam property. In September she wrote to Walter to discuss the topic of selling the house and buying another one right away in the Western zone. "It seems to be the only solution for Potsdam," she wrote, "as nothing really valuable such as jewelry could be gotten for the little money the house would bring."

By now, Walter had sold nearly all the furs to pay for expenses on the house. Hildegard suggested he sell the compass from the *Lahn* and other odds and ends.

Around the same time, Mamsell wrote to Hildegard telling her the Russians had barred her from the house. There were still quite a few things that should be removed, she wrote. But Hildegard trusted none of her relatives or friends in Berlin to safeguard her possessions, particularly the antiques. "They're the last valuables I have and I wouldn't want to lose them too," she told Walter.

It took two more years to arrange for the shipping of all the household goods—those remaining in the house and those in storage in Berlin—to New York. It wasn't until 1948 that Walter began sending crates weighing a total of nearly three tons to New York by American Express. The much fretted over Frederticiana collection, recovered from its safe haven in Munich, was sent as well.

Although she continued to doubt that Germany would remain divided for very long, Hildegard came to accept the inaccessibility of the house. She suggested to Walter that he explore the possibility of selling it. "Our other valuables wouldn't bring us nearly as much as the house would," she wrote. "But would the Russians allow it? Probably not."

Hildegard's time spent recovering the family valuables after the war may have been a distraction from the painful subject of Paul's death. She seldom spoke of his suicide, or of him much at all. In her letters she made passing references to being exhausted by the ordeal, and wanting to put it behind her. When she did talk of him it was with a tendency to romanticize. She rejected Germany after the war, she wrote to Walter, as she felt that the Germany she had been loyal to was dead, "not because it's been destroyed but because of what the people have turned into."

3: MAMA KEMPA

The Early Years of the Kindergarten

In the spring of 1951, Helga Kempa, a twenty-nine-year-old Kindergarten teacher, was looking for a job and a place to live when she
saw a newspaper advertisement for teachers at Kindergartens
throughout Potsdam. When she went to the town hall to see what
was available, she was given a list of facilities, and there was one
that caught her eye: a Kinderwochenheim run by the Free German
Labor Union, the union for state employees, was seeking a director.

Within minutes of arriving at the house, she knew she wanted to
work there. First, there was the setting: the property was on the
bank of the Havel River, at the foot of the Glienicke Bridge, and surrounded by trees. And the house itself was discreetly grand. With
the exception of some superficial damage left over from the war,
and incipient signs of neglect, the house was entirely intact, spared
the punishment of heavy bombing that many buildings in and

around Berlin had suffered. Although she did not have a trained eye when it came to architecture, Helga Kempa sensed there was something extraordinary about the house. She could tell that it was designed to fit the landscape, and although it was certainly not one of the biggest houses in that corner of Potsdam, she was struck by its incomparable stateliness.

To the right of the house was a tennis court, grown over with weeds and grass after years of disuse. The large garden behind the tennis court, scattered with various fruit trees, was also a jungle of weeds. To the right of the tennis court was a small, two-story carriage house built in the style of a Swiss chalet. The second story of the chalet appeared to be an apartment for servants. Directly in front of the villa on the bank stood another, very small house. She wondered if anyone was living there.

She got no response when she knocked on the front door, so she rang a small bell she found on a wrought-iron gate that had a "W" crafted into the ironwork. A woman came to the gate and showed her in through a back door. The first thing she saw after stepping through a back hallway was an elegant wide staircase, the steps lacquered white, with delicate metal bars in place for holding down a carpet. As she ascended the stairs, above her she saw golden stars plastered to the ceiling, which was painted a heavenly blue. She turned around to face a delicate figurine—a Madonna tucked into a small niche above the stairs. The rooms on the second floor were of a restrained splendor that Helga Kempa had never seen before. The most impressive was the main room: its high ceilings and ornate fireplace suggested a past of privilege and wealth, which the new Communist regime was doing its best to discard. The room now served as the day room and dining area for dozens of children.

Just as she was beginning to wonder where her quarters would be, she climbed a small spiral staircase to the third floor and found, tucked beneath the roof, an apartment. This, she assumed, would be hers if she took the job. It had three good-sized rooms, a kitchen, and a bath. She went out to the terrace, climbed a metal ladder to a smaller tower at the very top, and stood there, taking in the regal views across the river.

Kinderwochenheim, translated, means "weekly home for children." An alternative to traditional Kindergartens, where children could spend the entire week, the concept of a Kinderwochenheim was not widely known in West Germany; nor was it well understood. There weren't many Kinderwochenheims in the German Democratic Republic. But for as long as there were Kindergartens in East Germany there were also Kinderwochenheims. At their inception after the war, they were intended to serve the needs of women with irregular work hours, particularly those working a night shift. Many Kinderwochenheims were attached to factories. After parents deposited their children there on Monday morning they could see them during the week but they did not retrieve them until Friday afternoon or Saturday morning. It was a social arrangement that made a great deal of sense. In erecting such institutions, the state gave top priority to the socialist work ethic while reinforcing its commitment to universal child care. Children of single mothers who were completing their studies also attended such child-care homes. And when parents divorced, depending on the circumstances, social workers occasionally suggested the children be placed in a Kinderwochenheim.

As it happened, this Kinderwochenheim had been in operation for just a few months when Helga Kempa arrived. Two directors had already left, she was told, because they were unable to control all the children. This news barely fazed the new applicant. A hardy woman with plain, dark features, Helga Kempa knew true hardship. Her husband had died at the Russian front and when the war ended she and her parents joined the great treks of millions of Germans forced out of East Prussia and Pomerania. During the journey, she bore a child who died shortly after birth. When she arrived in Potsdam, she moved into a room she shared with four other family members. She became the only working member of her family, as her father was barred from teaching in the process of denazification (nearly 75 percent of teachers in wartime Germany had belonged to the Nazi Party), and for a time she supported them all. No wonder, then, that the apartment on the third floor of the villa at the bridge was more than Helga's most indulgent dreams had allowed. When offered the job, she agreed at once to take it. She would remain there for thirty years.

Neighbors who had stayed through the war told her a little bit about the history of the house. She heard that it had belonged to a Jewish banker and his family, but no one seemed to know what had become of them. She saw no trace of the family members, though signs of their wealth lingered. The walls were paneled in teak; elaborate parquet covered the floors in all the formal rooms upstairs; the ceilings were of molded plaster. The distinctive blue and white patterns of Delft tile lined the walls of the loggia and a small closet in the upstairs hallway. There had been a large library in one of the main rooms upstairs, where a grand piano had once stood. But that was all gone, and now the room was outfitted with a collection of small beds.

Mama Kempa heard that Russian soldiers had taken over the house shortly after the war. When the Free German Labor Union moved its administrative offices there in 1950, shortly after the Russians left, the place was filthy and had to be deloused. And the house still bore the scars of the war. Through the 1960s, its facade would remain pockmarked from the artillery fire during the last days of the war.

Although the largely residential area surrounding the house was not a direct target for bombs, the artillery fire nearby had killed an officer, a Captain Hermann, on the grounds of the house, and his chest of personal effects still stood on the third floor. Helga Kempa emptied the chest, painted it, and used it for years, first to store her own linens, then to store her daughter's toys.

The house at the Glienicke Bridge wasn't earmarked from the start as a Kinderwochenheim, or even as a child-care facility. Like hundreds of other villas abandoned during the war and put to public use, it evolved into one. When Helga Kempa arrived, there were about a dozen union employees in the house, occupying rooms on the ground floor. Because several of the women who worked there needed a place to put their children for the day, the rest of the house was turned into a day-care center. Gradually word spread that the state union was running a Kindergarten upstairs from its offices at the Glienicke Bridge, and more parents began depositing their children there.

As it turned out, the house made a spacious and convenient child-care facility. Many of the union employees were women, most of them widows who needed to find a place to put their children for the day or even the entire week, picking them up on Saturday afternoons. When Helga Kempa arrived, there were one hundred children, ranging in age from eighteen months to sixteen years; twenty of them stayed for the week. The entire first floor was reserved for the union employees and the rest was given over to the Kinderwochenheim. Everyone got their food from the big downstairs kitchen. The large room with the fireplace on the second floor was transformed into a dining room, holding twenty-five tables. Helga Kempa made her office in what she assumed had been one of the family's bedrooms.

Helga Kempa wasted no time making the apartment her own, filling it with her own and sundry possessions, many of which she had carried with her from East Prussia. She relished the privacy and the view. From her windows she could see the Glienicke Castle across the river to the north, and the Babelsberg Castle to the east. The backyard was filled with immense old trees. A weeping willow, an old oak and a beautiful red beech rambled across the yard, shading the house and grounds.

The grandeur of the house came out most noticeably in the loggia, a second-story breezeway with freestanding pillars. At one time an open-air room, the loggia now had one large window front. But the original vertically sliding window had been destroyed during the war, and replaced with unmovable glass. The wood around the frame had rotted from all the rain and bad weather. In her first years there Helga Kempa wanted to restore the entire loggia but, as was so often the case in East Germany, she had difficulty finding the proper materials and the loggia began to descend into amiable wreckage.

Helga Kempa took to the children and they took to her. It was a daunting job, but she had a great deal of patience, and an instinct for what children would respond to. She made an effort to know each child. They loved her, and called her Mama Kempa. Before long she was known throughout Potsdam as Mama Kempa, the woman who ran the Kinderwochenheim in the big house next to the Glienicke Bridge. Her entire life revolved around it.

A year or so after arriving, she fell in love with one of the union employees. They married and he moved into the upstairs apartment. A few years later they had a daughter. From her first day at the house, Mama Kempa's life was so idyllic that what was happening in the outside world, at least during her first few years there, escaped her notice.

Managing a hundred children wasn't easy. There was constant crying and screaming and running, and someone from the union downstairs frequently climbed the stairs to ask them all to quiet down. These requests incensed Mama Kempa, who had come to see her Kindergarten as the most important function of the house. "We can't tie them up," came her brusque response. "Either get thicker carpets for us or you'll have to move out."

The union did eventually move out, and the children laid claim to the rest of the house. Mama Kempa moved the bedrooms to the ground floor.

Gradually, the day children moved out and the place was devoted entirely to boarding children for the week. Gradually, too, with the exception of Mama Kempa's sanctuary on the third floor, the entire house became a place for children.

In inclement weather the house was spacious enough for the children to stay indoors for long stretches without bringing on foul moods. And in the spring and summer the garden became a children's paradise. During those warm months the children stayed outside in the huge backyard most of the time. They helped the teachers harvest vegetables and fruit. They stewed apples and pears and berries by the potful, pickled beans and cucumbers, and canned it all in huge five-liter jars. Mama Kempa saw to it that the children stayed well fed. The big kitchen downstairs was well suited to cooking in large quantities, and the meals kept two full-time cooks busy. There was always something on the stove or in the oven, and the children came to equate the kitchen with a kind of comfort that few of them had at home.

Mama Kempa belonged to the Communist Party, but only, she claimed, because after the war she was left with no choice. If she wanted to work, she said, she was required to join. Germans have an expression for this: "howling with the wolves." As she described it many years later, Mama Kempa had two sides. For years, she howled with the wolves but remained unhappy with and in the system. In her apartment upstairs, she listened to RIAS, the American-sector radio station, with the volume turned low so that no one downstairs could hear.

Josef Stalin, or rather his likeness, permeated the German Democratic Republic in its early years. The street that ran past the Kindergarten toward the Glienicke Bridge was renamed from Berlinerstrasse to Stalinallee. Ceremonial occasions for naming streets and squares after the Soviet leader, or for the erection of huge statues and busts in his likeness—some of them several stories high—were a staple of East Germany in its postwar era. When it came to infusing schoolchildren with a sense of the man behind the ideology, an image of Stalin was always close at hand. As an East German poet who was awarded the Stalin Peace Prize once put it, "Stalin is the best friend of my people." So overwhelming was the ubiquity of Soviet-style Communism that the East German leaders were overshadowed, their role so diminished that in many of the propaganda films they did little more than lead the masses in calisthenics.

On the day that Stalin died in 1953, Mama Kempa got word to call together the children and explain the tragic loss. As instructed, she told them that Stalin's heart had stopped beating, but the great leader was immortal, that his spirit would live on through this generation of children. She then led an impromptu memorial service. The teachers and children gathered in the large main room upstairs, and Mama Kempa said a few grave words of eulogy, followed by a minute of total silence. She looked up for an instant, just long enough for the bookkeeper to catch her eye and wink. It was all she could do not to laugh. She excused herself and left the room.

At other times, when she espoused a Communist line during a meeting, the other teachers took her to task. "They would say, 'What you said you don't even believe yourself.' I'd look at them, and we'd laugh and move on to another topic."

It was a fairy tale that prompted Mama Kempa's most courageous act of political defiance. In the early days of the German Democratic Republic, when the aim of education was to show children the virtues of the socialist world, fairy tales had no place. Operating under the slogan "we do not dream, we deal with reality," the GDR frowned on tales of princesses and kissed frogs in favor of socialist realism—stories that depicted workers at work.

In the Hitler era, the fairy tales of the Brothers Grimm had enjoyed a dubious distinction. The Nazis used them to further their cause, giving the tales a nationalistic and often anti-Semitic interpretation. "Like religion, the fairy tales are indispensable for the German human being in order to lead a brave, fertile and healthy life," wrote Rudolf Viergutz in a 1942 book about fairy tales. In language characteristic of national socialism, Viergutz called fairy tales "a true mirror of our German soul." After the war, as part of the effort to purge Germany of Nazi propaganda, the occupying powers ordered Grimm storybooks withdrawn from circulation in some cities.

In 1954, word got around that children were being taught fairy tales at the Kindergarten at the Glienicke Bridge. Mama Kempa was called in to the office of the director of education. But instead of fear she felt rage. She considered German fairy tales to be part of the nation's cultural heritage. They were stories that showed both the good and bad of a people. She told the stories in their full, un-bowdlerized form, complete with the violence and brutality contained in the original tales collected by the Brothers Grimm. Helga Kempa believed that the fairy tales fulfilled a child's need for fantasy, particularly in a place now so entombed in reality. And she refused to be party to the systematic snuffing out of the imagination. "I asked him whether he had heard fairy tales as a child," she recalled. "I said, 'I hope you had a mother or grandmother who told you fairy tales. And when they told you the stories, didn't you enjoy it?' He became uneasy, and began to squirm. I nearly started to cry." For days afterward, she couldn't sleep for fear that the authorities would come to the house to arrest her because of her intransigence in the matter. But nothing happened as a result of the meeting. She continued to tell fairy tales to the children.

The Wall Goes Up

Mama Kempa thought about her life in the house in terms of before the Berlin Wall and afterward, in terms of relative freedom and sudden imprisonment. Before the Wall went up the house was an idyllic setting for everyone. Through the 1950s the teachers were free to come and go. In summer there were frequent trips across the bridge to swim and picnic and hike around the immaculate grounds of the Glienicke Castle. A clutch of East German border guards and Russian soldiers were stationed at the bridge, and the teachers knew them all. So there was seldom a problem when they crossed over, sometimes wearing just their bathing suits. The more robust teachers occasionally even swam the 150 yards across the water and back again.

Nonetheless, Mama Kempa began scheming to leave. In the spring of 1961, she and her husband spent months in furtive preparation, sending their belongings piecemeal over the border to relatives in West Berlin. She said nothing to the teachers and hoped in turn that nothing would arouse their suspicion. She sent all of her good porcelain and linens, but to preserve appearances she kept her glass-front cupboards stocked with dishes of lesser quality. But just when their preparations were close to complete her husband lost his nerve. They abandoned the plan, at least temporarily. A few weeks later a trio of men—she assumed they were from the Stasi, the omnipresent East German intelligence agency—came to call at the house and asked to speak to Helga Kempa. They questioned her for several hours about what they suspected were her plans to leave. She denied everything, and pointed to her full cupboards, her commitment to her job, her membership in the party. Finally satisfied, they left.

Of course the Kempas had no idea that the border would be sealed so tightly in the course of one weekend, and that after that it would be too late. No one had guessed the lengths to which the East German regime would go to keep its citizens from leaving.

The construction began after midnight on Sunday, August 13, 1961. By midmorning, a barbed-wire barrier had been installed across Berlin. The usual Sunday peace at the Glienicke Bridge was broken by a frenzy of construction work. From her third-floor aerie Mama Kempa watched. Armed soldiers arrived in trucks and unloaded bales of wire, then unfurled it along the bank. She was most struck by the menacing silence with which they went about their task. It would take several weeks for Mama Kempa, like most East Germans, to grasp the permanence of the barrier. It didn't occur to her to do what others throughout East Berlin were doing: finding a weak spot in the wire and simply leaving. Border guards did not yet have orders to shoot escapees. Somehow, she thought, nothing could be quite as easy as simply walking away.

The teachers arrived at work on Monday to discover that everything had changed. There wasn't a concrete wall yet. That wouldn't go up for another twenty years, after escape attempts over the bridge and across the river made it necessary to fortify the area even more. But at the water's edge, one hundred feet from the front door, a tall and forbidding fence of dense mesh had materialized overnight. The area around the bridge was reinforced with more guards and gates, and high-powered lights were installed. In the months following the building of the Wall, more fencing was planted in the middle of the river, where the border actually fell. To comically domestic effect, two small and tidy guard houses were constructed on either side of the East German end of the bridge. The perfect finishing touch would have been a pair of flower boxes.

In the months leading up to the building of the Berlin Wall, relations between East and West had become increasingly strained, principally because the East was hemorrhaging people. In January of 1961 alone, ten thousand left; in July, a month before the Wall went up, thirty thousand left. West German, American, French and

British authorities sensed that East Germany, at the behest of the Kremlin, was planning a restrictive measure. But the unraveling of thousands of bales of barbed wire throughout the city in the dead of night was something few people knew about in advance. Khrushchev had given the final order at the urging of East German Communist leader Walter Ulbricht. Erich Honecker, then a young Ulbricht protégé and member of the party's central committee, had executed the order masterfully, with all the stealth the project required. Just the night before, unsuspecting East Germans had returned from a Saturday evening in West Berlin, spent at the movies, at the theater or visiting relatives. By midday Sunday a barbed-wire barrier stretched for miles along the Berlin border, while East and West Germans stood on either side and watched in horror and bafflement.

After the Wall was built, the area surrounding the house became completely still. The Glienicke Bridge was to become one of the most sensitive border crossings, its use restricted to diplomats and spies. Though Americans were more familiar with Checkpoint Charlie, the small guard house at the Berlin divide, the Glienicke Bridge's fame grew as it became the designated spot for exchanging captured spies between the Eastern Bloc and the Western world. The "Spy Bridge" became one of the Cold War's most enduring symbols. And there could hardly have been a more apt icon. Approached from either side, the span rose dramatically and suddenly, as if out of nowhere. West Berliners driving south encountered it after a long stretch of piney woods; what had been the most widely used link to Potsdam became a terminus.

An older generation of Potsdamers had seen the bridge as little more than a crossing into Berlin. To their children the bridge was something they knew of but never saw, as no one was allowed within five hundred feet of the area surrounding it without a special pass. The high-intensity lights kept the area as bright as day throughout the night. To block out the light, Mama Kempa installed black shades in the rooms where the children slept. She and her husband sat many weekend afternoons looking across the river into freedom, watching the patrol boats search for movement anywhere near the death strip, and ruing their aborted effort at leaving when there was still a chance.

For Mama Kempa the creation of two Germanys was something she would never recover from. "There were two souls in my breast:

a laughing one for the children and a crying one for my own life," she recalled years later. "We were an open jail, the whole GDR was an open jail. We were walled in in a nation that was growing more and more red."

Those who had left East Germany before the Wall went up were among the country's most educated and skilled. "We all knew where the ship was headed," Mama Kempa said. "To a bland equality. We were all looking at Russia, and we saw that Germany would be the way that Russia was under Stalin." But quasi-imprisonment wasn't the way that the East German regime liked to think of its walled-in nation.

As the Communist regime portrayed things, Germany had been cleaved by the Western enemies. The West had forced the division and now East Germany must protect its citizens. It was the fascists in the West who made war; the Wall was necessary to maintain peace. The Wall, whose official designation was *antifaschistischer Schutzwall,* or anti-fascist protection wall, was a shield against imperialist influences, its aim to prevent West Germans from sneaking in and spreading their invidious politics.

Restrictions grew so tight after the Wall went up that anyone who bought a toy raft was immediately suspected of planning an escape across the river. At the Kindergarten, all garden ladders had to be locked away at night so they couldn't be used as an escape aid. The universe was shrinking for all East Germans and the sense of imprisonment was particularly powerful at the Kindergarten. Then, as if to put one last nasty touch on the work of building the Wall, one morning in the mid-1960s a brigade of bricklayers arrived at the house and announced that they had been sent by local authorities to brick in the loggia in order to make the space habitable in the winter. Perhaps, too, they intended to limit the loggia's usefulness as a lookout.

Mama Kempa was outraged, and she tried her best to stop them.

"You're devils!" she cried. "This is a cultural disgrace."

They looked bewildered, and asked her what she meant.

"Just look at this whole house. It belonged to a Jewish family. What if they should ever return here, or sit in a boat on the river and see what's happened to it?"

The workers ignored her and set about their task. Mama Kempa decided not to argue any further. By the end of the day the open and airy loggia had been transformed into a dark box of a space, the two columns encased in red brick and transformed to pilasters. From the outside, the house had now lost all vestiges of its beauty. It looked wretched, even a little deranged.

In the 1970s Mama Kempa was told that the Kinderwochenheim was now required to feed a hot meal each day to the soldiers at the bridge. They would eat whatever the children ate. Every day at noon one of the soldiers arrived to pick up trays of hot food, occasionally stopping to chat with the cooks in the kitchen. An hour later he returned bearing the empty trays.

Mama Kempa encouraged the children to sing their songs— paeans to the socialist state—to the men at the bridge, and to take them gifts and flowers. At Christmastime every year, one of the guards, a middle-aged, roly-poly man named Herr Ostermann, came to the house dressed as Santa Claus. But usually it was all business.

The Building of the Socialist Personality

From the time the German Democratic Republic was voted into existence with single-slate elections in 1949, the task of caring for and educating children in East Germany was given to the state. Because they perpetuated the monopoly of the ruling classes, all private schools were abolished, all institutions were financed by the state, and every child's right to an education was established by the East German constitution.

Little was left to chance. East German educational experts asserted, logically enough, that the development of a human mind and personality is a lifelong process, and that the strongest foundations were laid in childhood. Moreover, the state held firmly to the belief that a child's education should be provided outside of the home from an early age. Therefore, children in East Germany were guaranteed an education that started at the earliest level.

The woman who did not work outside the home was a rare phenomenon. In the 1950s, women were placed under tremendous pressure to join the workforce, despite a relative dearth of childcare facilities. Women weren't just encouraged to work, but as participants in the collective endeavor of socialism, they were expected to do so. They worked in factories and stores, on collective farms and in schools. Even mothers with newborns were expected to work, and it wasn't uncommon for babies to remain in hospitals by themselves for weeks after their birth so that their mothers could return to work.

In the 1960s, the number of women in the workforce increased dramatically, but after the introduction of the birth-control pill, birthrates declined. To motivate young women to have children, in the 1970s the state instituted generous paid maternity leave policies. When a woman in East Germany went on maternity leave, she received her full salary for six months. After that, she received a percentage of her salary, with the amount dependent on the number of children she had.

There were ideological reasons for this as well. The state wanted to have children under its control from an early age so as to waste no time in educating them. In doing so, the state was more or less guaranteed the chance of producing an entire generation of dependent thinkers.

The officially declared mission was that it was beneficial for children to spend their days in a group with children their own age, and for them to receive proper and uniform nutrition and hygiene in a stable, predictable environment. Whatever the reasons given, parents often had little choice but to hand their children over to the state's child-care system.

As a result, the East German child-care system grew to be vast. By 1980, nine out of ten children aged three to seven had a place in a Kindergarten. State-provided child care that was nearly tuition-free was a way of life for East German citizens. At three months, children were put for the day in *Kinderkrippen,* facilities where they were cared for until they reached age three. After that, they entered Kindergarten, and stayed there until they entered school at the age of seven.

Margot Honecker, the wife of Erich Honecker, took the post of education minister in East Germany in 1963. (Her husband, ten years later, would become East Germany's leader.) The daughter of Communists who had been persecuted by the Nazis, Frau Honecker was a devout anti-fascist who became a devout young Communist and worked her way up through the ranks of the East German education ministry. As education minister she carried out her duties with an ideological fervor so strong as to appear Stalinist long after the discredited leader was expunged from the national psyche. Her carefully written education text, known as "the plan," was compulsory reading for all teachers. Copies were distributed to everyone, and teachers were expected to memorize its pages.

The obligation of every educator, according to the plan, was to raise children as *sozialistische Persönlichkeiten,* socialist "personalities." Such personalities were, according to the East German political dictionary, devoted to social patriotism, proletarian internationalism, and the protection and defense of the achievements of socialism. Teachers were expected to "build a content-rich, happy life and raise the children from an early age as socialist citizens." So important was this message that when Walter Ulbricht was depicted in propaganda films, he was often gazing over the shoulder of his daughter as she toiled at her homework. Socialism's future lay with East Germany's youth. And a squeaky clean youth it was: one aspect of an East German education was to train children to wash themselves in a prescribed way.

In their innocence, children were being dragged into a uniform system carefully designed by the grown-ups. The socialist education started at age three, in the Kindergartens. Every subject, every facet of the child's day, was to be imbued with socialism. Children were input/output vessels. Teachings on the virtues of socialism were expected to sink in right away, and the children were expected to understand and recite the data that had been fed to them. They were to be taught that music was good for socialism; it brought them closer to their "socialist environment." They were expected to regard such tasks as setting or clearing a table as significant duties for socialist citizens. "Tables don't set themselves," was the message of one early propaganda film that showed somber Kindergartners reverently arranging the mealtime cutlery.

Though playing was considered essential for the well-being of children, it was something to be carefully regulated and monitored. Dolls, miniature vehicles of the National People's Army and toy tractors were to be used in the course of understanding various aspects of a socialist society. Children were encouraged to look at countless pictures of workers working "to protect their socialist homeland," as the text put it, and to incorporate those images into their own drawings. In those pictures, children were told to study workers' facial expressions for signs of such qualities as courage and the willingness to work hard. In particular, they should see the joy the workers took in their jobs. Children were expected to know what their parents did for employment. They should understand that their parents went to work punctually every day and worked very hard, and that the function of everyone—construction workers, farmers, doctors, pharmacists—was to keep a socialist society going.

According to the plan, children were to be shown, by way of visits to war monuments, by hearing stories and seeing pictures and listening to working songs, how bad life was before the formation of East Germany and how courageous and stoic the worker was in his fight for socialism, for freedom, and against oppression and fascism. The children should be taught—through songs and stories, dances and toy figures—about the great accomplishments of people in the Soviet Union and other socialist countries. Teachers were to encourage the children to integrate the principles of socialism into their games, their conversations and their creative work. To assure that the plan was not undermined at home, they were to have the children play a form of show-and-tell surveillance, where, on Mondays, the children reported what had been discussed among the adults over the weekend.

Children were also to be taught that East German women fought for the peace and happiness of the children and that every year on March 8 in the German Democratic Republic International Women's Day was celebrated and women were honored for their work. On this day, children were expected to congratulate not only their own mothers but all women they knew.

Meal times were to be observed with military rigidity. Three meals a day were to be served, with three hours and thirty minutes between them. A midday nap of two hours was mandatory. Twenty to thirty minutes of sport were also required. At least three hours were to be spent outside, at all times of year. The room temperature of group playrooms, closets and bathrooms was to be carefully monitored.

In Frau Honecker's plan, children in Kindergartens were expected to become acquainted with members of the National People's Army. In films aimed at children, a great effort was made to humanize policemen and soldiers. Self-reliance and mutual help were the bywords of the state. Children were told that soldiers were necessary to protect them from the mercenaries in the West until the children were old enough to be soldiers themselves. Children sang songs with lyrics such as this:

When I grow up I'll be in the People's Army too
I'll load the cannons
I'll load the cannons

Sung by a group of golden-haired ten-year-olds in one propaganda film, this song was followed by an explanation from the narrator that the cannons belong to everyone. "We need them so we can protect you and you can grow up in peace," came the avuncular voice-over.

That, at least, was socialist education in theory. Although all had been instructed to teach by the Honecker plan, although the plan carried the weight of a directive from the state, in reality teachers in East Germany seldom adhered to it. At the Kinderwochenheim, the children sang songs of socialism, but only on official holidays. Toys were toys, not instructional tools. When Mama Kempa wrote reports to the education department, she peppered them with socialist pedagogical references, in contrast to the remarkably loose enterprise she ran.

Occasionally, however, it worked to the teachers' advantage to use the plan, particularly in awkward situations. The children at the Kinderwochenheim were told that the uniformed men at the Glienicke Bridge were there for their protection and for the protection of their socialist fatherland. What Mama Kempa and the other teachers didn't tell them was that when they grew older, should they try to escape across the bridge, or over the wall and across the river, these same men had orders to shoot to kill.

Mama Kempa knew firsthand about the order to shoot. Several times she had heard shots late at night, accompanied by shouts and screams. The most harrowing incident came late one summer night in 1975. Mama Kempa had been across the street for a visit to Herr Schmidt. Herr Schmidt was the resident watcher. His small house, just a few dozen feet from the bridge, stood recessed from the street and a bit apart from the other houses. With his binoculars he kept an unofficial watch over his neighbors' comings and goings.

When the Wall went up, a dozen or so houses, including the Kindergarten, had the misfortune of standing within the restricted border zone. This meant that the entire area was sealed off from the outside world. It was as forbidding as it looked. A crossing barrier in the street stopped all traffic. A sign with large block lettering warned pedestrians not to step beyond it. The heavy meshed wire fence that would later be replaced by a concrete wall was visible from a hundred yards away. A half dozen armed soldiers patrolled the area.

Several residents of the area had moved away, or had left during the war and never returned. Among those who had left were the Kampffmeyers, wealthy Jews who had fled the Nazis. The Villa Kampffmeyer, more conspicuously lavish than any other house, including the house at the bridge, stood just a few feet back from the bank on the other side of the street from the Kindergarten. The villa was now in the state's hands and as the years passed, trees on the expansive Kampffmeyer property disappeared and gray buildings resembling army barracks, cigar-shaped and slung low to the ground, took their place. It was known throughout the neighborhood that the Kampffmeyer property served as some kind of outpost for the state security police, or Stasi, in an intelligence function that was not entirely clear to the other residents in the area. Many of the houses in the restricted area were now occupied by high-ranking party members.

The people who lived within the border zone held to their own system. Those who chose to continue living there after the Wall went up were aware that they resided in one of their nation's most politically sensitive corners. That they should choose to remain in a no-man's-land surrounded by search lights, concertina wire, intentionally underfed guard dogs and watchtowers was an indication of how few better choices there were. Some chose to remain because that's where their homes were. Many had nowhere else to go. As one of the teachers put it, the worst thing about living in the border zone was that you grew used to it.

As with any other neighborhood, this one drew together with a sense of shared place. They formed their own community. They knew one another and often they knew one another's business. They could come and go as they pleased, but for outsiders to enter the area meant obtaining permission weeks in advance. Municipal upkeep all but ended in this neglected corner of Potsdam. Streets and sidewalks were left to crack and crumble, and buildings administered by the city received scant attention.

Mama Kempa's neighbor Herr Schmidt made certain that everyone knew of his connection to Erich Honecker. A man obsessed with the anti-fascist cause and the peripheral role he had played in it, Herr Schmidt could go on at some length about Brandenburg jail, where he had been imprisoned during the war for his anti-fascist activities. Honecker had been imprisoned there as well, and as Herr Schmidt told the story, the two were practically blood brothers. No one doubted that Herr Schmidt was a party member, and he and his wife always seemed to know everyone's business. But partly out of loneliness and partly because she thrived on gossip, Mama Kempa socialized with them anyway. One warm evening in high summer, when daylight in Potsdam lingers until 10 P.M., she walked across the street for a visit. The three sat on the Schmidts' open second-story porch, overlooking the barbed wire and the water beyond.

As she was leaving, shortly before midnight, she heard a commotion at the bridge—the sound of footsteps, then shouts of "Halt!" She knew someone was attempting to escape. She tried to cross the street at the foot of the bridge but a guard stopped her and told her to go a different way. Her only option was to retreat a few yards down the street and cross from there. When she got to within a few feet of the house, she saw a man lying on the street, his head facedown on the curb. Guards were bludgeoning him and he was pleading with them to stop. The warm summer air channeled his cries across the river, and a group of young people—they sounded like teenagers—taking a late night swim on the western side heard him. "Let him go! Give him his freedom!" came faceless shouts from the other world across the dark water.

Mama Kempa was horrified. As soon as she got back to the house, she telephoned the Schmidts. They must have heard the man's cries. "You must come over!" she told Herr Schmidt. "They're beating someone!"

"I hear it," he replied curtly. "He tried to cross the border. They should kill him." And he hung up.

There were other, equally harrowing incidents as well. If careless pedestrians ventured one step beyond the crossing barrier that marked the official border zone, guards arrested them and made them lean against the wall of the Kinderwochenheim that faced the border, their arms extended over their heads. Sometimes they were made to stand that way for hours. Occasionally entire families were forced to do this. "One day in 1967 or 1968 we saw a couple and their two children get arrested for trying to escape," Mama Kempa recalled. "We saw soldiers running everywhere. The soldiers were telling them to stop, that they would shoot. An officer who knew his children wouldn't be shot had taken them with him on his escape attempt. The entire family was put up against the wall of the house with their hands high. The soldiers' weapons were drawn. They had to stand this way for several hours. Then they were taken away, the parents in one jeep and the two children in another."

Unlike the earlier incident, this one had occurred in the middle of a weekday. When the children asked what was happening, the teachers were at a loss. It was times such as these that called for an explanation straight from the pages of Margot Honecker's education plan. They should have told the children of the family's faithlessness to the state, and perhaps seized the opportunity to expound on the menace across the border. After all, that's what they had done when it came to explaining the presence of the border guards. But this time they were at a loss. They said they didn't know why the people were standing there.

All Her Children

Through the years the house adapted itself to its function in a slow metamorphosis. Every year brought changes that made the house seem less like a villa and more like a place for children. Priceless oil paintings had long since been replaced by the children's drawings. A kitchen that once produced stuffed quail now served rice pudding. At once dilapidated and wholly functional, the house was losing grandeur but gaining soul.

Still, the house was showing signs of basic neglect. It contracted dozens of maladies. The luxurious parquet floors in most of the rooms had to be replaced with a more workmanlike wood because of dry rot that had spread throughout the woodwork from a chronically leaking roof and windows. Even with the best intentions, Mama Kempa was powerless to take care of the house as she might have wanted. She stood by helplessly as the stucco facade slowly chipped away. Several times she succeeded in getting the education department to schedule the facade for reconstruction but each time the work was delayed indefinitely because there was no scaffolding available.

Because it was located in the border zone, which made regular inspections more burdensome, the Kindergarten at the bridge was spared much of the scrutiny that other Kindergartens had to undergo. Ironically, this allowed Mama Kempa to run a looser ship than Kindergarten directors outside the border area. She allowed her staff to keep flexible work hours, to teach the children their favorite songs and tell them their favorite stories.

Mama Kempa took care of the guards at the bridge, too, most of whom were young men. If they needed an aspirin for a toothache, or a hot cup of coffee, they knocked at the door of the house. Ostermann, the guard who played Santa Claus, had stomach problems, and Mama Kempa ministered to him as she would to one of the children. When the night shift arrived at midnight, she occasionally gave them tea. "They were kids. They could all have been my children," she recalled. "You had the feeling they would rather have thrown away their weapons and gone over the bridge."

The guards also came to call her Mama Kempa. Every New Year's Eve, she put out coffee, Christmas stollen and oranges in the foyer facing Berliner Strasse, and through the evening soldiers wandered over to the house to help themselves to the offerings. Occasionally, when one of them had a birthday, Mama Kempa emptied a beer bottle and filled it with cognac.

In return for these small comforts, the guards displayed a soft side. When they cleared the death strip to secure the border and build runs for the German shepherds they used as watchdogs, the guards gathered whatever flowers they found growing wild in the sandy soil and left them at the door of the Kindergarten.

Mama Kempa's friends envied her living in a huge house directly on the water. But they didn't envy her the restrictive life. If they wanted to visit they had to submit an application five weeks in advance of the intended visit. Mama Kempa didn't want to have to do that. So the most significant gift that the guards extended to Mama Kempa was the nod and wink when she told them she was expecting company. Their only proviso was that the guests be gone before midnight. If 4 P.M. was a bad time because, say, they were anticipating an inspection, they told Mama Kempa to receive her visitors an hour or two later. When the time came for the guests to leave, Mama Kempa or her husband would go outside, look around, and give a sign that it was safe to go. She had the best relationship with Ostermann, who was posted most of the time in the small house on the bridge. He was the one she approached most often about receiving guests.

Mama Kempa was never caught in her circumvention of the rules, in spite of the nosy Herr Schmidt, who regularly sat peering out from behind his window curtains, a pair of binoculars teetering on the bridge of his nose. Once in a while he sent a report to the police to say that the guards had allowed visitors to the house at the bridge, and the guard in question would be docked his vacation or deprived of his assigned vacation spot. But that didn't stop the guards from helping Mama Kempa carry on her social life.

Mama Kempa was a perennial celebrator. She threw a party at any opportunity—a birthday, Christmas, Easter. That was when the house really came alive with her spirit. Days were spent decorating and cooking. Tables were put together in the big room with the fireplace, and the gatherings lingered into the night.

Through the years, Mama Kempa watched as other buildings around the Kindergarten were razed to improve the soldiers' *Schiessblick,* literally "shooting view." The small house on the bank of the East German side of the river, home to a local filmmaker, was torn down to make way for the death strip. The restaurant across the street was destroyed, and so was the carriage house next to the villa, where a fish smokehouse had taken up residence after the war. Mama Kempa was certain that someday her Kinderwochenheim would suffer the same fate. It made sense. Now that the other buildings were gone, the house stood out in conspicuous isolation. Ever in mind of the possibility of a military confrontation, the government needed a large circumference in the vicinity of the bridge for turning tanks around. The most frequently circulated story was that the house would be torn down and a guard's watchtower built in its place. Occasionally a rumor would circulate that the Kinderwochenheim was to be closed down in preparation for the demolition. Then the rumor would die and the threat would be forgotten. Still, for the thirty years Mama Kempa lived in the house, she felt there was a provisional quality to her life there.

Teachers at the Kindergarten came and went but one constant was Frau Krabbes. A small, round, somewhat humorless woman, Hannah Krabbes came to work at the Kindergarten shortly after the Wall went up. She was a favorite of the children, and a lover of gossip. Gossip, in fact, was a mainstay of the Kindergarten. Small whispers rippled through the house continuously, occasionally causing great rifts among the staff, and their source could often be traced to Frau Krabbes. For the twenty years she worked with her, Frau Krabbes remained allied with Mama Kempa.

For the thirty years that Mama Kempa ran the Kinderwochenheim, it was etched with her idiosyncracies. She was an emotional,

passionate woman, prone to melodramatic outbursts. The mood of
the household rose and ebbed with her moods. When she and her
husband fought, which was often, those in the rest of the house
knew about it the following morning, as soon as she descended the
wide stairs, still in her bathrobe.

In the 1970s, Mama Kempa's husband fell in love with a younger
woman and moved out. After that, a permanently somber mood descended on the house. Mama Kempa remained calm and loving
around the children but made life around the house unbearable for
the teachers. She was quick to become angry with them for something as trifling as failing to water the plants according to her precise
schedule, and she seldom contained her wrath. They came to dread
the dark side of her temperament. And they had unfocused suspi-
cions of her: she claimed to have no relatives in the West, but she
frequently received packages from there—shipments of coffee,
chocolate, sewing fabric and other things that were scarce in the
East.

Then, in the late 1970s, Mama Kempa's daughter, son-in-law and
granddaughter, who had been living upstairs with her, applied to
the East German authorities for permission to leave. It was a scan-
dal. Others snubbed them, not only for their unpatriotic act but out
of fear of being associated with them. Mama Kempa's daughter, a
schoolteacher, lost her job as a result of the request. In the mid-
1980s, they were finally allowed to leave.

In 1981, Mama Kempa turned sixty and the time came for her to
retire. She asked Frau Krabbes if she would like to apply to take her
place. But the dour Frau Krabbes, apparently more comfortable in
her lieutenant's role, declined. Several weeks later Mama Kempa
heard that her replacement would be a woman named Helga Neumann.

After she retired, Mama Kempa continued to live in the upstairs
apartment. She took an immediate dislike to her replacement, a severe, nervous woman. For her part, Helga Neumann appeared to
feel precisely the same way about the outgoing director. Frau Neumann was polite enough at first, but as soon as the keys to the
house passed hands, Frau Neumann made Mama Kempa feel unwelcome. Not only was Frau Neumann aflutter most of the time, but
she avoided eye contact. Mama Kempa wondered whether she was
an informant for the Stasi. In lieu of any hard evidence, Mama
Kempa could offer only a few facts which, by themselves, were

hardly incriminating. Frau Neumann's husband, she pointed out years later, was a career officer in the East German army. And because of the heavy military presence there, Potsdam was known to be a "Stasi Stadt," absolutely infiltrated by the secret police. But when Frau Neumann heard about Mama Kempa's musings more than a decade later, she flatly denied having had anything to do with the Stasi.

That Mama Kempa would even wonder whether Frau Neumann was a Stasi agent can only be understood against the backdrop of the times. It wasn't until nearly a decade later, after the Berlin Wall fell, that the extent of the Stasi's presence in the lives of East Germans would be made public: some 100,000 East Germans acted as official informers, and many more had a looser arrangement with the agency as unofficial collaborators, feeding occasional morsels of intelligence to Stasi contacts. East Germans spied on co-workers, neighbors, friends and relatives. Some did it for money; others did it out of fear. Through the years the Stasi collected more than a hundred miles of records, maintaining a file on one out of every three East Germans. Though they may not have known the full extent to which the Stasi was into their lives, East German citizens certainly sensed its presence. The most sophisticated espionage organization ever created, the Stasi was everywhere. And in an area as politically sensitive as the one circumjacent to the Glienicke Bridge, it would not be surprising that the Stasi should plant an informer at the Kinderwochenheim. In Mama Kempa's view, Helga Neumann seemed just the type to be easily intimidated by the Stasi.

By the time Helga Neumann started her job, the Kindergarten was once again a mix of day and weekly children. Seeing to the weekly children's needs was becoming more of a challenge. Kinderwochenheims had come to be associated with East Germany's *Asoziale* element, the social outcasts—alcoholics, the unemployed and citizens otherwise disenfranchised from East German society who had no other place to send their children. Unemployment and alcoholism often went hand in hand in East Germany. Because both problems were officially nonexistent, the state went to extraordinary lengths to keep its social pariahs as invisible as possible, providing them with housing—often superior to that of their working compatriots—and other essentials of life.

To be an *Asi* (pronounced AH-see) was to be considered not just invisible but incapable of caring for your children seven days a week. But neither did the state consider it appropriate to take the children of such people away from them entirely. If these parents weren't able to care for their children all of the time, they should be able to care for them some of the time. Placing them in a Kinderwochenheim seemed the best compromise. At a weekly child-care facility, the children would come to know daily rhythms, eat regular meals and bathe once a day. The weekend, a slice of the week as hallowed in East Germany as in West, was thought to be an ideal time to try to put children back in the home.

Children who were placed in Kinderwochenheims often had problems adjusting. They were leading, in effect, double lives. For five days of the week they had one home and for the remaining two days they had another. Fridays were usually spent in anticipation of being retrieved for the weekend, while Mondays were a period of readjustment to the ways and rhythms of the school. Children who lived their weekdays in Kinderwochenheims were considered "special," the way abused children are special. Some of them were slow learners. Others were difficult to discipline. And many developed strong attachments to the teachers. To be a teacher at such a school required the patience and calm of someone able to play surrogate parent from a comfortable distance.

Helga Neumann was neither patient nor calm. But she was unwavering in her dedication to her work. Her copy of Margot Honecker's education plan was dog-eared and underlined. She could quote verbatim from its pages, and she expected the other teachers to be able to do so as well.

Soon after her arrival, for no reason that Mama Kempa could discern, Frau Neumann went about rearranging all the rooms in the house. She moved all the beds upstairs, and moved her office downstairs. She removed the table coverings and various knick-knacks that Mama Kempa had placed around the rooms to make the house cozier and replaced them with a more austere brand of interior decoration. And to complete the marking of her territory, she removed most of the curtains and replaced them with window coverings of her own choosing.

Mama Kempa went into a quiet rage over the new director. Frau Neumann was a woman who had over time been stripped of her certitude. East Germany had gradually eroded her sense of self. Through the years, Frau Neumann seemed to grow increasingly dependent on being told what to do. In turn, she exercised her authority over the staff at the Kindergarten with ironclad rigidity. Not only did she rearrange the rooms but she instituted an inflexible work schedule.

Frau Neumann was not a party member. Occasionally while seated with the others in the garden—it was only in the garden now that the women spoke their minds, as they had grown worried that the walls of the Kindergarten were bugged—Frau Neumann expressed some gentle opposition to the state. But, as Frau Neumann herself admitted many years later, she did not dare speak her mind to a greater public. "Had I done that I wouldn't have been a Kindergarten director," she said. "I'd have been given a job as a cleaning woman." As Mama Kempa saw it, Helga Neumann's silence amounted to a tacit endorsement of the state. The millions of silences like hers throughout the GDR were, in their aggregate, what kept the state propped up.

Mama Kempa had the feeling that Frau Neumann was trying to force her out. She was no longer comfortable having her granddaughter play with the other children. Mama Kempa had been accustomed to eating lunch downstairs with the other teachers even after her retirement. But now she no longer felt welcome dining with the others. Eventually, Mama Kempa moved out of the house entirely. A few years later, in the late 1980s, word filtered back to the teachers that she had followed her children to West Germany. The third-floor apartment was then occupied by Edgar Brunke, the caretaker, and his wife, and all traces of Mama Kempa's three decades in the house gradually disappeared.

4: ULRIKE

A Young Rebel

By the early 1980s, more than two thirds of the forty or so children at the Kinderwochenheim at the Glienicke Bridge were weekly children. One teacher there, Ulrike Weichelt, believed that the children who stayed the week were different, needier somehow, and that they deserved special attention. She noticed this particularly in the afternoons, when the day children's parents came to fetch them. A gloom crossed the faces of the weekly children. Some of them got angry and demanded to know why they had to wait until Friday for their parents to come. "Your mother is working in the week so she can be with you all weekend," was the explanation they seemed most willing to accept. But those with parents who drank heavily and neglected their children knew enough not to believe it.

The teachers did a lot of talking among themselves about families like these, shaking their heads disapprovingly. When the parents did arrive on Friday afternoons—and they always came, even if they were the last and even if they were inebriated—the teachers handed the children over to them as if against their better judgment.

Ulrike Weichelt was the only exception to this. She spent hours talking to the most down-and-out parents. Time was one thing they possessed in abundance and on the days that Ulrike worked the late shift, they sat out the afternoons with her upstairs in the loggia, telling her of their hardships.

Ulrike worked at a conspicuous remove from the rest of the teachers. Her habits made the other teachers, several of whom were as old as her own mother, shake their heads in bewilderment and irritation. Occasionally they treated her as if they wondered how she could possibly have been allowed in the door. They shook their heads and whispered about her lifestyle. She was living with a man and had two children with him, but she wasn't married to him. This wasn't so unusual in the German Democratic Republic, but her colleagues, saddled as they were by tradition, looked askance at the arrangement anyway. And her way with the children was hardly more acceptable to them. Her ideas were different. She resisted their adherence to strict schedules and she had the children call her by her first name, a rejection of authority the other teachers found intolerable.

Ulrike's incongruous presence at the Kinderwochenheim was felt by the children as well. They sensed that she was different from the other women. They knew that when she was in charge they could get away with more. The other teachers punctuated their days with a succession of Nos and regarded Ulrike as overly permissive. Ulrike, on the other hand, saw her approach as one that fostered creativity and expression. When it came to drawing, for instance, she told the children to draw whatever pleased them. And she balked at the nearly constant attention paid to hygiene.

For all their disapproval, the other teachers held a cranky respect for Ulrike's passion for children. She could be counted on for unbounded patience after her colleagues had long since lost theirs. The others approached their jobs with a tired resignation. Ulrike, perhaps because of the energy of youth, arrived each morning as if it were her first day on the job.

Ulrike came into her profession after a few false starts. She was born in 1964 in Halle, an industrial city two hours south of Berlin by train. When she was a year old, her family moved to Kleinmachnow, a leafy village on West Berlin's southern border that was one of the more desirable places to live in East Germany. Part of its attraction is that Berlin is only a few minutes away. Moving there had actually been a tremendous stroke of luck. The Weichelt family was by no means a family of political privilege, and most of Kleinmachnow's residents were just that. Party functionaries and military officers and members of the East German secret police lived in spacious houses and small villas in Kleinmachnow that had been abandoned by well-to-do Berliners who fled Communism or, before that, the Nazis. The house Ulrike lived in with her parents and her younger brother was a simple but roomy two-story home. Not long after they moved in, an elderly couple living upstairs moved out, and the Weichelt family took over the entire house. This was a luxury that few East Germans had. Not only was the house spacious, but there was a terrace in the back, with a yard and garden. Ulrike had her own small bedroom upstairs. By East German standards, Ulrike's childhood was idyllic.

Their street dead-ended about one hundred yards to the north at the Berlin Wall. There was no traffic up and down the street, save the occasional National People's Army vehicle. Beyond the Wall was Zehlendorf, one of West Berlin's most affluent areas. While Ulrike was growing up, she regarded the stretch of Wall by her house as a fixture in her life, like her parents' garden. She and her brother often played at the Wall's base without thinking much about what was on the other side. She knew it was the West, because her parents told her so. And she could hear its sounds—ambulances, loud motorcycles, barking dogs. She had no great desire to go there. Yet she knew she would go there someday, if only for a brief visit. Somehow she equated going over to the other side of the Wall with the other things one does when grown up, like drinking beer and getting married and having children.

As a child, Ulrike was quiet and unsure of herself. She was small and fragile, and she felt uncomfortable in her own skin. She lived in her own world, sitting alone for hours in her bedroom, painting small watercolors of the view from her window: two poplar trees in the distance and a large pear tree in the well-tended garden. Or she just stared out the window at the lights on in the house across the way, wondering what her neighbors—particularly the son, who was Ulrike's age—might be doing at that moment.

Her mother stayed home with the two children and kept them out of Kindergarten, which was just as well with Ulrike, who was exceedingly shy around other children. Frau Weichelt worried about her daughter incessantly, which made Ulrike withdraw more. Her father, a landscape gardener, was seldom at home. Ulrike's strongest memory of him at home was breakfast time, when he sat in somber silence over his food, and left immediately after eating.

When she entered school, Ulrike was an apathetic student, and her grades reflected her attitude. The one regard in which she followed her parents' example was in her political leanings. Her parents weren't exactly anti-Communists, but they avoided the party, and so did she. Even so, she belonged to the Freie Deutsche Jugend, or Free German Youth, the Communist youth group, and she attended the requisite three or four meetings a year. As a member of the FDJ, she was given a brilliant blue shirt with a yellow flame sewn on the left sleeve, but she seldom donned the uniform. By and large, politics bored her.

Later, when Ulrike heard more about the West, she was curious, if not eager to go there. Her family watched Western television, which was broadcast into the country by West Germany. Of the East German households that owned television sets, all but the most ardent party members watched the programs that television signals sent drifting over the border. Officially, however, no one was supposed to watch Western television (Erich Honecker, in keeping with a promise of increased leniency, lifted the ban when he became Communist Party leader in 1971), and state officials risked losing their jobs if they were found to have done so. If teachers suspected any child of having been influenced by Western television, they were obligated to report the transgression to the authorities. Younger children were occasionally subjected to the Sand Man Test. Every evening in East Germany at ten minutes before seven, the Sand Man came on the air to throw sand in children's eyes to make them sleepy and to tell them to go to bed. A slightly different version aired on Western TV. Teachers would ask their pupils if they had seen the Sand Man, then ask the child under suspicion to describe the face of the big clock that filled the screen at the end of the program. If the child said the marks on the clock were small lines, instead of the small dots shown in the Eastern version, then it was confirmed that Western television was being viewed in that household.

The most popular television show in East Germany was *Dallas*.

The American soap opera was more than idle entertainment; it was a national preoccupation. Every Tuesday evening at 9:45, millions of East Germans tuned to a Western channel and sat in thrall to the machinations of the Ewing family. In one East German border village, residents even gave each other nicknames from *Dallas,* and a similar show, *Dynasty.* J. R. Ewing, the evil, heavy-drinking caricature of a Texas oilman, his manipulative, equally alcoholic wife, Sue Ellen, and his benevolent brother, Bobby, provided East Germans with their view of Americans. In fact, the East German government couldn't have asked for better advertising. As much as the regime frowned heavily on the viewing of Western television, the portrayal in *Dallas* of Americans as crass, coldblooded mercenaries only reinforced the Communist message.

But *Dallas* bored Ulrike. Even the Western commercials, with their colorful seductions into the land of material wealth, didn't faze her much. To her it seemed a world of make-believe. She knew that the goods she saw in the advertisements wouldn't be in any East German stores the next day. This was something she simply accepted. It wasn't so much deprivation she felt as it was frustration at others' preoccupation with things Western. The only television ad that affected her was one that promised total escape. It was a Cinzano commercial, and it showed tanned, muscle-bound young men and lithe, equally sun-kissed young women on a bepalmed island of unspecified location, playing volleyball and lounging and swirling their Cinzano glasses. It looked so calming. Her greatest wish was to be on that island.

In East German propaganda films, schoolchildren were depicted as ideal youths, blank slates either listening attentively to a teacher or cavorting through fields, drenched in sunlight and song. Often they were shown in the uniforms of the Free German Youth—short pants and blue kerchiefs—in an exaggerated salute, their right hands palm-up, straight over their heads.

It wasn't until children reached an age at which they began to think for themselves that teachers were taught to use more subtle tactics in the classroom. If a class of fourteen-year-olds expressed skepticism toward the *a priori* benevolence of Communism, the teachers were told to encourage discussion, since hard-line party dogma in response could backfire. At this age children must be reasoned with and drawn out; teaching an ideology to adolescents required a more enlightened approach.

Frau Fabig, one of Ulrike's teachers, had no talent for this method. A devout party member who had spent some years in Castro's Cuba, Frau Fabig taught the class called "Instruction in Citizenship," a uniquely East German line of political teaching. The primary purpose of the class was to impress upon young students the inherent goodness of socialism and the evils of capitalism. East Germany, she tried to convince her students, was the best, most advanced, most important country in the world. Frau Fabig's students, however, grew weary of her impassioned dogmatism. Ulrike, now fourteen, and a handful of others started a provocation campaign, disagreeing with everything she said regardless of what they thought of it. The class objected so consistently to everything Frau Fabig tried to present as dogma that their truculence finally sent her running out of the classroom one day, crying, "I am a Communist! I am a Communist! Even if you don't want it, I am a Communist!" Ulrike heard years later that Frau Fabig had gone mad and committed suicide.

Ulrike found that her fellow students fell into two categories: the budding *Mitläufer,* or unquestioning fellow travelers, and the habitual nay-sayers. By the time she experienced Frau Fabig, Ulrike had firmly established herself in the latter camp. But the nay-sayers didn't necessarily nurture an ideological stance because they believed in it. It became a point of pride for them to resist whatever a teacher said, regardless of what it was. Whenever it came to a comparison of East and West, Ulrike could predict who would take which side.

Ulrike's apathy in school was fed by the lack of a challenging curriculum. It was certainly broad enough. She took compulsory lessons in math, chemistry, biology, physics, music, German, Russian, English and literature. But the teachers at her school had a tendency to give good grades because the performance of their students was viewed by the state as a reflection of their own abilities. So with a minimum of effort Ulrike managed to make high marks. English was the only subject that bewildered her. Russian, by comparison, which every East German child was required to learn, seemed much easier. The history lessons were simply irritating. All modern historical developments, or so the teachers would have the students believe, had their roots in the 1917 revolution in Russia. America, Ulrike learned, was a place that had committed genocide against natives who had a legitimate claim to the land, imported slaves from Africa and, in spite of emancipation, continued to oppress blacks and other minorities well into the late twentieth century.

Ulrike grew to detest living at home. Her father was home less and less, and his absences took a high toll on her mother. Ulrike took refuge in her friends and her brother, Frank, a consistent ally. The worse things got, the more sister and brother stuck together. Frank took her out with his friends. Sometimes she stole out of the house late at night by climbing onto the roof and jumping into the backyard.

Ulrike's grades were good enough to qualify her to continue her studies at the most advanced level and prepare for a professional degree. But her parents wanted her to get some job training right away, and not to bother with the tedium of advanced studies. That suited Ulrike fine. Her primary interests centered on boys anyway. From age fifteen, she was seldom without a male in her life. By this time, she had become a rebel at home. When she decided to do something, she seldom consulted her parents first. One of the most difficult encounters with her mother came when, at age sixteen, she announced that she was planning to go on a camping trip with a boyfriend her mother objected to. Frau Weichelt did what she could to forbid it, but Ulrike had already developed such a contrary streak that it was no use.

In 1980, she entered a training program at a factory near Potsdam, not far from her parents' house. The plant manufactured microchips for various pieces of Eastern Bloc technical equipment, but as far as Ulrike could tell, no one appeared to be doing much real work. Mostly, the workday consisted of a succession of breaks, during which a great deal of alcohol was consumed on the sly. She spent most of her time brewing coffee, reading books in the library and helping the others distill spirits. There was a hairdresser on the premises who seemed to be the busiest employee of all.

After two years, Ulrike left the factory with a certificate as a trained chemical technician, and she decided to go on to become a chemical engineer. She enrolled at a girls' technical school in the city of Magdeburg, an hour's drive southwest of Berlin. It was a terrible experience from the start. Magdeburg was a filthy city, and the curriculum, heavy in math and physics, was too difficult for Ulrike. Still worse, she had nothing in common with the other students, most of whom were young women from such places as Nicaragua and Africa. For them it was something different and exciting. But Ulrike couldn't stand the place. Whenever she could, she spent weekends in Potsdam with friends.

Ingo

During one of her trips to Potsdam, in 1981, Ulrike met Ingo. At thirty, Ingo was thirteen years older than Ulrike. He had a strong face offset by gentle green eyes, and at five foot six, he wasn't much taller than Ulrike. He was a musician, philosopher and iconoclast. But mostly he was a *Gammler,* a cross between a beatnik and a hippie. They met one night at the Stube, the sole public gathering spot for young Potsdamers. Ingo noticed Ulrike immediately. In her long dress and dark wooden beads, she looked the perfect bohemian. As he put it years later, he "took her in."

Ulrike was put off by Ingo at first. When a group went on a camping trip in the mountains of southern East Germany near Czechoslovakia, a constant downpour kept them from hiking. The men took the bad weather as an excuse to sit in a bar and drink beer all day, which disgusted the women. Ulrike decided Ingo was just like all the other men she knew. But once the rain stopped, the group set out on its hike and Ulrike was attracted to the sturdy, quiet side of Ingo. She began to see something in this small, serious man.

Ingo was the only one in his family to leave his hometown of Erfurt, a provincial capital deep in the heart of East Germany, and pursue a university education. Although he had wanted to become a cook, there was no cooking course offered that year, so following his father's steps he studied Marxist philosophy at the renowned Humboldt University in East Berlin.

While growing up, Ingo was part of an extended and elaborate underground music scene in East Germany. He and his friends were particularly fond of the Beatles, the Rolling Stones, Bob Dylan and Donovan. Because they were considered sufficiently left-wing, Pete Seeger and Joan Baez were officially approved, and their records were sold in East German stores.

Records were difficult to come by, but there were inventive ways to get them. One of Ingo's friends made a practice of listening to West German radio show contests where records were given away as prizes, then writing to the winners, explaining that he was a deprived East German and asking for the record, just in case the winner wasn't so keen on the prize. Sometimes the request brought results, and occasionally it brought more than one copy of the same record, which he passed on to Ingo.

Ingo held a more jaded view of the West than many of his friends. Like Ulrike, he hadn't spent much time pining to go there. But when word of Woodstock traveled through Ingo's network of friends in 1969, he dreamed of going. In his adolescence he lived for the packages that came from his grandparents in West Germany, as they usually contained at least one record. Each time the grandparents sent word that a package was on its way, the entire household worried that it might not make it through customs. Ingo was especially disappointed when *Revolver,* a Beatles album he had been looking forward to, never showed up.

Ingo was the son of loyal party members, and he took part in all the compulsory youth groups—the Free German Youth and Young Pioneers. Like many East Germans, Ingo's parents came to Communism as a reaction against fascism. They believed that Communism was the only system that nurtured peace, friendship and heroism. Ingo's mother had a largely emotional tie to Communism. Ingo was certain that she had never read any Marx, and that if she did it would bewilder her. His father, on the other hand, the director of a local secondary school, passed an intellectual's love of Marxist theory on to Ingo.

Ingo was also an accomplished guitarist, and for years he and a circle of friends cultivated an interest in Irish folklore and folk music. In the late 1970s, he was part of a larger group that assembled every Thursday night to help establish a folklore culture in the GDR. They were helped by a small group of Irish musicians living in West Berlin, who visited East Germany on day passes.

Ingo's was a mild, measured form of dissent, certainly nothing to attract the attention of the authorities. He and his friends came up with the idea for a club. They called it the Stube, or pub. There was to be no cover charge at the Stube, and they would test the limits of the state's patience by cutting themselves into the mold of East Germany's *Liedermacher* (songmaker) scene, where poems—many of them subtly critical of the state—were put to music. It would be in the spirit of Wolf Biermann, the singer and poet who had moved to East Germany from Hamburg in the 1950s but had then rankled the state with his critical lyrics once too often and, in 1976, been forbidden to return after a concert in the West.

Ingo and his friends got permission from the city to have a regular Thursday evening "cultural" gathering and moved into the third floor of an old building in the middle of the city. The Stube's interior decorating was haphazard. Lumpy old sofas and rickety chairs both stolen and borrowed served for seating. There was a makeshift stage and a small bar, which served one kind of beer and one kind of red wine and one kind of white wine, none of it very good. But no one in East Germany ever paid attention to the quality of the drinks anyway. Since no one owned a car, supplies were hauled in on small children's wagons.

Gradually word of the Stube spread and young people started coming from all parts of East Germany on Thursday evenings. The Stube was also known to be a favorite place for the Stasi to do surveillance. The agency was known to spy on groups it considered dangerous, whether they were political activists, subversive poets or musicians. Everyone knew that by having anything to do with the Stube, they were attracting the attention of the Stasi and their names would probably end up in a Stasi file. But that wasn't much of a deterrent. The Stube was able to attract some of East Germany's most talented artists. One of the high points came when the novelist Christa Wolf gave a reading from her work.

When Ingo and Ulrike met, he was teaching Marxist theory at a local school for training nurses and Kindergarten teachers. Classes met six days a week, and every Saturday morning a group of his students came to fetch him for class so that he wouldn't oversleep. The attention Ingo's students paid him made Ulrike a bit jealous, but she took comfort in his now constant reassurance that he had eyes only for her.

Ingo became Ulrike's universe. She dropped out of the school in Magdeburg and moved in with him. She was sure that she would live with him forever. She loved his apartment, one small room overflowing with books and records and cooking equipment. It was the antithesis of her parents' orderly house.

Ingo introduced Ulrike to his collection of friends, musicians and drinking buddies: André, a friend who, like Ingo, had managed to avoid doing compulsory military service; and Ingo's best friend, Lutz, a quiet, wiry fellow musician who was in awe of Ingo's ability to talk for hours to a circle of rapt friends about politics. Ingo grew particularly impassioned about the virtues of Marxism after he had had a few drinks. As Lutz described it years later, Ingo may have been long-winded, but he was so articulate in his long-windedness that listening to him expound on politics was like sitting down with a good text.

Ingo also introduced Ulrike to Wolfgang and the scene at Langerwisch.

For all its proximity to Berlin, Potsdam had remained partly rural. And just outside the city limits was some of the GDR's most pristine countryside. Langerwisch was a tiny village about five miles from Potsdam. It consisted of a few stores, a few dozen houses, a handful of farmhouses and Wolfgang's place.

Everyone in the village knew about Wolfgang. He was different from the rest of the villagers. Short and stout with a long beard and Ben Franklin glasses, Wolfgang was considered an outsider. He was a native Potsdamer, born in 1946. His mother, who was half-Jewish, had stayed in Potsdam during the war, protected by her non-Jewish husband. Wolfgang's grandmother died at Auschwitz, but he rarely spoke of this with his family, and never spoke of his family's background with his friends. All that Ulrike knew of him was that he was from Potsdam and had been one of the primary organizers of the Stube. He always seemed to have a different woman around him. He moved to Langerwisch in the late 1970s to get away from the city, to work the land and build a refuge for his Potsdam friends. He bought a dilapidated eighteenth-century adobe farmhouse with a thatched roof in the middle of the village.

The house was known throughout the village as the "Family Hilltop," because before Wolfgang arrived three large families lived in it. But the house had fallen into such disrepair it was nearly uninhabitable, and he set about rebuilding it with a passion. At first his friends thought he was crazy to buy such a ruin. But when he invited friends from Potsdam and East Berlin to help with the task of renovation, and they saw how beautiful the setting was, they changed their minds. From atop a small knoll on the property was a view across fields that stretched for miles. In the milder months, during spring and summer, Wolfgang's friends brought their tents and their children and stayed for the weekend. While the men worked on the house, the women supervised the children and baked cakes and sat and talked. Ulrike loved sitting for hours with her closest friends, talking about their children.

The other villagers looked slightly askance at Wolfgang. While they kept their gardens in immaculate condition, his was a bit wild and overgrown. They were particularly wary of the entourage of scruffy friends he imported from the city on weekends. They didn't and couldn't understand what it was that Wolfgang was trying to achieve. He was trying to build a microscopic version of what the GDR was failing at so conspicuously: a bearable form of socialism. The tight-knit community around Wolfgang didn't necessarily want to move to the West. In fact, wanting to go west was considered uncool. They wanted a kind of socialism they could live with within what one well-known East German writer called the *Dreckhaufen* (pile of filth) that was the GDR. They were on the fringes of a more visible dissident movement of Third Way Marxists and democratic socialists who opposed the Honecker regime's mangling of socialist ideals. But Wolfgang, Ingo, Lutz and the others in the group made a point of staying out of politics. If they were searching for affirmation, they did so by turning inward. For many East Germans, what they did in private mattered more to them than what they did in public. For Wolfgang, Ingo and Lutz, it was enough to build a tightly wound community of their own, marginal to be sure, but unassailable.

When the Langerwisch weekends were over, everyone drove back to Potsdam and East Berlin and returned to their matchbox apartments and their tedious jobs and waited for Thursdays at the Stube and more weekends in Langerwisch. Like the Stube, Wolfgang's place attracted Stasi surveillance. Whenever there was a collection of cars outside Wolfgang's bearing East Berlin or Potsdam license plates, the Stasi was sure to keep tabs on the goings-on.

Ulrike was as much bewitched by Ingo's circle of friends as she was by Ingo himself. Everyone in Potsdam seemed to know him. There always seemed to be someone dropping by to visit. On music nights, the tiny apartment was packed with people and their instruments. The chaos couldn't have made Ulrike happier.

She was out of work now, and sooner or later the authorities were bound to catch up with her. Unemployment was simply not permitted. She decided she would work with small children, as a Kindergarten teacher, and in 1983 she enrolled in a course for a Kindergarten certificate. The curriculum consisted of lessons that might be expected in the course of preparing a child educator: child psychology, education and health. There was also the compulsory smattering of Marxist-Leninist teachings. In contrast to the difficult times she had with teachers like Frau Fabig, this time she enjoyed the lessons. Her teacher seemed open to discussion, and she was glad for the chance to go home and talk with Ingo about what she had learned.

A Teacher Out of Step

Any child in need of a spot in a Kindergarten was entitled to one; regardless of how crowded a place was, an effort was usually made to find room. By the time Ulrike decided to become a Kindergarten teacher in 1983, Potsdam was badly in need of more teachers. Ulrike was placed in a new facility in the middle of a housing project called Am Schlaatz. One high-rise was indistinguishable from the next, the walls were paper thin and shortly after they were completed in the 1970s, the buildings began to show signs of wear. Roofs leaked, electrical wiring shorted out, pipes rusted. But because of their central heating, which eliminated the bother and work of constantly feeding a coal-burning oven, such "new" buildings were among the most popular in East Germany. The Kindergarten that Ulrike was assigned to was the first in the development, so it was oversubscribed from the start. Most of the children were known to be the offspring of Stasi officers and party members, as those were the people who lived in the complex. But Ulrike tried to overlook that. Five-year-old children couldn't be held responsible for their parents' political convictions.

The pay was miserable. Ulrike started out at East Germany's equivalent of minimum wage—390 marks a month for forty-five hours of work a week, far below the 1,200 mark national average wage. But that didn't matter much. As was the rule in East Germany, Ingo's rent was a nominal 30 marks a month, which enabled Ulrike to put her pitiful income to groceries and clothing.

Ulrike loved the challenge of her new job. She liked working with small children. There could be as many as thirty children to a group with two teachers, but even that didn't faze her much. Ulrike paid little attention to Margot Honecker's education plan. As someone with a broad creative streak, Ulrike was appalled by some of the regimentation she saw—the drawing of trees, for instance. It was unacceptable for the children to draw trees in any way that deviated from the specified form. The goal wasn't to teach them to draw what they saw, in whatever form that pleased them, but to learn the technique of tree drawing as set forth in Frau Honecker's book. Making it still more difficult for the children to draw trees was the fact that there were few trees visible from the antiseptic confines of the high-rise. But Ulrike saw that as an opportunity. If they couldn't see trees, then the children should draw the trees of their imaginings. They needn't necessarily have leaves, or even a trunk. She encouraged them to draw crooked trees, branchless trees, leafless trees, dwarf trees and trees that didn't look like trees at all. Ulrike's approach was a far cry from social realism's teachings on artistic representation, and it provoked some nasty looks from her colleagues. She ignored them.

Instead of being encouraged to explore negative emotions when they arose, which struck Ulrike as the only respectful way to raise a child, children were simply ordered to play peacefully with the others.

It was usually the younger children who expressed interest in setting the table for meals. But according to the education plan, only the older children were allowed to do so. By the time the younger ones were old enough to do it, they had lost interest. "So they were first disappointed when they wanted to do something and weren't allowed to, and then they had to do something they didn't want to do," Ulrike later recalled.

Even though the Kindergarten at Am Schlaatz was running out of space, it didn't turn any children away, and the work grew increasingly difficult. It seemed to Ulrike that as more children arrived, teachers began to take more time off. Weakened by the stress, perhaps, the teachers seemed to catch the children's colds and flus more than usual, and they took more sick days. Several went on maternity leave.

The teachers who remained picked up the slack from those who were absent, and Ulrike believed that the added strain made them more susceptible to illness. What started out as a delightful challenge had turned into a nightmare. All of Ulrike's ideas about what a Kindergarten should be—a place that nurtured children's creativity—were shattered. Within a year of her arrival, there were sixty children to a group. Giving the children individual attention was impossible. After a certain point, the most she could do was station herself at the door and try to see to it that the children didn't run away. In such numbers, though she was loath to admit this to herself, the children even frightened her. She asked the city of Potsdam to put her in a different facility, preferably a smaller place with fewer children per teacher. Because of her relative inexperience, her prospects were dim. Ulrike was beginning to wonder if this career, too, would prove a disappointment.

That year, Ulrike stopped taking birth control pills. A few months later she was pregnant. She would be twenty when the baby was born. In East Germany this wasn't considered particularly young. In fact, most women began having children in their early twenties.

Ulrike's first pregnancy was a blissful time. Four other friends—all around her age—were pregnant as well, and they formed a tight circle. Ulrike was certain she would have a girl, and she and Ingo decided on Maxi for the name. When she gave birth to a boy, they were at a loss for names, and finally settled on Philipp. It was standard practice in East Germany to keep mothers in the hospital for at least a week even after uncomplicated deliveries. Ulrike had to stay in the hospital for ten days. Ingo visited her every day. He always showed up looking a bit disheveled, as if he needed a shower, and it made her worry that he was squandering the days. But when she and the baby got home, she saw that he had been building a loft bed for them to sleep in, making room for the baby's crib underneath. Ulrike breast-fed Philipp and was paid "nursing money"— about $5 a month—by the state for doing so.

Once the children arrived, the same group of women spent their "baby year" together. They ate breakfast together every day, and they exchanged baby clothes and baby-sitting duties. The children made friends with one another. When visitors came from West Germany, they couldn't believe that women that young were having children. For her part, Ulrike was amazed to hear them say they would feel as if life were passing them by if they had children that young. The way Ulrike and her East German friends saw it, women who waited until they were in their thirties to have children were going to let their best years be taken up by childrearing. It seemed far better to get it out of the way early.

Philipp was an easy, quiet infant, almost too quiet, Ulrike thought at times. After six months of relative calm, Ulrike went back to work at Am Schlaatz. The overcrowding had gotten worse, and the work was more stressful than ever. She took Philipp with her every day, and he stayed next door in the Kinderkrippe for infants. With the baby, the ninety-minute journey to work seemed more strenuous. They had to take two trams and walk long distances each way. The harsh Potsdam winters were particularly unforgiving. But Ulrike did it uncomplainingly, and she seldom thought about alternatives. Neither she nor Ingo knew how to drive. Even if they did, and even if they had the 15,000 marks (a year's worth of their combined salaries) to spend on a Trabant, the underpowered People's Car, they would have to wait at least ten years before getting one. On the contrary, Ulrike considered herself fortunate. Philipp was right next door, which made nursing him easy. Her heart went out to the children she was meant to look after, who were spending their first years lost in a crowd.

Not long after Philipp was born, Ulrike and Ingo moved into a new apartment. Cavernous by East German standards, the five-room apartment was in Ulrike's favorite neighborhood in all of Potsdam. Called Potsdam West, the new neighborhood was tucked into a corner of the city untouched by the war. The streets in Potsdam West were lined with grand old apartment buildings, villas, poplars and lime trees. Ulrike's street, Lennéstrasse, named for the nineteenth-century landscape architect Peter Joseph Lenné, abutted the lavish grounds of the Sanssouci Park. In summer, the large leafy trees along the streets dampened both light and sound. The quiet of the neighborhood was broken by the occasional two-stroke splutter of a Trabant. In winter, when the trees were bare, Ulrike could see the Sanssouci Palace from her living room window.

After six months back at work, in 1985 Ulrike got word of an opening at another Kindergarten. This facility was a Kinderwochenheim. Ulrike had learned a bit about such facilities but had never actually seen one, much less considered working at one. The Kinderwochenheim, she learned, was next to the Glienicke Bridge, a part of Potsdam Ulrike did not know, as it was in the heavily guarded border zone. She decided to go have a look at the place. As she approached she saw that there was no way to get to the house. She was halfway up the garden in the back of the building when she was stopped by a gate, and by signs warning all pedestrians and automobiles to turn back at once. One of the teachers inside the house must have seen her and guessed her reason for being there because she saw a woman emerge from the front of the building and exchange some words with one of the guards. He then waved Ulrike in.

If she hadn't grown up so close to the Wall she might have been more spooked by its proximity now. It stood no more than fifty feet from the house, a ribbon of concrete lining the bank on either side of the bridge. Anyone from deeper inside East Germany, where the Wall was more of an abstraction, might have gotten a fright from such a close encounter with it. For Ulrike, it wasn't so much the Wall itself that she found nerve-wracking as the brace of guards she saw at the bridge. Her friends were just beginning to start to go to the West, or try to go to the West, and the first postcards were now arriving from England and Ireland. Now she wished she could go over, if just for a day, just to see it.

Ulrike was greeted at the front door of the house by a woman wearing an apron, which made Ulrike wonder whether this might be a cook. The woman introduced herself as Frau Krabbes, one of the teachers, and explained that Frau Neumann, the director, was on vacation. It was a warm sunny September day, but the house was dark and cool. Unlike the other Kindergarten, where there wasn't a tree in sight, this building was surrounded by tall solid trees that conspired to block out the daylight. Ulrike sensed a warmth and coziness that presented a comforting contrast to the nearby guards at the bridge.

There was something charming and old-fashioned about the place. Children were running up and down the stairs and in and out of the back doorway leading to the garden. All of the teachers were wearing aprons decorated with flowers, throwbacks to the pictures of Kindergarten teachers in aprons Ulrike had seen in her outdated schoolbooks published in the 1960s. In fact, from what she could tell, all the teachers looked old enough to have posed for those pictures.

And there was something chaotic about the place. The children were livelier than the ones she was accustomed to, and their liveliness added to the general sense of disorder. The women who worked there had tried to give the house a homey look, with curtains on all the windows and curtains drawn across the miniature closets in the front hall. Nothing had been put together with precision, but everything aspired to domesticity.

Frau Krabbes seemed to assume that Ulrike would take the job. She showed her around the house and explained how they handled the children. She showed Ulrike a small closet where the toys were kept, and how to lock them up. While Ulrike was standing there, the children descended on the closet and lined up for their toys. The rule, Frau Krabbes explained, was that the best-behaved children got the best toys to play with for the day.

Ulrike left enchanted but a bit frightened at the prospect of work-ing there. She had heard that the children came from Asi families, and such children were known to be difficult. As she had learned from her previous job, the children from normal households were difficult enough. Still, she was happy to take the job. It was an im-measurable improvement over the place she was working. Even the daily journey would be far easier, as the Kindergarten at the bridge was a twenty-minute bicycle ride away from her apartment.

On Ulrike's first morning of work she was relieved to be greeted this time by two young women closer to her own age. They imme-diately took Ulrike onto the back terrace and brought out coffee and cake. There was a hint of celebration in the air, and one of the women explained that Frau Neumann was out for the week, taking a cure at a spa east of Berlin. Ulrike still hadn't met this Frau Neu-mann, but she had the impression that things at the Kindergarten were much more relaxed during Frau Neumann's absences.

The children were playing in the huge backyard and seemed en-tirely self-sufficient. Ulrike's two new colleagues kept an eye on the children but didn't police them. Ulrike was struck by how well this old place catered to children's needs. The makeshift playground equipment and the large trees were all they needed to occupy them. The trees, in particular, were all-consuming, multipurpose objects. Their branches served as a jungle gym; huge exposed roots were a perfect balance beam. The leaves were just beginning to fall, and the children were already gathering them into jumping piles. In groups of two and three they approached the three women and Ul-rike asked them their names. They were open and friendly and in-quisitive. With no hesitation, they addressed her in the informal *du*.

Frau Neumann returned the following week. She was the same age as Ulrike's mother—in her late forties—and had jet black hair that Ulrike decided must be dyed. She wore horn-rimmed glasses. There was a pinched expression fixed on her face, and she held herself in a forward pitch. She was friendly to Ulrike, but there was no warmth in her manner. She had difficulty making eye contact. In-stead, she crooked her neck slightly and shifted her glance sideways and downward. With Frau Neumann's return came a noticeable shift in mood. The teachers were more aware of schedules and regula-tions. And it was as if someone had turned down the volume on an amplifier, because there was less general noise. Frau Neumann, Ulrike heard, suffered from frequent severe headaches.

One of the things Ulrike liked most about the Kinderwochenheim was the regular meals that the cooks prepared each day. She liked to see that the children had something they could count on, and she loved the smell that came from the kitchen at certain times of day. Meals were simple, to be sure, and predictable. You could tell what day of the week it was by the food served. Breakfast on Mondays consisted of a piece of dry bread (dry because it had been bought on Friday) and jam, and the warm meal at midday was a bowl of noodles. On Mondays after their naps, the children got freshly baked cakes, garnished with fruit from the garden, either fresh or preserved. On Tuesdays and Thursdays there was always some kind of cooked pork or beef for lunch, and on Wednesdays and Fridays the cooks prepared a rice or noodle pudding, or a light soup. Suppers in the Kinderwochenheim were the same as they were throughout both Germanys. The light meal of the day consisted of bread and cheese and cold meats. On special days, such as a birthday, the child's parents were expected to furnish a cake, and the Kindergarten provided a sparkling fruit juice.

The children never seemed to get enough to drink. Health regulations called for two liters of liquids a day, but the teachers seldom provided that, as it was too difficult to keep taking drink breaks.

The enclosed loggia on the second floor was Ulrike's favorite place. As the official break room, it was the one place where she occasionally saw the other teachers relax. Every day after the midday meal, after the children were put to bed for their two-hour nap, the teachers sat in the loggia and drank coffee and tea and smoked and talked. To keep the room extra warm, Frau Neumann had insisted that the caretaker, Edgar Brunke, drill large holes in the thick plastic radiator covers. Frau Neumann had done her best to decorate the room. She installed a couple of bedraggled house plants, a few posters and a set of graying laced curtains. The tall ceiling of dark walnut lent a coziness to the room. When Ulrike began working the night shift, in summers, after she put the children to bed, she sat at the window and drew the scene outside: the casino at the Glienicke Castle across the way; the boats on the water; the beautiful Sacrow church on an island in the middle of the river, an orphan of the division of Germany and now abandoned.

Ulrike came to realize that she was simply different from the other teachers, even the younger ones. She had ideas that were often at odds with those of the others, and she approached the concept of educating small children more openly than the others did. It baffled Ulrike that there was so little room for experimentation.

The others' intense interest in particulars irked her as well. The smallest detail—a slight change in the menu, say, or the rearranging of beds—could provoke a week of discussions. And then there was the close attention they paid to one another's personal lives. Each was obsessed with the other's relative position in the closed universe that was East Germany. Who had the larger garden plot? The more coveted vacation destination? Whose husband had the better job? Who had a television, a car, a telephone? Who had better access to Western goods? When they took rare and brief, officially sanctioned trips to West Germany, they catalogued them not so much by what they saw or how they felt but by what they purchased. "That was the time I bought those skeins of wool." Or, "I bought a petticoat on that trip." Then again, their preoccupation with details saved them from thinking about leaving for good, or trying to leave for good. All of them dreamed of going over the bridge once and for all, but no one ever did anything about it.

The Bridge

By and large, Ulrike and the other teachers were spared the task of explaining to the children the significance of the border, but Ulrike soon learned what it was like to work so close to a spot as sensitive as the Glienicke Bridge. She had arrived at the Kinderwochenheim just after a mass exchange of political prisoners had taken place on the bridge, and she heard about the incident in engrossing detail from the other teachers. The span was now known as the "Spy Bridge," a place of prisoner exchanges—the latest use of a bridge which had had many uses through time, both practical and symbolic.

The Glienicke Bridge had first gone up around 1660, a narrow wooden span over the Havel at the river's narrowest point before widening into the Jungfernsee to the north and the Tiefensee to the south. Those were the days of the Grand Elector Friedrich Wilhelm, when all of Potsdam was in the hands of Prussian aristocracy, whose intention it was to enhance the area surrounding the Havel. The original bridge was intended to provide the Grand Elector convenient access to adjacent Berlin, where he had his hunting lodge across the river in the woods at Glienicke. Then, in 1687, the road leading from Berlin to Potsdam over the Glienicke Bridge was converted into a wide avenue, called Berliner Allee. In 1777, another wooden structure was built in place of the original bridge, this one with a drawbridge. Eventually, the bridge over the Havel was to become a vital link in the road stretching the length of Germany—from Aachen on the Belgian border all the way to Königsberg, 1,000 kilometers away in East Prussia.

Fifty years later increased traffic over the bridge required a change. The wooden bridge was replaced in 1834 with one of red brick. Its architect was Friedrich Schinkel, the official architect of the Hohenzollerns. Schinkel applied his skills in the modern technology of brick structures, while at the same time meeting the aesthetic requirements of Friedrich Wilhelm IV and his brother, Prince Carl: a series of Roman arches, with one arch in the middle of the span serving as a drawbridge. The Schinkel bridge was one of the first to be designed to be both a work of art and fully functional, serving well the area's growing transportation requirements. One design concession Schinkel had to make was to allow two small control points to be built on the bridge, in order to keep errant soldiers from crossing into Berlin.

What many considered an aesthetic crime occurred in 1908. The bridge was destroyed and rebuilt. A steel span, the latest in steel technology, replaced Schinkel's artful brick. The new bridge—140 yards long and 30 yards wide—came under sharp criticism. It held nothing of the former bridge's romance. When speaking of the Glienicke Bridge, Germans referred to the old one and mourned its loss.

Depending on your vantage point, Berlin began or ended at the Glienicke Bridge. When Germany was divided in 1949, the bridge became a terminus. Precisely in its center was painted a white line marking the divide between East and West.

For reasons that eluded West Germans entirely, and remained a mystery to many East Germans as well, East Germany's official name for the bridge was the Bridge of Unity. The answer lay in a speech given in 1949 by the Brandenburg minister in the newly formed GDR. The bridge, he announced, should serve as a constant reminder of the socialist fight for unity of the fatherland. In 1977, the East Germans declared the Eastern side of the bridge a historical monument.

Rather than unity, the Glienicke Bridge came to symbolize the chasm between East and West. The large notice at the foot of the Western side of the bridge that warned pedestrians and automobiles that they were leaving the American sector of Berlin was more than a sign. It was a powerful indictment:

"Glienicke Bridge. Those who gave this bridge the name 'The Bridge of Unity' also built the Wall, erected barbed wire, and built death strips. With that they hinder unity."

After the division of Germany, the Glienicke Bridge was heavily restricted. It was open only to French, American and British diplomats working at the military missions in Potsdam, all of them in the Berliner Vorstadt. East Germans were not allowed to cross at all. As one joke put it, the Glienicke Bridge was the longest bridge in the world: a sign on the Potsdam side read "Berlin—28 kilometers."

A constant battle raged over upkeep of the bridge. In 1984, the East Germans briefly held the bridge hostage, closing it to diplomatic traffic. West Germany had renovated the Western half of the bridge and, arguing that the GDR never used the bridge, the East German government was now demanding that the West refurbish the Eastern half as well. The West Germans eventually capitulated.

The first famous spy exchange at the Glienicke Bridge took place in 1962. Two years earlier the spy plane of U.S. pilot Francis Gary Powers had been shot down over the Soviet Union. Powers was exchanged at the Glienicke Bridge for Soviet agent Colonel Rudolf Abel early one winter morning. After that, spy exchanges—at the bridge and elsewhere—became something of a business arrangement between East and West.

Twenty-two years later, on a beautiful clear morning in early summer, two dozen Westerners who had been imprisoned in the East were released at the bridge in exchange for four convicted spies from the Eastern Bloc. The teachers watched from behind the curtains of the upstairs loggia, as the vehicles carrying the two sets of prisoners stopped at the center of the bridge, as diplomats and lawyers from each side waved and signaled to one another, and as the weary-looking prisoners walked to freedom on the opposite side. The event hadn't made it into any East German newspapers, but the teachers had seen enough official events take place at the bridge over the years to be able to imagine the significance of this one.

And five months after Ulrike started to work there in 1986 came the most spectacular exchange in the history of the bridge. From all the preparations taking place the teachers knew that something extraordinary was about to happen. For days beforehand Stasi agents were in the house, checking its security and setting up watch posts. One of these was Frau Neumann's office, as it had a direct view of the street and bridge. In fact, the hulking presence of the house at the Glienicke Bridge was difficult to overlook at times such as these. During politically sensitive episodes it was necessary to turn the house inside out to make certain it harbored no one suspicious. As harmless and innocent as a house full of middle-aged teachers and preschoolers might seem, the authorities decided to err on the side of caution.

Anatoly Shcharansky, a Soviet Jew and human rights activist whom the Soviets accused of being an American spy, had been a political prisoner since 1977. The negotiations leading to his release had taken eight years. Shcharansky was one of the Soviet Union's most valuable trump cards when it came to trading prisoners. When it finally became apparent that Shcharansky and three others were to be exchanged for five Eastern Bloc agents at the famous Spy Bridge, the event attracted dozens of journalists and spectators.

The day was still dark on a frostbitten Tuesday morning in February 1986 when Western newspaper reporters and camera crews began to gather on the West Berlin side of the bridge. A handful of Stasi agents, some of them sharpshooters holding rifles, were stationed on the ground floor of the house. They gave strict instructions to the teachers to stay away from all windows for the day. But they stole upstairs anyway, and from the loggia they had a clear view of everything. The white line dividing the two nations had been dusted with snow the night before, and the guards had swept it clear. At 10 A.M. the teachers watched as a silver-blue minibus rolled up and parked on the Western side. It was followed by a gray BMW a few minutes later, which was followed by a Red Cross ambulance. The ambulance was followed by two Mercedes, one charcoal gray and one gold. They both parked dead-center on the bridge.

Of all the teachers, Frau Krabbes remembered most clearly the image of Shcharansky as he crossed from East to West. Mostly, she remembered what a small man he appeared to be, not much taller than herself, made smaller still by an oversized black coat and the large furry hat on his head. And she would never forget the famous, playful little leap he took over the white line dividing East and West, just before climbing into the U.S. ambassador's limousine and being whisked away to the West Berlin airport.

Still, none of the teachers was aware of the global importance of the episode. News of the exchange spread around the world. It was the lead story on television news, and *Der Spiegel,* the West German weekly magazine, made a cover story of the event. East German accounts of the exchange, however, were sparse. The official East German news agency disposed of the event in a few dozen words: "On the basis of agreements between the USA and the Federal Republic of Germany as well as the USSR . . . and the GDR an exchange of persons who had been arrested by the respective countries took place on Tuesday, February 11, 1986. Among them were several agents." Had the teachers not been able to view the event from their second-story perch, chances are they'd have had no idea it happened.

With the exception of the occasional official occurrence at the bridge, Ulrike was seldom confronted with graphic reminders of the Cold War. This changed one Monday morning in 1986 when Mandy, a friend who had applied to leave East Germany, was arrested, separated from her husband and daughter, driven through the streets blindfolded and kept in an East German prison for a year. Her husband was also arrested. Her daughter was placed in an orphanage. Ulrike found out years later that although neither Mandy nor her friends knew where she had been taken, she was sitting in a prison on Lindenstrasse, in the middle of downtown Potsdam, just off the pedestrian zone where Ulrike did her shopping. The prison had scores of small, cold cells, each with a toilet (with the flush chain on the outside of the cell) and a slot for delivering food trays.

From the outside, the building that housed the prison looked much like an ordinary office building. Ulrike walked past it daily without giving much thought to what was inside. (After the Berlin Wall fell, Potsdam's landmark preservationists used the cells as oversized file cabinets for storing their archives.) Mandy was released after a year in prison. She was reunited with both her husband and three-year-old daughter. They were lucky. After a brief stay in the orphanage the child had gone to stay with her grandmother. Many other political prisoners, and those who had fled the GDR, had lost their children in forced adoptions. Instead of being bought out by the West, as many other East German political prisoners were, Mandy and her husband were sent home. Mandy became increasingly bitter. Eventually she was allowed to leave East Germany and moved to West Berlin. For Ulrike, recalling Mandy's arrest years later was like driving back through a dense fog to a place she had once been: she knew the lay of the land, but many of the details, including her own reaction to the incident, now escaped her. In most countries, the unexplained arrest of a close friend would be deeply disturbing. As Ulrike explained it years later, most of the time she and her friends took things in without thinking much about their significance. "It was a defense mechanism. I tuned things out and now they play back like a film with no context," she said. "It wasn't exactly a conscious act of looking away. It was more like a vacuum."

Crossing the Line

Ulrike worried for the children who stayed the week. They were different from the day children. Even their names were different. From the time she started working there she noticed an unusually high number of American names among the weekly children—Mike, Danny, Nancy, Ronny—all taken from the American television programs and films the parents watched on Western TV, perhaps in hopes that their children might have a better life than theirs. At the same time, these children were starved for attention. Like the other Kindergarten, this one was seldom fully staffed. Someone was always sick, or on vacation, or taking her monthly "household" day: every female worker in the GDR was entitled to one day a month for tending to the needs of her home and family. Ulrike worried occasionally that because of the scant attention they received and the unhappy homes they came from, when they grew up they might be left vulnerable to recruiting efforts by the Stasi, taken under the agency's wing and made to feel wanted and needed and protected. But she was learning to be less concerned about other people's children and more concerned about her own. Philipp was now attending the Kindergarten as a day student. He had been a quiet baby and now he was a sullen, withdrawn little boy. Ulrike decided he was lonely. Perhaps what he needed was a sibling.

By early 1987, at age twenty-three, she was pregnant with her second child. It was around that time that Ulrike applied to take a short trip to West Germany with her mother. Theoretically, at least, she qualified for the trip because her grandmother in Düsseldorf in West Germany was celebrating her eightieth birthday. An aging relative's birthday was considered a special event for which the state usually granted short-stay visas.

In order to get permission Ulrike needed a recommendation from Frau Neumann. And although Frau Neumann knew that Ulrike was by no means loyal to the state, she also knew how much the trip meant to Ulrike, and she put in a positive word. For a teacher to travel west, even for a short visit, was frowned upon. Who knew what kind of ideas she might bring back and infect her students with?

But Ulrike was considered a safe bet. She had a child at home, she lived with the child's father, and she was pregnant with a second. All of this was considered by the authorities to be sufficient incentive for returning.

She got permission to go for a week.

The train left at 5 A.M., and her father drove Ulrike and her mother to the Friedrichstrasse station in East Berlin. The station was heavily guarded and the wait seemed interminable. It was like a dream. Ulrike half expected one of the guards to pull her out of the line and tell her a mistake had been made and she wouldn't be allowed to travel after all. A thick white line was painted on the platform. It was forbidden to cross over the line: that was the West. Just standing there made her feel like a criminal.

They finally boarded, and the train pulled away from the station. When they reached Wannsee, Ulrike was tempted just to get out, to walk away from her life with Ingo and Philipp, from the Kindergarten and the children there, from all her friends and the Stube and the Thursday night music. It was a fantasy she had had many times. She might start a life somewhere in the West with her new baby, perhaps work at a Kindergarten in West Berlin. As the daydream ran through her head, the Wannsee station had come and gone.

It was hard for her to imagine that she was on one of the very trains that had been forbidden for so long, one of the lacquered trains that hurtled regularly past Potsdam on its way to West Berlin. She was eager to taste something Western right away. Since she could use her Eastern marks to pay for food on the train, she bought juice and toast for breakfast.

After two hours, the train came to a stop at the Helmstedt border crossing, which divided East and West Germany, and guards examined their passports to check the exact time the passengers had left West Berlin. After that, the Eastern guards disappeared, and West

German conductors in dark blue uniforms were the only ones left. Ulrike was surprised by her own relief.

Ulrike looked out the window for the remainder of the trip. The landscape was benign, the buildings totally unsoiled. When the train traveled through the heavily industrial Ruhr section she was struck by how clean even the smokestacks looked.

Her mother's brother picked them up at the train station. He was the relative who had always been known simply as the uncle from the West, who sent packages and visited once in a while and told jokes and watched soccer and went to pubs and laughed a lot. Ulrike suddenly felt conspicuous in her secondhand maternity overalls. Certainly no one in the West was this sloppily dressed.

From the moment they arrived, Ulrike and her mother were treated, perhaps unintentionally, like the poor, half-witted relations from the East. Immediately, they were presented with gifts of used clothing: sweaters and skirts and coats. Ulrike decided her aunt and uncle must have spread word of their visit and taken up a collection of sorts around the neighborhood. Though the secondhand gifts embarrassed Ulrike, even humiliated her a little, there were some items of clothing she would continue to wear for years afterward.

Their relatives appeared to expect something of Ulrike and her mother. They expected them to be astounded by the abundance and selection and quality of everything on the other side of the Wall. But Ulrike wasn't astounded. She was disappointed. Yes, there were more things around everywhere, and they were all more colorful and sturdier and fancier than anything in the East. It was all just like what she had seen in Western magazines and on Western television. She was surprised to see how quickly she became used to it all, to her uncle's large, comfortable, quiet car that he drove at what seemed to be recklessly high speeds, to the variety of meats and cheeses and chocolates, and to the bottomless pot of coffee. If she had brewed so much coffee in one week at home she'd have used up a month's wages. A pound of coffee in the GDR cost $20. Here a pound of fresh beans cost $3.

Prices for other goods, however, seemed inordinately high. Ulrike and her mother were accustomed to paying 25 cents for a loaf of bread. Western bakeries charged $3. Twelve pounds of potatoes cost 50 cents in East Germany and the price hadn't changed in twenty years. Potatoes in West Germany cost six times that.

The village outside Düsseldorf where Ulrike's grandmother lived was a dull place. People spent most of their days inside stuffy, over-heated rooms, awash in inactivity. Sometimes they walked small dogs. They watched a great deal of television and ate a great deal, and it all made Ulrike very tired. She had dreamed of going to at least one rock concert during the week, but saw that that would be impossible. Nonetheless, she was comforted by the musty smell of the furniture and the sheets, which reminded her of visits to her grandparents' house in Zwickau when she was a small child, before her grandparents moved to the West. Her grandmother had all the old family furniture and Ulrike slept in a large antique bed that her grandparents had owned for many years.

After a few days, Ulrike was beside herself with boredom. There had to be more to West Germany than this. Nobody displayed any curiosity about life in East Germany. Instead, they acted as if they already knew all about it and wanted to know how she could stand it. How could she bear standing for three hours at the butcher? And how did she live without a deep freeze? After all, didn't she have to freeze anything she was able to buy right away, since who knew when it would show up in the stores again? Ulrike didn't bother to tell them that she would have trouble finding a deep freeze even if she wanted one. She had the feeling that all they wanted was confirmation of their own lives through their fantasies about Ulrike's miserable one. And that's when the anger set in. Ulrike stopped being polite and started to defend her small socialist country, as if it were a defenseless child.

"I've never stood for three hours at the butcher," she told them. "We cook Chinese and Indian and Mexican food. And there's enough. There's enough. A tenth of what you have here is enough."

The next disappointment came when a relative asked her to sign some papers. He said he wanted to take a tax deduction and needed her to sign a document saying she had stayed at her relative's and had taken a gift of over $600. She hadn't stayed at her relative's house and she hadn't taken any gifts from him. Taxes existed in East Germany, but they were structured differently, and she had no understanding of what he was trying to do, though she sensed there was something improper about it. Despite her misgivings, she signed the document anyway.

Her week in the West was passing and she was sitting in stiflingly warm living rooms, drinking coffee and helping with the dishes. She wanted to see something.

One of her grandmother's neighbors, a young woman from Brazil, heard that Ulrike was a Kindergarten teacher and offered to take her to a local Kindergarten. Ulrike was appalled by what she saw. The children ate breakfast whenever they felt like it, and they went home for lunch, because the mothers were at home! Ulrike couldn't understand why, if a woman had the luxury of staying home, she wouldn't keep her children with her all day. The teachers at the Kindergarten explained that the primary purpose of the Kindergarten was for the children to have social contact with other children. The teachers were Ulrike's age, but few of them had children of their own. With her bulging stomach, Ulrike thought to herself, she probably fit their stereotype of the fertile East German woman. Ulrike was overwhelmed by the many materials the children had at their disposal. There were dozens of different varieties of construction paper and pencils and crayons. The place was as orderly as a toy store.

The concept of a weekly Kindergarten was alien to these West German women. When Ulrike explained that it was a cross between an orphanage and a regular Kindergarten, they were at once intrigued and aghast. How could children be separated from their mothers like that for an entire week? This seemed like no solution at all. Ulrike tried to remain polite. She reminded them that most women worked and many of them worked night shifts, so that they were unable to care for their children during the week.

The teachers also asked Ulrike if it was true that children in East Germany were raised in an authoritarian manner, that three-year-olds were made to march to nationalistic songs, and sit quietly through lectures on Marxism. Ulrike could only laugh. In her mind's eye, she saw the unruly mob of kids, and the teachers trying to lure them down from trees with the promise of a delicious snack. It was difficult to get those children to sit through anything, she said. In fact, her Kindergarten was far more chaotic and its children given far more rein than the children at this one.

Near the end of the week, Ulrike and her mother took the train into Düsseldorf, and they went into a large department store. The entire store was a series of shoe departments, or so it seemed. It was all just too much. How could anyone possibly need so many shoes? Suddenly and simultaneously, they sat down amid one of the shoe displays and burst out laughing. If she hadn't been able to laugh with her mother just then, she would have cried.

The worst part of the visit to Düsseldorf proper was the number of panhandlers and prostitutes on the streets. Of course she had been taught in school that homelessness and prostitution were two of capitalism's most insidious by-products. But like all the other propaganda, she had largely ignored it. On one of the street corners she saw a young man playing the violin. This, she decided, was wonderful. Playing music on the street had always been one of Ulrike's dreams, and she and Ingo had even tried it once in the center of Potsdam. The East German police had hauled them away and detained them for several hours of questioning. But here was a man who was attracting little or no attention, while a passerby dropped the occasional coin into his violin case. But then she realized this wasn't really street music in the way she had envisioned it, because he was doing this to get money for food. And as she listened more carefully, she noticed that he didn't play particularly well. She became more depressed than ever.

She and her mother stopped in a pizzeria, and Ulrike ate a pizza with tuna and fresh mushrooms. Both ingredients were rarities at home, and it was then that she began to miss Ingo. She wished he could have been there to share some of the culinary adventures she was having. In spite of her defensiveness toward her relatives, she secretly delighted not just in the array of foods, but in how convenient they were to buy. She wanted Ingo to see it all, too.

Ulrike came up with her own solution to her boredom. She decided to leave a few days early and, on the way home, to visit friends in West Berlin who had fled the East two years earlier. She called them from her grandmother's and asked them to meet her train. Her visa made no provision for such a stop, but she decided to take the risk. Her train arrived at the Zoo Station in the center of West Berlin. Both friends were waiting for her. Ulrike had precisely twenty-four hours to spend there. Before she had a chance to say what she'd like to see, one of her friends said, "Let's go to the Glienicke Bridge." He said he did it frequently, just to look at what he had left behind.

The drive down to Potsdam seemed to take forever. As they wended their way south, the bustle and din of the city gradually died down, and the landscape grew bucolic. Ulrike thought it eerie. She was sure that around each corner they would run into the Wall. But she never saw it.

Finally they approached the Glienicke Castle. From the loggia of

the Kindergarten Ulrike had only had a glimpse of one small building on the castle grounds—the casino. Now she was able to see the
entire castle of the Prussian Prince Carl. Then the bridge came into
view. In contrast to the other side, on the Western side there were
just two guards, and a large sign warning them that they were leaving the American sector. They parked a safe distance from the
guards and walked over to the left of the bridge. Ulrike stood looking at Potsdam. It was a bleak, stagnant landscape. Nothing moved
but streams of Trabis, the anemic East German autos. She had already grown accustomed to the Western cars, and the Trabis looked
like small gray phantoms.

Then she walked over to the right of the bridge and climbed up a
small set of stairs to a lookout platform of sorts. It was a familiar
platform to her because as she was growing up she had had to suffer people from the West peering from such a perch over the Wall
into her neighborhood.

She was startled that she could see not just the house but a window on the second story that she and the children had painted with
butterflies. She thought of Frau Krabbes there, and Frau Neumann.
By this time, the children were up from their midday naps and probably playing in the back, while the cooks were lathering rolls with
marmalade. One of the kitchen staff had probably just mopped the
floor. She felt like calling out to them.

She didn't want to stay long at the bridge; she had only twenty-
four hours, and wanted to see as much of West Berlin as the time allowed. She called her friend Mandy, who was living in West Berlin
now. Mandy wanted to show Ulrike how wonderful everything in
the West was. As far as she was concerned, nothing was better than
the West, and nothing was worse than the East. But Ulrike couldn't
function. She couldn't eat what Mandy was cooking for her. The
prostitutes along the Kurfürstendamm upset her, and so did the
homeless people. She wanted to go home.

The Wall Comes Down

Benni, another boy, was born to Ulrike and Ingo in late 1987. As an
infant Benni was energetic where Philipp had been quiet, almost
phlegmatic. Ulrike took a year off to be with him. Many of her
friends were also taking a second baby year. In some ways, it was
like old times. They ate breakfast together and looked after one an-

other's children. The intensity of Ulrike's friendships with other women occasionally outstripped what she had with Ingo. Her relationship with Ingo was relaxed and predictable. But she was able to confide in her friends in a way that she couldn't with Ingo. She ascribed it to the fact that he was a man who, regardless of the preachings of equality through socialism, treated her as a member of an inferior sex. When Ingo got drunk, he called women *Weiber*, an antiquated word that when used in the 1980s was considered demeaning.

By the time Benni was a year old and it was time to go back to work, Ulrike sensed a growing restlessness among her friends. More and more of them were talking about the West as if it were a better place to be. Ulrike was surprised to hear some of them say they were thinking of applying to leave. Few of them did, but their discontent made her uneasy.

The dissatisfaction Ulrike's friends were feeling was reflected throughout East Germany. In 1989, an unprecedented wave of open opposition to hard-line Communist regimes swept across the Eastern Bloc. In Poland, Solidarity was legalized; the playwright and political dissident Vaclav Havel became president of Czechoslovakia; in Hungary, hard-line leaders were rejected and Hungary removed the electrified fence bordering Austria. By the summer, East Germans were streaming across the Hungarian border and into Austria.

But at the Kindergarten, nothing changed. Ulrike returned to work after her baby year to find her co-workers as set in their ways as ever. If they were aware of the dissident movement now building within East Germany they didn't show it. Perhaps they were afraid that if they so much as admitted to knowing about it, they would be placing themselves in danger. That summer at the Kindergarten went by like all summers. The children and the teachers spent most of their time outside in the garden. The warm weather had a relaxing effect on everyone. In those months the teachers migrated from the loggia to benches in the garden, where they sat for hours talking among themselves like nannies in Kensington Gardens while the children played around them. When parents arrived in the late afternoon to retrieve their children and saw the teachers on duty deep in conversation, it made them wonder whether anyone was watching the children. Some of the more concerned parents thought that although it was fine for the children to have a garden as wonderful as this one to keep them amused, that shouldn't excuse the teachers from organizing games and activities with them.

By early in the fall of 1989, Ulrike and Ingo were hearing about demonstrations throughout East Germany, and weekly demonstrations in Leipzig, with chants of *"Wir sind das Volk"* (We are the people). Thousands were taking to the streets to demand a share of Gorbachev's glasnost, and the freedom to travel. New Forum, the pro-democracy group, became a formidable organization.

Rumors spread of orders to shoot the Leipzig demonstrators. In the week leading up to October 7, an official holiday marking the fortieth anniversary of the German Democratic Republic, the Stasi occupied the Kindergarten, apparently fearful of what might happen in the vicinity of the bridge. A handful of Stasi agents stationed themselves in Frau Neumann's office around the clock. They brought in their own food and asked only for the use of the downstairs bathroom next to the kitchen. They accepted the women's offers of coffee. The children were told to stay away from the men and the teachers tried to continue working as if there was nothing out of the ordinary happening. As it turned out, the Leipzig demonstration proceeded peacefully and the precautions at the house had been unnecessary.

Ulrike and Ingo were at home playing Irish music with friends the night the Wall fell. Ingo's best friend, Lutz, was the last to leave, at about 11 P.M. An hour later the doorbell rang. Lutz was back.

"Have you heard the news? The Wall is open!"

"Are you crazy?" Ingo asked.

"Turn on the television!"

They turned on the television and watched, mesmerized, as the events unfolded. At the Brandenburg Gate, where the Wall was deep enough to stand on, people were dancing on top. And someone had taken a pickaxe to the Wall itself.

"Let's go over and see for ourselves," Lutz said. He had heard that the Glienicke Bridge was open.

But Ulrike and Ingo told Lutz to go without them. They had the children to worry about. Ulrike was still attending school for her Kindergarten teacher's certificate and had to be at an early morning class. She and Ingo went to bed.

That night, Frau Krabbes was on night duty at the Kindergarten. Night duty at the house—a rotating obligation—was a dreaded part of the job for all the teachers. It required struggling to stay awake and alert in the dark silent house, on call to fitful sleepers through the night. At eight o'clock, she put the children to bed and settled herself on a small couch in the loggia. Late that night the telephone rang, amplified through the house like a school bell. It was her husband, telling her the Berlin Wall had fallen. She didn't believe him. She looked out the window. There were people milling around the bridge. She thought it must be an escape attempt. She worried that someone would get shot. But there were no shots. After an hour, the people dispersed.

Early the next morning, as Ulrike walked to her school, she was startled by the number of people out on the street. It seemed as if they had been up all night. "I'll never forget it," she said later. "People were absolutely euphoric. You had this feeling you could go up to perfect strangers and hug them." It was possible to cross over the bridge, but it was necessary to go to the police and get a visa first. Hundreds of people were lined up outside the police headquarters.

It was all very confusing. Ulrike and Ingo weren't sure if they actually needed visas to go over the bridge. Everyone they asked had a different answer. Nobody, including the border guards, seemed to know precisely what the rule was. The first night at the various border crossings had been like a sweater unraveling: one stitch came out and the whole thing came apart. First dozens, then hundreds, then thousands of East Germans had presented themselves at border crossings by the hundreds and told border guards that travel restrictions no longer applied. The guards let them through, first at Bornholmer Strasse in the north, then at Checkpoint Charlie and Invalidenstrasse. Ulrike heard that a large gymnasium in Potsdam had been converted into a visa clearing house, where dozens of policemen sat at tables stamping passports.

Ingo had no great desire to go to West Berlin immediately. In fact, the only thing that made him consider going was the fact that he had a good friend he had grown up with in Erfurt who had left East Germany a few years earlier and settled in West Berlin. When they wanted to see each other they met in Czechoslovakia. The idea that he might travel just a couple of miles to see his friend intrigued him.

But Ingo didn't want to go alone. He wanted to go with someone who knew something about West Berlin. The last time Ingo had been in the West was 1961, just before the Wall went up. From all that he could tell, it was an intimidating place. So early that evening he and a friend set out on their bicycles. At the bridge there were masses waiting to go. It was dark out, and as they crossed, a crowd of West Germans, not yet allowed to travel over the Glienicke Bridge in the reverse direction, greeted them, clapping and cheering and shouting "Bravo!" Some of them were offering open champagne bottles to drink from. It seemed to Ingo very strange, almost embarrassing, that the rich West Berliners should be treating their poor relations as if they were emerging from four decades in prison.

The first thing that struck Ingo were all the Western cars parked at the side of the road: VWs and Mercedes and Opels, Mazdas and BMWs. Ingo was accustomed to Trabis and Wartburgs and Ladas. As soon as people crossed over into Wannsee, they stopped Western cars and hitched rides into the city. The buses and taxis were taking passengers up and down the four-mile stretch from the bridge to the S-Bahn station and charging no fare. Ingo and his friend took the S-Bahn up to Schöneberg and walked to the friend's apartment. Ingo was certain that he would be the first friend from the East to arrive. But there were already four old friends from Erfurt there who had driven through the previous night to Berlin.

They stayed just two hours and then took the S-Bahn back to Wannsee, and rode their bicycles back over the bridge. By this time it was close to midnight and the crowd at the bridge had thinned. They rode their bicycles home in the darkened, quiet Potsdam streets.

Ulrike decided it was more important to go to a party at Wolfgang's in Langerwisch that Saturday night than to rush off to West Berlin. But when they arrived in Langerwisch, there were far fewer people there than usual. Many were in West Berlin; others were too exhausted from having spent the previous two days there.

For days afterward it seemed that no one was working. Ingo's classes were poorly attended, and the only topic of conversation at the Kinderwochenheim was the recently opened border. West Berlin pubs were pouring free beer to East German patrons. Over and over Western television cameras captured jubilant East Germans pouring beer over one another's heads, or holding up Western 100 mark notes. Ingo was beginning to feel a bit ashamed of the behavior of his compatriots, lunging into television lenses singing *"Deutschland Deutschland über alles."* Reports started to emerge that the pub owners were beginning to regret all the beer they gave out, as their customers drank themselves into stupors and passed out on the pub floors, or filled the toilets with vomit.

The thing that impressed Ulrike most were the double-decker

buses that went from the bridge to the Wannsee station. The GDR buses were all filthy and half broken, but these were as tidy as her mother's house, with soft cloth seats. And the rides in the Western buses were so pleasant. Total strangers were chatting like old friends. In contrast to the sour-faced drivers in East Berlin, the West Berlin drivers were laughing and inviting passengers to board their buses for no fare. What she didn't know was that West Berlin bus drivers had a reputation for being among the surliest of the city's public servants. Ulrike had caught them in a temporary state of good cheer.

When Ulrike went to a West German bank and picked up her 100 deutschemarks in "greeting money," which every East German was entitled to, she resolved to spend it on something ordinary. Many of her friends were returning from West Berlin with portable stereos. She bought some fruit, and a few small toys for Philipp and Benni.

Of course there was no way to really know what the effect of the falling of the Wall would be, but Ulrike was beginning to see some signs. On the following Monday she went to work at the Kinder-wochenheim. She was on the early shift that week and it was still dark when she arrived at the house. The barrier gate was gone, ripped away by the first crowds. Inexplicably, it now lay in a corner of the garden at the front gate. And at the very spot where people had been arrested, or shot, if treading there, they were now strag-gling back over the bridge in the early morning after a night in West Berlin. The soldiers at the bridge had flowers in their uniforms.

The mood among the teachers that Monday was quiet. Ulrike wasn't surprised. She knew that most of them more or less believed in the system they lived in. Frau Neumann, in particular, married to a military officer, had never once questioned the authorities. It was known among the others that Frau Neumann's younger son had fled to the West some months earlier and that she had been extremely distressed by it. On that Monday, no one admitted to having been over. They talked cautiously about how it might be a good idea to go over and have a look at the West. Ulrike sensed Frau Neumann's unease. As director of the facility, it was her responsibility to repre-sent a certain loyalty to the state. Ulrike had the impression that everyone was maintaining a bit of a front. Everyone said they didn't trust what was happening. Frau Neumann said she didn't want her other son to go over because she feared the West might not let him return.

That night after work, Ulrike left Benni at home with Ingo and took Philipp over to visit Michael, the same friend Ingo had visited on Friday. There was still a crowd from Erfurt there. Ulrike and Philipp went with everyone to play billiards, then spent the night there. This time, in contrast to her Berlin visit a year earlier, Ulrike shared the others' happiness. This time she had her son with her, and they didn't necessarily have to go back.

Ulrike was curious to see how her five-year-old son would react. Philipp expressed no interest in all the colorful things in the stores. But he became truly excited by the double-decker buses, doors that opened automatically, escalators and riding on the S-Bahn. Philipp had always been difficult to predict. Nonetheless, his lack of interest in the toys surprised his mother. Ulrike took him to a toy store and told him to pick out whatever he wanted, and he didn't even want to go inside. "It was very strange," Ulrike recalled. "It was simply too much for him." He seemed much more taken by the different fruits: the bananas, and the kiwis, and the different varieties of pears and oranges.

Although life continued as normal, there was something dream-like about those first few weeks. One of the words heard most frequently was *Wahnsinn.* Craziness. For a place so dependent on established order, this was too much to fathom. Potsdam was already painted with the first coat of free enterprise. Three days after the Wall fell, a defunct state-run television store reopened on one of Potsdam's main boulevards. For sale: nothing but kiwis. In subsequent months along the central pedestrian mall, the city's shopping area and a long strip of typically gray East German shops, Western businesses quickly moved in. A well-known chain of bakeries opened a store, and a number of fast-food kiosks materialized. When an ice cream stand opened, there was always a line of customers.

Philipp's indifference to the new freedom to go West was much like that of other children in the Kinderwochenheim. They didn't seem to notice that everything in their immediate vicinity had changed completely, that where it was once dead quiet, cars were buzzing by, or standing in a traffic jam waiting to go over, and that pedestrians were constantly milling around the bridge. Nor did they notice that the guards had disappeared and the small houses for the soldiers now stood empty. The children continued to play with toys they had always played with. Nothing they had was quite as pretty or bright or new as Western toys, but it didn't seem to matter to them.

Now, instead of comparing gardening plots, the teachers at the Kinderwochenheim were paying attention to one another's attire, to what the others were driving and buying. One teacher, who the others suspected was married to a Stasi agent, had traded in her acrylic sweaters and pants for cotton leggings and oversized tops. After the currency union in July of 1990, which gave Easterners the Western marks they needed to buy Western products, most of them bought Western cars—a VW Passat for one, a Ford Fiesta for another.

The time following the opening of the Wall came to be known as the *Wende* (pronounced VEN-da), which means "turning." It can mean turning a car, or the turning around of a nation. Wende became a shorthand for conveying all that turned and changed and churned in the weeks before and after the Wall came down.

By the time the two Germanys were reunited in October 1990, Ulrike and Ingo were extremely uneasy. A nationalist overtone had crept into conversations. After the Wall fell and leading up to unification, "We are the people" had been replaced by "We are one people." That slogan, taken up by Kohl's Christian Democrats, made it onto Trabant bumpers throughout the GDR. Both Ulrike and Ingo were put off by the constant celebrating of Kohl and the West. At first, in the days immediately after the Wall fell, West Germans stood at the border with tidings of bananas. But after a while Ulrike found it downright embarrassing that people were eating bananas so greedily. It didn't surprise her when westerners began to mock easterners for their appetite. The banana became a symbol, first for the euphoria of the first few weeks following the Wall's fall, then for the distasteful aspects of unification. Westerners began to ridicule eastern Germans for seizing the opportunity to dissolve the borders between the two nations not out of a desire for democracy but out of a desire for fresh fruit. When a television reporter asked West German Otto Schily, a founder of the environmentalist Green Party, to sum up the reasons for German reunification, he pulled a banana from his suit pocket.

With undisguised contempt, West Germans began calling East Germans "Ossies," and East Germans turned around and started calling West Germans "Wessies." Ossies became the butt of many a joke at the hands of better-dressed, better-traveled, better-fed Wessies.

Banana jokes became commonplace ("How do we know Ossies are descended from apes? From all the bananas they eat!"), as did jokes about Trabants:

"How do you double the value of a Trabi? Fill it with gas."

"What do you call a Trabi on a hill? A miracle."

"How many workers does it take to assemble a Trabi? Two. One to fold and the other to staple."

"Why does a Trabi need a rear defroster? To keep your hands warm when you're pushing it."

Wessies began to send out unambiguous signals that they were no longer so keen on having the Ossies in their club, which produced this joke: "Ossi says to Wessi: 'We are one people!' Wessi responds: 'So are we.' "

Ulrike couldn't bring herself to eat any bananas. She had managed to remain happy and healthy for twenty-five years without any bananas. Why start eating them now? Three-year-old Benni, on the other hand, turned into a veritable banana snob. He loved bananas but insisted they be uniformly yellow and turned up his nose at the slightest evidence of brown specks.

At border crossings shortly after the Wall fell grocery-store chains distributed bags filled with basic foodstuffs that had been scarce in East Germany—not just bananas, but coffee and chocolate as well. East Germans were furious when they found that some of the food was old inventory that the stores needed to get rid of.

Ulrike and her brother, Frank, had grown distant with the fall of the Wall. He had left for the West shortly before the Wall fell and gotten married there. But the marriage fell apart and Ulrike found that the two of them had less and less to say to each other. He was becoming more and more obsessed with himself and his own difficulties. Now Ulrike felt that she was nothing more than the "poor Ossi" sister and he the "besser Wessi."

Ulrike had always liked other East Germans. But now she was beginning to wonder if she really did. The women she worked with at the Kinderwochenheim were becoming pettier than ever. They had perfected the language of victimization. As if to exaggerate the stereotype of the *Jammer-Ossi*—the constantly complaining East German—they complained about the high prices that reunification had brought with it, the greater quantities of garbage that western products generated because of all the unnecessary packaging, and the increased bureaucracy put in place to receive medical care. It was wrenching to go through such rapid change, to have an entirely new system suddenly imposed on them. They spoke wistfully of the many eastern food products that had disappeared from the stores and been replaced by more expensive western foods that didn't taste as good. The western ketchup was too sugary. Western pickles weren't as crisp as GDR pickles.

They were embittered and frustrated, and debilitated by self-concern. Their husbands were unemployed or facing unemployment. Women in reunified Germany had even more reason to be nervous about their jobs. East German women had worked mainly in jobs that were the first to be eliminated—in education, industrial production and administration. Frau Zierke, a teacher in her fifties, said that three of her friends—so devastated by the effects of reunification—had committed suicide.

Even after the Wall came down and there was no longer a need to fear anything from speaking one's mind, the teachers didn't talk with one another about their political opinions. No one said how she had voted in East Germany's first free elections in March of 1990, when East Germans voted overwhelmingly in favor of reunification, and the conservative Christian Democratic Union carried a sweeping victory. Perhaps it was because their lives now amounted to a lot of broken promises, first of the socialist state, then from Herr Kohl. Perhaps they were embarrassed to admit that they had brought this upon themselves. They had voted for Kohl's party but didn't say they had—which left them free to complain about it.

If it is the nature of Germans to be divided against themselves, then reunification was the perfect incitement to battle. Each side railed against the other—easterners were stupid and lazy, while westerners were arrogant and obnoxious. Wessies were behaving in the same awkward manner around Ossies as they would around someone in a wheelchair: staring at them was wrong, but looking away was wrong, too. And at the same time that eastern Germans were glorifying the past, western Germans were busy demonizing it. Western Germans fostered some peculiar myths about the former East Germany. Some had a vague basis in truth (all East Germans had kept a stash of thousands of marks under their beds) while others were complete fabrications (it was against the law for East German couples to touch each other when they danced).

Reunification was a bit like Halley's Comet—something that comes along once a century and by studying its physical properties you can learn a lot about your own universe. But rather than seize the chance to learn more about itself, each side focused on the differences. For forty years the two Germanys had been different, although superficially so. They wore different clothes, they vacationed in different places, they gave their children different names. At the same time, when the west looked at the east, it saw a more undiluted form of itself, purer in its Germanness after forty years of suspended animation. Western Germans resented the "reunification tax" deducted from their paychecks to help their seventeen million poor cousins rebuild eastern Germany. Easterners latched on to a new slogan: "I want my Wall back."

Most of Frau Neumann's fears and complaints centered on the Kindergarten. It was more expensive to maintain it now. Everything—from lightbulbs to construction paper—cost more. In the GDR days, parents had paid a nominal sum—about $10 a month. Although they were required to pay much more now, many of them failed to do so and Frau Neumann felt uncomfortable dunning them. The education department provided $200 a month for the children's toys and equipment, and another $50 for office supplies. But when she needed something beyond that allowance she had to request it from the school district. Recently, for instance, she had had to ask for the money for lice medication, as the children had contracted lice. At the same time, the parents had become more demanding consumers. They held the Kindergarten up to western standards and expected more from it—better food, better equipment, more field trips. Frau Neumann, who was doing her best just to keep the place running, resented the extra demands. She began having severe migraines.

Of all the teachers, Frau Neumann was most uneasy in a reunified Germany. She had spent her fifty years first in a war-torn country, then had become a victim of geography. And now, when the disappearance of Communism should have made her breathe more easily, she fretted all the more. Freedom frightened her. If flexibility or optimism had once been in her nature, East Germany had long since squeezed it out of her. Ulrike wondered sometimes what kind of woman Helga Neumann would be if she had lived her life in West Germany.

The toll of reunification was particularly pronounced on those eastern Germans considered asocial, who were losing the social safety net provided by the GDR. Children parroted their parents' worries: "My father says everyone is going to lose their job." "My mother says we need the Wall back." Children told of heavy drinking at home. One Monday morning the teachers arrived at the house to hear that one desperate father had killed himself over the weekend by jumping from his upper-story apartment window while his children stood nearby and watched.

But there was one aspect of reunification that pleased Ulrike. For years she had managed without a telephone. She and her best friend, who lived across a large courtyard, had devised a complicated system of signaling with their window shades and lights. Now she and all of her friends applied for telephone lines to their homes. Ulrike knew that Telekom, the German telephone company, was overburdened and that it might take several months before she got one. On the other hand, under the Communists she hadn't even bothered to apply because it could take two decades.

In late 1991 the telephone was installed. Ingo, however, considered the addition to the household a great nuisance. As soon as it was installed, the phone rang constantly—and always for Ulrike. If she wasn't home, Ingo answered the phone only after a half dozen rings, and, having never learned telephone etiquette, he answered with a great deal of gruffness. He complained to Ulrike that he was becoming her secretary.

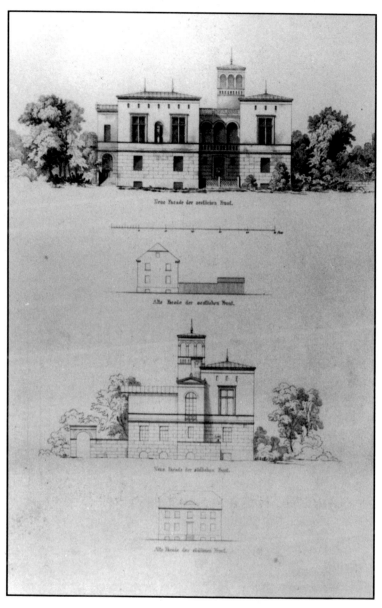

Ludwig Persius's original drawing of the villa he designed for Kurd Wolfgang von Schöning, a courtier to Prussia's royal Hohenzollerns in the 1840s. The villa was later the home of three generations of the Wallich family. (Courtesy of Dirk Heydemann)

ALTHOUGH HILDEGARD REHRMANN WAS NOT PAUL WALLICH'S FIRST CHOICE, IN MARRYING HER HE FINALLY ENDED HIS QUEST FOR A NON-JEWISH WIFE. (Courtesy of the Wallich family, London)

PAUL AND HILDEGARD IN THE 1930S. THE PHOTOGRAPH CAPTURED PAUL'S CAUTIOUS AFFECTION FOR HIS WILLFUL SPOUSE. (Courtesy of Karl-Heinz Tornow)

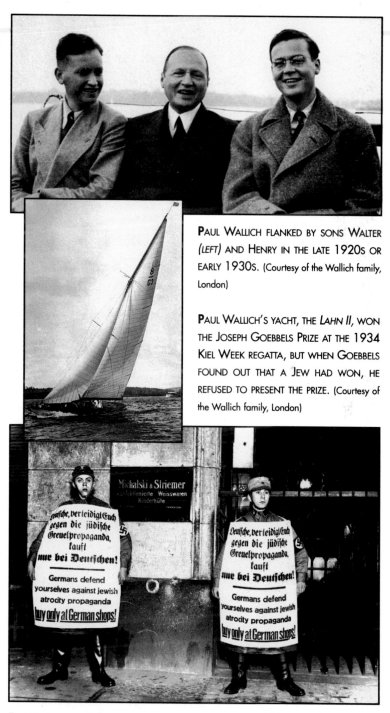

Paul Wallich flanked by sons Walter *(left)* and Henry in the late 1920s or early 1930s. (Courtesy of the Wallich family, London)

Paul Wallich's yacht, the *Lahn II,* won the Joseph Goebbels Prize at the 1934 Kiel Week regatta, but when Goebbels found out that a Jew had won, he refused to present the prize. (Courtesy of the Wallich family, London)

The boycott of Jewish businesses spread quickly after Hitler seized power in 1933, but Paul Wallich could not bring himself to leave Germany. (Landesbildstelle Berlin)

ELEVEN YEARS AFTER THE END OF THE WAR,
THE CENTER OF POTSDAM WAS STILL IN
RUBBLE. (ULLSTEIN-ROEHNERT)

MAMA KEMPA IN THE 1950S WITH FOUR
OF HER CHARGES AT THE KINDER-
WOCHENHEIM.

CHILDREN FROM THE KINDERWOCHEN-
HEIM PRESENT FLOWERS TO BORDER GUARDS
AT THE GLIENICKE BRIDGE IN THE 1960S,
AS DICTATED BY MARGOT HONECKER'S EDU-
CATION PLAN.

FRAU NEUMANN (*LEFT*) AND ULRIKE WEICHELT AT A PARTY AT THE KINDER-WOCHENHEIM IN THE 1980S.

ULRIKE SERENADES A GROUP OF CHILDREN AT THE KINDERWOCHEN-HEIM AT BEDTIME.

MARGOT AND ERICH HONECKER CELEBRATE EAST BERLIN'S 750TH BIRTHDAY IN 1987. MARGOT HONECKER TOOK A PARTICULAR INTEREST IN EDUCATION. IN JANUARY 1989, ERICH HONECKER PROCLAIMED THE WALL WOULD "STILL BE STANDING IN 50 OR 100 YEARS." (LANDESBILDSTELLE BERLIN)

ARCHITECTURE STUDENT
DIRK HEYDEMANN WAS
AT THE WALL THE NIGHT
IT CAME DOWN. DIRK
GAVE HIS PICKAX TO
AN EAST BERLINER,
WHO ACCOMPANIED
EACH BLOW WITH THE
WORDS, "THAT'S FOR
ALL THE YEARS!" (PHOTO
BY DIRK HEYDEMANN)

THE OPENING OF THE BERLIN WALL GAVE DIRK HEYDEMANN THE OPPORTUNITY TO
EXPLORE THE HISTORY OF THE GARDEN BEHIND THE WALLICH VILLA. (COURTESY OF
DIRK HEYDEMANN)

THE VILLA IN THE SPRING OF 1990, AS SEEN FROM THE BERLIN SIDE OF THE HAVEL RIVER. THE GLIENICKE BRIDGE IS IN THE FOREGROUND. ALTHOUGH THE BORDER HAD BEEN OPEN FOR SIX MONTHS, THE WALL ITSELF WAS ONLY PARTIALLY REMOVED. (COURTESY OF PAUL WALLICH)

CHRISTINE AND PAUL WALLICH TRAVELED TO BERLIN IN 1990 TO FIND THE HOUSE AILING. (COURTESY OF PAUL WALLICH)

MONIKA HAGEN, FRESH OUT OF LAW SCHOOL WHEN SHE BEGAN WORKING AS A CLAIMS OFFICIAL, DECIDED THE FATE OF THE WALLICH VILLA AND MANY OTHER PROPERTIES IN THE FORMER EAST GERMANY. BY 1994 SHE HAD MOVED INTO THIS MODERN NEW OFFICE. (COURTESY OF MONIKA HAGEN)

CRISTINE WALLICH AT HOME IN MCLEAN, VIRGINIA, IN FRONT OF A RELATIVE'S PAINTING OF THE VILLA SCHÖNINGEN. (PHOTO BY THE AUTHOR)

ULRIKE IN A CONTEMPLATIVE MOOD ON THE MAIN STAIRCASE THE DAY THE KINDERWOCHENHEIM MOVED OUT IN LATE 1992. (PHOTO BY BERND GURLT, POTSDAM)

5: THE WALLICHS

Hildegard's Extended Family

When Hildegard had decided to move from California to New York in 1947 to be near her older son, Henry was working at the Federal Reserve Bank in New York.

In 1940, without so much as an undergraduate degree, Hildegard's enterprising eldest son had convinced Harvard's economics department to admit him as a graduate student. "I was particularly weak in the area of theory, having never seen an elementary textbook," Henry later wrote. But Harvard gave him credit for "every conceivable earlier activity remotely associated with economics," and he received his Ph.D. four years later. He then joined the New York Fed as its Latin American expert. Economists had been in great demand during the war (nearly as much as riveters, Henry once noted), and the boom continued afterward, with economists sought after by universities, government agencies and financial institutions.

His successful start in a career notwithstanding, as a foreigner and partial non-Aryan Henry did not feel completely secure in his situation in the United States in the postwar years; in the political climate of the time, he was unsettled by his brother Walter's open expression of his socialist views to mutual acquaintances.

At the New York Fed Henry met his future wife, Mable Brown, also an economist there. They married in 1950. Soon after his marriage Henry took a teaching position at Yale, and he and Mable had three children in fairly quick succession: Christine, Anna and Paul.

Hildegard, who had now created something of a peripatetic life for herself, moved to New Haven as well. Her influence on the household and its routines was strong and immediate. She spoke excellent English, but in her presence the children were expected to speak German. In Potsdam, the family had always eaten a cold supper on Sunday nights because that was the servants' night off. Even after she moved to the United States, Hildegard ate a cold supper on Sundays. So did her grandchildren. Christmas in New Haven was a carbon copy of Christmas in Potsdam when on Christmas Eve the children descended the stairs to find a tree laced with slender lighted candles. Christmastime suppers usually consisted of herring salad, black bread and boiled eggs.

As a young child, Henry's eldest daughter, Christine, already spoke fluent German. And while the family was in Germany during Henry's sabbaticals, German was Christine's primary language. When she returned to the United States she encountered a painful lesson in assimilation. Christine was direct and forthright as a child, even pushy at times. Her mother, who had learned German since her marriage, applied a German expression to it. She said Christine had *Ellenbogen,* or elbows. When Christine was still quite small, she addressed strangers on the street in loud German phrases. When she went to kindergarten at age five, her English was halting and flawed. Some of her classmates taunted her, and called her a Nazi, which was particularly hurtful.

Christine described her childhood in New Haven as a "1950s German upbringing." Her father, she said, "wasn't the Fred MacMurray style of husband, coming home at five, changing his clothes and barbecuing." Henry was hardly an attentive father. He had inherited his own father's traditional views on children—they were all right as long as the sound was turned down. His attitude lent credence to the family legend that he once jokingly advised his brother Walter that the way to be absolved of responsibility for infant care was to come close to dropping the baby a few times; one was then sure to be liberated from all further obligations.

The New Haven house in which Christine and her siblings grew up was a large airy Victorian Gothic structure a short walk from a river. It wasn't until much later that she noticed a pattern in her father's taste in houses. They were always near water, and there was always a view of some kind. In New Haven, he turned the master bedroom, which contained a large picture window, into his study. When Christine finally saw the Potsdam house in 1990, she understood why.

Everything Henry's family did had to be approached with thought. Like his grandfather, Henry was a wine connoisseur and kept a huge wine cellar consisting mostly of German wines. But he derived as much pleasure in knowing the origin of the grapes and the method by which they were grown and harvested as he did in drinking it with his meal. "The same with music," Christine recalled. "He would say, 'Let's read the libretto. Who wrote it? What was it all about?' "

Christine knew that her household was different from those of her schoolmates. There was no television in the house. The rule was that the family would acquire a television after the youngest child learned to read. "And that meant the encyclopedia, not ABCs," Christine said. "My father did not go to baseball games or take us to the circus. The nature of the pursuits we did as a family were different. They were Sunday walks, going to art museums, taking four-year-olds to the opera." Shopping malls were another taboo.

When they reached adolescence, all three children were sent to Kent, an Episcopal boarding school in northwestern Connecticut. The school emphasized "moderation in all things and constancy of purpose," said Christine. Christine's stay there overlapped slightly with Anna's, which overlapped with Paul's. But even when they were there together, the siblings didn't have much to do with each other. The children didn't often travel home. Instead, every other weekend Mable drove to Kent and took them out to lunch.

While growing up, Christine was perhaps more attuned to what her father did for a living than most children were. Particularly when the family was living in Frankfurt while Henry was on sabbatical from Yale Christine became accustomed to frequent visits from European and American economists. Some of them were to remain lifelong acquaintances and colleagues of Henry's. Many years later, when she, too, became an economist, Christine was in regular touch with people she had met as a toddler in the 1950s. For years afterward Christine remembered the hats they wore, their "funny German suits with animals around the neck. The hats with veils and the hatpins and feathers."

While in Frankfurt, Henry worked on a book that became his seminal work: *Mainsprings of the German Revival*. First published in 1955, the book was the definitive work on the origins of the German economic recovery after World War II. In it, he expressed concerns about Germany that he rarely, if ever, discussed with his own children. "The present political and cultural vacuum in Germany compels one to speculate what might fill it," Henry wrote of postwar Germany. "[The] existing condition appears unstable and in danger of being displaced by some new enthusiasm. God help Germany and the world if it is again the wrong one."

Christine's memory of her father was of a man utterly absorbed in his work. His work was his life. "He was the man with the tape recorder," she recalled. "He would come home, and be pacing his study dictating speeches or notes for classes. Or he would sit in his study with a yellow pad and electric typewriter." Especially after President Richard Nixon appointed him to the Federal Reserve Board in 1974, Henry led an intense work life. In his twelve-year tenure as a member of the Board of Governors, he established a reputation for his intellectual rigor, his wit and his somewhat austere manner. His colleagues counted him among the foremost economic thinkers of his time. He was known mostly for his conservative streak, and his intolerance of inflation.

The more Henry worked, the less his children saw of him. An ordinary briefcase was too small. He carried work documents between home and office in an oversized salesperson's case, made to carry paint samples. He arrived every day by 7 A.M., and was still at work at 6 P.M.

As a father, Henry was distant and reserved. His son, Paul, recalled that there were two occasions on which Henry took him aside for what Henry considered a serious talk. Both times it was to talk about economics. He remained silent on most aspects of his personal background. If Christine asked him specific questions, his answers were vague. He never talked about his father and Christine was never quite sure why. "Paul Wallich to me as we were growing up was a portrait in my father's study," she said. It was a cold portrait, and its austerity made Christine think he must have been a severe or unhappy man. Hermann's portrait hung in Henry's study, too. His face seemed to have more character. Indeed, Henry talked freely and proudly about his grandfather Hermann, and his rise to the pinnacle of the German banking elite. On the subject of his own father he was surprisingly reticent.

Occasionally Henry did reminisce about his earliest years, up to age fifteen, during the Weimar Republic. One of his favorite stories was about hyperinflation, and the time Hildegard sent him off to riding lessons with a 5 billion mark note. He also told his children a little bit about his days at Oxford. But he seldom referred to the period from 1933 to 1944, when he was in South America, New York and Harvard. His reminiscences picked up again when he started work at the New York Fed. Henry's silences were always a mystery to his children. When he did occasionally talk about the years in Argentina and Chile, he spoke in highly impersonal terms. "I learned where he lived, and some of the things he ate and saw," Christine recalled. "But he said nothing about himself. He talked only about things." They could only guess at the effect Hitler had on Henry's career.

Henry was perhaps most open with his brother, Walter, despite the differences between them. Henry had developed into a conservative economist and Walter, a journalist with the BBC in London, had strong leanings to the left. On the few occasions that Walter visited Henry at his office at the Federal Reserve Board, Henry's coworkers could hardly believe that the two men—one an open and friendly Briton with an impeccable British accent and the other a reserved American with a tinge of German accent—were brothers.

Despite advancement in their chosen careers, Henry and Walter felt that their education had suffered as a result of their forced departure from Germany. The German government ceded the point, awarding both brothers compensation for damage to their education.

Hildegard talked quite a bit about the family, but she, too, remained strangely silent on the topic of her husband, Paul. Christine couldn't recall one mention of Paul by her grandmother. Instead, Hildegard grew misty on the topic of her beloved brother, Walter, the painter who had died in World War I. In fact, World War I and the difficult conditions it brought to Germany were one topic Hildegard frequently dwelt on. She talked about the difficulty of nursing Henry when she wasn't eating well enough herself, and about the difficulty of trying to get food for Walter, whose delicate constitution didn't tolerate all foods.

Hildegard remained a strong influence on her family even as it was strewn across the globe. The children were expected to speak when spoken to, to kiss their grandmother upon her arrival, and to rise when adults entered the room. She seldom raised her voice. It was simply accepted that her word was law. When Henry's family lived in Germany, Hildegard visited them there, and when Henry and Mable traveled, Hildegard stayed with the children. On vacations to Germany Hildegard stayed in the same hotel as the family and took all her meals with them. Hildegard also provided the glue for her twelve grandchildren. She insisted that they write to one another regularly. When she visited a branch, she took small gifts from the branch she had just left.

Hildegard's children and grandchildren regarded her and her itinerant life, which she maintained well into her dotage, with both awe and trepidation. Whenever she visited London, Walter would become physically ill a few days beforehand, usually with a stomach complaint that his wife ascribed to nerves. For years Hildegard terrorized Walter's wife, Muji, accused her of trying to starve her or, still worse, poison her. Walter had married Muji in 1956. An intelligent, headstrong Spanish woman several years Walter's junior, Muji developed an immediate dislike for Hildegard, who dwelt on her daughter-in-law's lack of formal education. Through the years, Muji came to demonize the doyenne of her husband's family, and to express a distaste in general for all things German. Her attitude had a long-lasting effect on her children.

One of Hildegard's grandchildren once compared her to the main character in Friedrich Dürrenmatt's play *The Visit,* which is about a wealthy old woman who returns to her hometown village to wreak revenge on her childhood sweetheart, who wronged her decades earlier. Although Hildegard had never sought summary vengeance for past misdeeds, her ability to strike fear into those she visited made the comparison an apt one.

As she advanced into old age, Hildegard began to lose her faculties. There was something wraithlike and pitiful about her. When she stayed with Walter's family in their large house in London, after each meal she would disappear upstairs briefly, then return to her seat at the dining room table and wait for the next meal. Hildegard loved dogs, but disdained cats, and could occasionally be seen giving her foot to the family cat in London. After her senility worsened, the London Wallichs once observed her kicking her handbag at the base of her chair, which she had mistaken for the cat.

Walter and Muji had five children: Erica, Robert, Kathy and a set of twins, Walter and Peter. Their father had little hesitation about informing them of their Jewish heritage. He apparently saw no reason to tell them anything but the truth about their grandfather's death, and he occasionally expressed rage over it. Walter's children later recalled an incident that occurred when they were small. On a walk one day in their neighborhood in north London, the family came across a swastika spray-painted on a wall. Walter's temper flared and he said, "It's exactly this that made your grandfather tie weights around his waist and throw himself into the Rhine." At that moment, Walter seemed offended and enraged at something that drove his father to suicide. At other times, his children sensed a silent anger at Paul himself for lacking the courage and energy to leave Germany when he still could.

Between their mother's general dislike of Germany and their father's sad experiences with his homeland, the British Wallich children knew little that might endear them to Germany. They remained neutral, at best, and had a much greater affinity for Spain, their mother's native country, than for Germany. To reinforce the family's bond with Spain, Walter and Muji bought land outside El Escorial in central Spain, built a house and took the children there for summers. The children loved their maternal grandmother. Their memory of their other grandmother included stories of, worst of all, prejudices in her family.

Stories circulated among her grandchildren that while Hildegard was a girl, the family dog had been trained to perform a clever trick. A biscuit was held out to the dog. Say "It comes from Christians," and the dog took the biscuit. Say "It comes from Jews," and the dog turned away.

Henry remained very reserved on the subject of the family's Jewish heritage, particularly in his professional circle. A few years after Henry's death in 1988, when a magazine article mentioned the circumstances of Paul's death, Christine got a call from Helmut Schlesinger, the head of the German Bundesbank, Germany's central bank. He told Christine that in the thirty-five years he had

known Henry, he never had an inkling that the family had been persecuted. Christine's own guess was that Henry remained silent on
the topic, particularly among his German colleagues, because he
believed it might have colored the way people treated him.

For a long time Paul's death was a mystery to his three American
grandchildren, Henry's children. For many years, Christine wasn't
sure how he had died or why he had died. It was Mable who took
her eldest child aside one day when she was ten years old. "She ba-
sically said, 'You may hear this from somebody else and you may be
upset by it, so I'll tell you,' " Christine recalled. Mable told Christine
that her grandfather had killed himself and that it had to do with the
Nazis. For years Christine thought Paul had shot himself. It wasn't
until fifteen years after that conversation with her mother, when she
was talking with Fritz Körte, one of her Argentine cousins, and
brought up the topic of their grandfather's death that she learned he
had drowned himself.

And it wasn't until she went to England to attend Cambridge and
heard the story from her British relatives that Christine learned that
her great-grandparents had been Jewish and raised their children as
Protestants. Until he read Paul's memoir, published as a commemo-
ration together with Hermann's by the Deutsche Bank in 1978,
which contained his suicide notes to Hildegard and to Henry, Christine's younger brother, Paul, thought his grandfather had died from
the lingering effects of an injury he sustained during World War I.

Christine and the House at the Bridge

Of Henry's three children, Christine was the only one who developed a strong attachment to the house in Potsdam while she was
growing up. She grew up looking at a watercolor of the house that
hung in the family's foyer in New Haven, painted by a distant relative at the turn of the century. The house itself dominated the painting, and it was surrounded by the accoutrements of bucolic
elegance: a dinghy floating daintily in the water; the Prussian flag
flying from atop the high tower; and three large pots holding exoti-
cally tropical plants outside the front door. The house in the painting offered the benign promise of a family intact and thriving.

Christine continued the Potsdam traditions in her own household
in McLean, Virginia, serving meals on china engraved with the ini-
tials "H.W.," which her uncle Walter had salvaged from the Potsdam

house. In obstinate denial of the fact that suburban Washington in the latter part of the twentieth century bears little resemblance to nineteenth-century Prussia, Christine also planted some of the same trees and shrubs that had been in the Potsdam garden.

The generation of the Wallich family that Christine knew was intact only in pockets, strewn as it was all over the globe. And whether it was thriving was debatable. In their many years of corresponding, Henry and his brother, Walter, had occasionally discussed the family's relatively precipitous ascent and decline in wealth and status. In the course of one generation, the family had descended from opulence to middle-class comfort. The war had reduced Hildegard's fortune considerably, and her children's inheritance was diminished accordingly.

As a journalist with the BBC, Walter was not destined for a great independent fortune. And as a professor of economics, then as an economist in the public service at the Federal Reserve Board, Henry had also chosen a field far less lucrative than his father's and grandfather's. Obviously, neither of them would live as their father had. While Walter seemed concerned by this, Henry took the view that they had entered socially respectable professions, and he encouraged his brother to enjoy the rewards of the middle class.

Christine had visited the Potsdam house many times in her imagination. Her grandmother had taken her on extended verbal tours. And several times over the years, while the Berlin Wall stood, she had actually gone to Berlin to see it. The first time she went was as a teenager, by herself, during her first long trip through Europe in the 1970s. She stayed with cousins in West Berlin and they drove her to the Glienicke Bridge, the closest she could get to the house.

The Glienicke Bridge had long since become a fixed part of the landscape, and Christine had heard about it for years. Whenever she told West Berliners that her family had a house in the East and told them it was at the Glienicke Bridge, they knew precisely where it was. After all, the Cold War was quite literally being played out in their backyard. But when she mentioned the bridge to her American friends, it meant little. If she mentioned spy exchanges, they tended to confuse the bridge with Checkpoint Charlie, the famous border crossing between the two Berlins and the venue for the opening pages of John le Carré's *The Spy Who Came In from the Cold*.

When Christine arrived at the bridge that first time, she saw that it was impossible to get very close to the house. The best view came from standing on the opposite bank of the Havel. So Christine stationed herself on the edge of the water, next to a fast-food kiosk that served the weekend visitors to that sylvan southern edge of Berlin. While standing there, she recalled years later, she felt "a tremendous sense of loss. I was very struck by the situating of the house," the guard towers and the impenetrable fencing across the river. She was startled when her relatives told her that there were mines in the water.

While her cousins' attitude toward Germany and the family property there was realistic, occasionally even a shade bitter, Christine's was romantic. Standing on the bank of the river, she gazed for a long time at the house that stood hostage on the opposite side of the water, its cupola peering over the Wall. The house was no more than two hundred yards away. It was so close, in fact, that if Christine had called out, people sitting inside could have heard her through an open window.

The house in Potsdam signified her father's home, but it also came to stand for a time when her family was in one place, unaffected by what was to come. Gradually, too, the Potsdam villa had come to represent less a house in Germany than Germany itself.

Christine did not spend much time pondering the possibility of living to see the house return to Wallich hands, but she nurtured an attachment to it nevertheless, partly because she knew that the house in Potsdam symbolized the family's past prosperity. And Germany had become for Christine and her siblings a kind of second home. The family's frequent trips there, particularly those made when the children were very young, gave them a sense of belonging in two places.

Christine collected signs of her father's attachment to Germany like so much memorabilia. She thought it no accident, having seen the family villa on the Havel, that her father had always chosen to live in houses that were near water. Not only was the house in New Haven near a stream, but so was the house he and Mable bought in McLean, when Henry was appointed to the Federal Reserve Board in Washington. Christine noted that two books which occupied a prominent place in Henry's library were Thomas Wolfe's *You Can't Go Home Again* and *Look Homeward Angel*. The family cars carried vanity license plates—Lahn I and Lahn II, after the family sailboats. If Henry's children could not experience the feeling of *Heimat* firsthand, they could at least experience it through their father.

Henry Seeks His Past

Heimat is a German word that defies precise translation. It is more a feeling than anything else. It can mean place of birth but also the place where one feels most at home. It can be a country, a region or the village that had been home to a family for centuries. It was often the feeling of Heimat that held Germans in their towns in East Germany even when they still had ample opportunity to leave before the Wall went up and it was too late. The strong identification with their Heimat prompted many Jews to stay in Germany until it was too late, and others to return to Germany after the war.

Henry's sense of Heimat was manifest in his urge to revisit the home of his childhood. Though he seldom spoke of it to his children, he tried for years to obtain a visa from the East German government so that he might revisit the house in Potsdam. Finally, in 1979, he succeeded, and he and Mable spent several days in East Germany. There was little that looked familiar. He was pleased to see that the ornate Nikolai Church in the center of Potsdam still stood. But the beautiful City Palace was gone, and in its place was a large, modern, poorly built hotel. The street where the family's house had stood, Neue Königsstrasse, had been renamed Berliner Strasse, although, Henry noted ironically in a later journal of the trip, "the street unfortunately doesn't lead there." In fact, it seemed that most of the streets had been renamed.

Henry and Mable thought they might get a better view of the house from the Potsdam side. But they were able to reach only the middle of the garden wall before encountering the heavily guarded border zone, and a barrier warning unauthorized persons to stop in their tracks. From what Henry and Mable were able to see, it appeared the house was being used as a child-care center of some kind. There were no children around, but there were signs suggesting their presence: the paths running through the stately garden were gone, as well as the stone benches, and the entire garden had been transformed into a playground, with rubber tires serving as various pieces of gym equipment, a crudely constructed toy ship and a swing set. The fact that everything was rusted led them to believe that the facility had been there for quite a while.

Henry remembered that lime and chestnut trees had hidden the house. But they were gone and the house stood in plain view. The house appeared to be much darker in hue than he remembered.

And from the curtains in the windows it appeared to be occupied on all three floors. Although he and Mable stood there for at least fifteen minutes, the guards didn't seem to take much notice.

Henry wanted to look for Paul's grave. Paul had been buried alongside Hildegard's parents in a cemetery only a mile or two from the house, the city's oldest graveyard. Deserted and in terrible condition, its gravesites and tombstones were grown over with grass. After a grave-by-grave inspection, they found nothing. They searched for an office that might be able to tell them where the graves were, but found no buildings open. Depressed and defeated, they left.

They left Potsdam at the place where they had entered, and at the border control, Henry asked the guard—with the Faustian devil in mind, he noted wryly in his journal—whether it was an East German law that one must exit by the same place one had entered.

A few days later, after driving out to visit the old country estate in Jerchel, Henry and Mable drove back toward Potsdam, this time approaching it from the Western side, and they took up the familiar station at the kiosk on the bank.

Their view of the house was much better from the Western side of the river, mostly because the East Germans had cut down all of the tall trees around the Wall and death strip. Henry was pleased to see that the lion of copper alloy—one of his favorite features of the house—seated inside an arch in the garden wall, was still in good shape. He was also glad to see that the Pallas Athene was still keeping a quiet vigil in her small arched niche on the outside wall.

Henry wanted to have another try at finding his family's graves. He and Mable drove back to the old cemetery in Potsdam and this time found two helpful women working in the office who told them exactly where to find the graves. But when they arrived at the site, instead of marked graves they came upon what appeared to be a workshop for building gravestones. They approached a stone mason at work there. He told them that he had been over the site with his shovel and gathered all the tombstones he could find, and pointed to a collection of tombstones nearby. They inspected all of them. Paul's was nowhere to be found.

Henry never would enter the Potsdam house. In 1985, at age seventy-one, he went to see his doctor because he was having trouble remembering things. He thought he might be losing his mind. The doctor advised him not to worry about it. He was just getting older.

A few months later, while at a conference in Asia, he collapsed. He was flown back on a government plane, and entered the hospital for tests. He was diagnosed with a brain tumor.

After surgery he eventually returned to work. He was noticeably weak, but insisted on continuing to work. One day, while walking past a stack of his own papers and speeches, he remarked sadly, "Did I really write all of this" His secretary put the pile of papers away so he wouldn't have to pass them again. When Henry died in September 1988, Mable searched for something to inscribe on his tombstone. She found an Alexander Pope quotation he had circled in Bartlett's: "A Mighty Maze, But Not Without a Plan."

At the time of Henry's death, Hildegard had been in a nursing home near New Haven for sixteen years. For the last several years of her life she was gravely senile. When her son Walter visited her in 1976, she mistook him for her brother Walter. Hildegard died in 1989, at the age of 101, having outlived her three children. Both Walter and Christel had died earlier, Christel of a brain tumor and Walter of pancreatic cancer.

Shortly before the Berlin Wall fell, the family lawyer, a man with the unfortunate name of Hans Frank (a different Hans Frank, a Hitler crony, had been the Nazi Party lawyer and governor of Nazi-occupied Poland), looked into the possibility of seeing the Potsdam house returned to the family. A German-Jewish emigré who had been Henry's lawyer in the 1940s and remained the family lawyer even after he became partner at a successful corporate law firm on Wall Street, Frank was of two minds about the Wallichs. He was loyal to Henry, as the two had known one another as young men newly arrived to the United States from Germany. On the other hand, he was sharply critical of Henry's father, Paul, whom he had never known but whom he had read about. He thought that Paul embodied the worst kind of German Jew—one whose desire to assimilate not only overshadowed all else but, in the end, killed him.

Christine and Paul Enter the Maze

It was with a mix of apprehension and excitement that Christine set out with her brother, Paul, for Germany in April of 1990, five months after the Berlin Wall fell. When Christine was in fifth grade in Germany in 1961 during one of her father's sabbaticals from Yale, her class had carried on a correspondence with a fifth-grade class in

East Germany. When the Wall went up that summer, the connection was suddenly broken. Now the lines were open again, communication and travel possible again. Might it be that she and her brother could now visit and explore the house that had been till now only a picture on the wall, a family legend, a fabled villa seen from an opposite bank? And was the impossible now possible? Might the house now be restored to its rightful owners?

Christine was not alone in her hope of repossessing the past. Other Western owners of East German properties had soon learned after the Wall fell that their properties had become accessible once again. But they and Christine would also learn that the return of property, the question of what belongs to whom, had become a central and contentious debate on the way to a reunified Germany, a protracted soul searching. It seemed that all of East Germany was up for grabs, and the question of rightful ownership maddeningly vexed.

Property rights in Germany had become elastic from the time that Hitler came to power in 1933, beginning with the systematic expropriation of the properties of Jews in the name of Aryanization. The Soviets, occupying East Germany with the dissolution of the Third Reich in 1945, had subsequently undertaken their own program of expropriation, for reasons no less vehemently ideological. This time the victims of property seizures weren't the Jews but the Junkers, Germany's landed nobility. In the four years of Soviet occupation, some eight million acres were seized, about a third of eastern Germany's total land area. In that time, too, virtually all of the aristocrats, stripped of their estates and seeing what Communism would mean for the nobility, fled eastern Germany for the newly democratic West Germany.

The Wallichs' estate in rural Jerchel fell victim to the Soviets. The property spread over some 1,500 acres and accounted for about a third of the entire village. Paul and his sister, Ilse, had inherited the farm from their parents but signed it over to their spouses in 1936, presumably to protect it from the Nazis. Ilse and her husband, Oskar, stayed at Jerchel through the war. But shortly after the war, in 1946, they were stripped of the property in the first wave of Soviet land reform. They were promised title to twenty-three acres but never received the actual deed. The 1950s brought the forced collectivization of farms, and the Jerchel farm was one of them. Whatever Ilse and Oskar still had claim to was wiped away.

The Wallich descendants knew only vaguely what had become of the Potsdam house since Henry and Mable's trip there a decade earlier. In early 1990 Hans Frank, the New York lawyer who, with Mable, was co-executor of Hildegard's will, wrote to Mable to report on a visit he had made to Berlin. According to real estate brokers he had consulted there, the value of the Potsdam property was approximately $950,000, for approximately 20,000 square feet.

Frank told Mable that the house itself was in such poor condition it should be torn down. The property was being used as a kindergarten "and the legal difficulties to remove the tenant are formidable," he wrote.

Christine and her brother had a clear agenda for their trip to Berlin. They wanted to see the house in Potsdam, as well as the old family estate at Jerchel. They also meant to inquire into getting both pieces of property back, although they weren't quite certain how to go about it. Hans Frank suggested they get in touch with a young Berlin lawyer who had been an intern at Frank's firm the previous year. So one of their first visits was to the law offices of Knauthe & Partner on the wide, posh Kurfürstendamm.

The tall and confident young lawyer with the aristocratic name of Frank Walter-von Gierke greeted Christine and Paul enthusiastically. Almost immediately he suggested they speak with a local developer, who had made the original appraisal and was interested in acting as their agent in selling the property.

However, Christine told von Gierke that the family had no immediate intention of selling the property. Yet she and Paul agreed to pay a visit to the real estate firm.

Brandel & Co. was one of the largest and most successful real estate firms in Berlin. The real estate business had made a few people very rich over the years. Before the Wall fell, West Berlin was a well-guarded investment secret. After World War II, the population of the combined Berlins fell steadily, from 4.4 million in 1939 to 3.4 million in 1989. Berlin was on the map, but in the minds of many West Germans it didn't exist. One of Brandel's specialties was drawing West German investors to the divided city by enticing them with generous subsidies and tax breaks offered by the West German government. When the Wall fell, several firms that knew their way around the city's real estate scene cashed in on some quick speculative deals. The Wallich property was one of hundreds of such promising pieces of land. The villa itself had become an eyesore and needed extensive renovation, but Brandel had seen worse, and the location was excellent.

Brandel's proprietor was a man in his middle years named Lothar Collberg. Herr Collberg spared no expense appointing his lavish Kurfürstendamm offices and took pride in giving visitors guided tours of room after room filled with priceless antiques. Herr Collberg ran a tight ship. An intercom system ensured that none of his many assistants would travel far from their boss's quarters before being summoned into service: to fetch coffee, make a telephone call or accompany an out-of-town visitor to the nearest taxi stand.

When Christine and Paul arrived at the Brandel offices, they met not with Collberg himself but with one of his lieutenants. He told the two young Wallichs that the firm thought it could sell the house for a minimum of 1 million marks (about $625,000).

Christine politely repeated to the man what she had told the young lawyer—that the family was still undecided about what to do with the property. After that, the conversation shifted to more general topics.

The next day, Christine and Paul made the drive through Wannsee and over the Glienicke Bridge to the house. The most striking sight when they drew close was the Wall, running parallel to the property close to the house, not more than fifty feet from the front door. Large cranes were in the midst of lifting sections of the concrete from the border strip to truck away.

The house's exterior was a mess. Its stucco facade was crumbling and in some places it had disintegrated completely, leaving red brick exposed underneath. The house did not appear to be abandoned. Parked alongside the garden wall were a few cars, small Trabants that looked like they were made of tin. Colorful flowers and bumblebees cut from paper were taped to the upstairs windows, suggesting the presence of children.

They noticed right away that the property appeared to be far larger than they had expected. Paul decided to pace it off. The concrete slabs of wall had never been intended for use as a capitalist surveying instrument, but Paul seized the opportunity to turn them into one. Using his size nine shoe to approximate twelve inches, he walked the length of one of the sections and used that as a rough guide to estimate the size of the property. From Paul's rough measurement, the property appeared to be more than double the size they thought it was. And that didn't even include the adjacent unbuilt plot with the garden. When Paul walked that, the total was closer to 75,000 square feet, or nearly two acres.

Then they decided to ring the bell. There were two bells to choose from. One was labeled "KWH" and the other "Brunke." They rang the one for "KWH." The heavy oak door was opened by a short and stout middle-aged woman wearing an apron over a plain blouse and skirt. Her expression was one of skepticism and bewilderment.

Of the two siblings, Christine had the better command of German, so she did the talking. She explained that she and Paul were the grandchildren of the family that had owned the house before the war, and they were interested in seeing the house.

The woman frowned, motioned for them to come into the entrance hall and told them to please wait. She disappeared into the dark hallway. Christine and Paul used the privacy to survey their surroundings. The floor of the foyer they stood in looked as if it had just been mopped. The floor's brown and yellow mosaic tile obviously dated from the days of their grandparents.

A few moments later another woman appeared. She seemed slightly younger, and she, too, was wearing an apron. Her face was somewhat pinched, and her short straight hair appeared to have been dyed jet black. Her bangs reached down to the rim of small eyeglasses with thick black frames. She seemed less skeptical of the two Americans but more guarded by nature. She answered their questions but offered little information on her own. She introduced herself as Frau Neumann, the director of the facility. When they asked what kind of child-care facility this was, she told them it was a Kinderwochenheim, and explained its purpose.

Christine and Paul maintained a polite fiction about their reason for being there, acting as if idle curiosity had brought them to this newly accessible corner of Potsdam. Paul later described the visit as laden with a "strong performance aspect to it. We were very careful with what we said because we didn't know if we'd mess things up."

And just as politely, Frau Neumann didn't inquire after their intentions for the house. But they suspected she wasn't fooled. Since the Wende, eastern Germans everywhere had begun to fear the return of western property owners. By the time the two American Wallichs arrived in Potsdam, it was fairly clear that those who had been stripped of their property either by the Nazis or later by the Communists would have some claim to it.

Frau Neumann told them she could take them through all the

rooms of the house except the back bedrooms on the second floor where the children were taking their midday nap. Christine removed her shoes, Paul followed suit and the two of them tiptoed up the wide staircase after Frau Neumann.

The first sight to greet them was a tall arched window at the end of a short hallway. From the window they had an unobstructed view across the river to a Tudor-style castle atop a hill. Frau Neumann explained that they were looking at the castle named for the Babelsberg section of Potsdam.

Directly next to the large window was the door leading to what must have served as the great central hall of their grandparents' home. It was at once simple and grand. The original oak floors in a herringbone pattern were largely intact, and Paul was taken aback to see the grandeur of the molded ceiling. For the first time since entering the house, he suddenly realized in concrete terms how far his family had descended from the wealth his grandparents and great-grandparents had enjoyed. He was living in an apartment on the Upper East Side of Manhattan that would have fit inside that main room. He mused to himself that in his grandparents' day his own economic status would have qualified him to use only the servants' entrance.

The ornate ceiling had been defaced by a fluorescent lighting fixture that dangled precariously from three long chains. The room's marble fireplace had been transformed into a puppet theater. Tiny chairs and tables covered with construction paper furnished the room.

Many aspects of the house reflected the ad hoc nature of maintenance and repair that was common practice in East Germany. Inferior materials and sometimes the wrong materials had been used to make repairs or build things or decorate a room. Cheap mustard yellow linoleum in a mottled pattern covered many of the floors. Translucent curtains with a filmy texture covered most of the windows. For all the warnings issued by the men back in Berlin, the interior of the house was in remarkably good repair. Its worst offense, said Paul, was that it had "very carefully been kept in a taste that appalled."

Several of the rooms had been given over to specific functions. One large room—a former bedroom, perhaps—had been turned into a bathroom with a dozen miniature sinks and pint-sized toilets with seats of orange plastic. Small hand towels hung neatly from individual hooks. The house was so quiet it seemed to be inhabited by an army of miniature ghosts. Next to the bathroom were two closed doors. Frau Neumann quietly pushed one of the doors open and Christine and Paul peered in to the semidarkness to see a dozen or so short narrow beds occupied by small children. A woman sat in a chair at the other end of the room, apparently keeping watch. Some of the children were sleeping; others were wide awake, staring at the ceiling or whispering, waiting until they could get up again.

The end of their tour brought them to the loggia in the center of the house. The wide-beamed ceiling of a hard dark wood was framed by a wall of blue and white tiles. These two features, along with two large columns that appeared to be embedded in the outside wall, served as some of the few reminders of the house's former grandeur.

"And who is Brunke?" Christine asked, recalling the second name on the bell.

Herr Brunke, Frau Neumann said, was the caretaker. He and his wife lived in an apartment on the third floor. She did not offer to show them that part of the house.

Paul thought, This is the house my grandfather died for. He had occasionally turned the scenario over in his mind. If Paul and Hildegard had remained married and left the country successfully, the Nazis would most certainly have taken the house. In killing himself, Paul thought he was ensuring that his family and his property would be left alone, that they needn't "resist placing the Nazi flag" outside the house. Paul had even heard that there had been discussion of the two divorcing, which would have given them a better chance of preserving the property.

Frau Neumann then took them downstairs to the kitchen and adjacent servants' quarters. There were several women gathered there, for what appeared to be a midday break. Two of them were busy buttering rolls piled high on a platter for the children's post-nap snack. Just then, they began to hear voices and saw children running past the kitchen area into the backyard. Frau Neumann invited Christine and Paul outside as well. By this time there were about thirty children running through the large backyard, playing and chasing and climbing on tires. Christine and Paul both noticed several large trees in the yard, particularly a spectacular tree with auburn leaves that were just beginning to emerge. They were beginning to feel the conspicuousness of their presence as the house sprang back to life after its midday rest. They thanked Frau Neumann for her time and headed for the door. As they were leaving they passed small freestanding closets of laminated wood veneer, where tiny jackets hung side by side on hooks labeled with names: Norbert. Benni. Michael.

6 : MICHAEL

*I*n 1989, when the teachers first heard about the new child coming to the Kinderwochenheim, they were a bit put out. His name was Michael Schneider and he was three years old. They knew little about the boy himself but they knew his older sister, Katrin, well. Now six, she had been there for three years, and she had been a problem from the start. Katrin wasn't a troublesome child in the typical sense. She was, for the most part, polite, well-mannered and quiet. But they had been unable to toilet-train her. Now she was six and still wetting not just her bed but her clothes as well. As she grew older, her incontinence became a source of embarrassment for her, a subject for ridicule by the other children, and an increasing irritation to the teachers. She had also been slow to learn to speak properly and articulate her thoughts.

The teachers attributed Katrin's problems to her situation at home, one of the worst they had seen in their years of taking in the children of troubled parents. Katrin was the child of alcoholic parents and the teachers had seen plenty of that. But hers was an extraordinarily unhealthy environment. Both parents drank heavily and the mother often became abusive, not toward Katrin but toward her husband. When Katrin was an infant, her mother began leaving the apartment for days at a time to be with other men. The mother was loud and boisterous and openly contemptuous of her timid husband. Whenever the mother left, Herr Schneider despaired. Never able to hold down a job for more than a few weeks, he mostly stayed at home and drank.

It surprised the teachers to see that even when Frau Schneider was at home, it was usually Katrin's father who delivered her on Monday mornings and picked her up on Friday afternoons. He often arrived very late on Friday afternoons, just as the teacher on the late shift was beginning to wonder if he would come at all. But he always arrived.

Some of the stories about the Schneider household the teachers heard were spun in highly dramatic form by Frau Neumann, who had gotten her information from the social worker assigned to the family. And some of the facts surrounding the case they saw for themselves, during periodic visits to the Schneiders' apartment. Frau Neumann was the one with the authority to decide if visits to a child's home were called for. If a child began to display signs that the situation at home was worsening—black-and-blue marks or increased aggression—or if the child said as much, Frau Neumann and one of the teachers occasionally went to see for themselves.

When Katrin turned five, her bed-wetting got worse. She told Frau Neumann that she was living with her mother in a different place. She also told Frau Neumann that she now had a baby brother, who was living with his father. It was now Frau Schneider who dropped Katrin off and picked her up. She was usually drunk, or so it seemed to the teachers, and she was usually accompanied by different young men. So Frau Neumann decided to pay her a visit. She found that Frau Schneider was keeping a tidy enough household, but she seemed to have nothing to do. There was little in the apartment to suggest the presence of a small child. In spite of the appearance of order, Frau Neumann had the sense that this wouldn't last. She was right. A few months before Katrin's sixth birthday, Frau Neumann got word from the social workers that the Schneiders had reconciled, and the entire family was living again under one roof. This, they suspected, wouldn't last long either.

Katrin was not an attractive child. She was plump, and she had her mother's round face, small, deep-set blue eyes and a flat, slightly hooked nose. Her awkwardness made it difficult for her to get along with the other children. She struck the teachers as a particularly needy child; she latched on to anyone who offered the slightest bit of affection. And she was so phlegmatic that the teachers occasionally called her an *Esel,* or donkey.

When her brother arrived at the Kindergarten three years later, the teachers braced themselves for a difficult child. But they were astonished to see that the little boy was nothing like his sister. His face betrayed none of the trouble around him. His charm spread across his face and his large, bright green doe eyes shone with benign mischief. He was small-boned and fragile, and his olive complexion was offset by hair the color of wet sand. Michael was a charmer, and he displayed an impish joyfulness from the moment he arrived, appearing to have none of the emotional burdens that darkened Katrin's life. He was unusually well-spoken for his age, and had no trouble taking care of himself. Someone had apparently toilet-trained him properly at an early age. In many ways, he seemed the model child.

At the same time he had a contemplative side that the teachers found intriguing if occasionally frustrating. He had an eerily cerebral way about him, and often expressed himself as an adult might. If confronted with a rule he disliked, he would look pensive for a while, then might remark, "Well, no, it really isn't that way at all," and follow with a logical, remarkably well-reasoned argument. Then again, he could take forever to put on a pair of shoes or, in the middle of pulling on a jacket, suddenly seem lost in thought.

Michael was extremely small for his age, and his spareness was worrisome. It wasn't until several months after his arrival at the Kindergarten that he started gaining weight. Shy at first, he carried with him a sense of vulnerability that made others want to protect him. The teachers and the other children called him by the diminutive "Micha."

Micha was resilient nonetheless, in a way that his sister wasn't. He possessed none of Katrin's need for affection. Instead, he was a self-contained, private person. Occasionally, however, he fought with the other children. The arguments were usually over a toy that Micha refused to share. As the teachers interpreted his behavior, he had so few things of his own that he became possessive of everything that came within his grasp. Whenever he got into one of these disputes, he screamed in a high shrill voice, a bit like the midget Oskar from Günter Grass's *The Tin Drum,* whose screams shattered glass. Frau Neumann's headaches couldn't tolerate Micha's occasional screaming outbursts, and she disciplined him severely when they came.

The two siblings gave credibility to the notion of a throwaway first child who shields the second from the ugliness of the adult world that surrounds them. Katrin seemed to bear alone her parents' chaos and sorrow, as if to free her brother of the burden. She had a tough side, and could occasionally come out with surprisingly strong language. "You should see the schnapps my father can put away!" she would say with no apparent prompting.

The relationship between Katrin and Micha was cautiously loving. They never knew when they might be taken from each other. So they erected their own barriers, like two adults, weary of disappointment and afraid of getting too close. Katrin's protective side emerged when Micha got sick. If he became ill in the middle of the night the teacher on night duty would fetch Katrin and she would come sit on the edge of her brother's bed and stroke his head.

At home on weekends, they stuck close together. They were different from the other children in the building and they knew it. Other parents told their children to stay away from the two Schneider children, especially the older one, whose pants were always soaking wet.

Occasionally the estrangement from other children carried over to the Kindergarten. When other children had birthday parties, Micha and Katrin, who the others knew would be unable to come up with any gifts, were seldom invited. Micha didn't understand it. One afternoon, as one of the children was handing out invitations and passed Micha over, he asked of no one in particular, perhaps himself, "Why am I never invited?" A teacher standing nearby didn't know how to respond. She said nothing. And he didn't seem to expect an answer, from her or anyone else.

Micha seemed unusually attached to his father. He talked about him often, and every Friday fretted over his expected arrival. As the afternoon wore on, he grew increasingly fidgety. But he had a self-protective veneer. Perhaps to preempt any ridiculing for having such a conspicuously ne'er-do-well father, Micha occasionally announced to strangers in a strong, matter-of-fact voice, "My father always comes very very late to pick me up. Sometimes just when the Kindergarten is closing."

The teachers were wary of Herr Schneider. They had no sympathy for him. They were put off by his inability to say more than a few words at a time and appalled by his apparent illiteracy. Whenever they gave him a form to sign, he did so in an undecipherable scrawl. They considered his drinking a sign of weakness and his constant state of unemployment not merely illegal but immoral as well.

Herr Schneider's inability to hold on to a job qualified him to receive a monthly welfare check. At the same time, he and his wife were put under the care of a social worker. Social workers in East Germany were called *Fürsorger,* or caretakers. Theirs was a much more matter-of-fact mission than that of their counterparts in West Germany. They did little in the way of counseling. Their job was to see to it that the families they looked after had a place to live, and to assess how capable these families were of caring for their children. A social worker possessed greater authority than was allowed in the West. An East German social worker had the power to decide that a child be placed in an orphanage or a weekly Kindergarten, or be put up for adoption. In the West, such a decision was made by a court of law.

There were very few recipients of a social worker's care in East Germany, and they had to meet a strict set of requirements. Most were people who hadn't worked for several years.

It was next to impossible to lose a job in East Germany. Somehow, everyone got pulled along in the system. If anyone really fell through the social safety net, it was considered as much a stigma for the state as for the individual. People like Herr Schneider, who simply didn't work, or couldn't work, did fall through. Many of them were alcoholics.

Alcoholism was a well-hidden problem in East Germany. Alcohol abuse became particularly acute in the 1980s. But the East German government regularly denied that alcoholism existed, trotting out statistics showing that the disease was far worse in Western countries such as France and West Germany, a result of manipulative advertising campaigns waged by the alcoholic beverages industry, alienation of the working class, and a system more interested in profits than in maintaining the health of its citizens. Any alcoholism in evidence in East Germany was explained away as a vestige of Germany's bourgeois past.

But East Germany's statistics reported only a small fraction of the actual number of alcoholics in East Germany, and the attempts to keep the problem hushed up only compounded it. There were laws banning the consumption of alcohol at the workplace, but few supervisors complied with them; they were often drinking on the job as well. Drinking was a leisure activity that gave people, especially men, a sense of solidarity. There weren't many state-owned pubs, but many people gathered to drink in private homes on a regular basis. Even the state sometimes seemed to encourage citizens to drink, with organized drinking parties for its workers.

Prominent party members were also indulged in their love for the bottle. If a party official drove drunk late at night and plowed his car into a lamppost, he was given a new car the following day and the damage repaired quietly and quickly. In the accident report, no mention of alcohol would be made.

A small number of outspoken physicians and social workers in East Germany worked for years to get the government to acknowledge in hospital reports the existence of alcohol abuse. Finally, in 1978, the Ministry of Health designed a policy for treatment and prevention. Still, there remained scant incentive to seek treatment.

Most of the state's efforts to curb the problem focused on the workplace, as more than half the absenteeism among workers was attributable to alcohol. But employers, conspiring in collective denial, often refused to cooperate. Herr Schneider's problem, however, was so acute that it was impossible to overlook. He was absent from his various jobs at least half the time, and when he did show up, he usually wasn't sober. So he spent a great deal of time out of work.

Unemployment was illegal. An alcoholic who stopped working was put on notice for "loafing." Some were sent to prison, and when they came out they were given another chance. To keep them out of public sight, many were given nice apartments—dwellings that others would wait several years for. But if they failed again, their support was cut off entirely. Monthly rents were so low—about $20—that if they shirked their payments, the state looked the other way. Occasionally the social workers would help them find furniture and necessary appliances.

The disenfranchised in East Germany—the Asoziale—were pariahs and they were treated that way. Unemployed alcoholics were required to register weekly with the authorities. If they failed to do so, they were threatened with imprisonment. But they remained a hidden statistic. Occasionally they fell through the cracks entirely and were ignored by the system.

Herr Schneider was in some regards an exception to the stereotype of the Asi. Of the two parents, he was the more responsible. His wife exhibited little or no interest in her children. She was constantly off with a different man. Sabine Reisenweber, the social worker assigned to the family, even bumped into Frau Schneider once in a while in downtown Potsdam, seated on the lap of a stranger on a public bench. Herr Schneider was the one who cared for the children as best he could. At times he would find work, usually some form of unskilled labor such as loading and unloading warehouses. For several months he was employed as a night watchman, but again his drinking got him fired.

The Schneider family first came to the attention of the Potsdam social workers in 1988, when the social work office received a letter of complaint from other residents in the Schneiders' building. The building's occupants had composed a collective letter to the Potsdam Youth Agency. The families that signed the letter said they were worried about the Schneider children. The parents stayed at home most of the time, slept until all hours, didn't pay their rent and disturbed the entire building with their constant fighting. Furthermore, the children were not being sent to their Kindergarten regularly. A few of the residents had visited the apartment and encountered complete disorder. Dirty diapers lay on the kitchen floor, and the Schneiders used the hall toilet, shared by others on their floor, as a waste bin.

Another complaint came a few months later, in early 1989. Katrin, now six, was attending the Kindergarten only sporadically, and her mother appeared to go away for days at a time. Micha was kept clean, but soiled diapers lay all over the floor. The neighbors were worried that the Schneiders were turning the building into a health hazard. And now the father's half-sister, just out of jail, had moved in and she and the children's parents remained inebriated most of the time.

In response to this news, the social workers organized a meeting of the building's residents. More than a dozen people attended, including a party representative. Frau Neumann from the Kindergarten was there. Frau Schneider admitted to the group that she had been irresponsible, and that she wasn't watching over her children properly. She promised to be more conscientious, and in return she asked her neighbors if they would keep an eye on the children whenever they could. They agreed to do so. Frau Schneider also promised to look for a job.

In March of 1990, the Schneiders were given a large top-floor apartment on a quiet street lined with tall trees and historic villas near the Sanssouci Palace. It was the same neighborhood that Ulrike lived in. Katrin had just entered school and was now living at home. From what the social workers could tell, the marriage had improved—or, rather, the couple was going through another rinse cycle. Frau Schneider claimed to be a changed woman. She spoke of nothing but wanting to be with her husband and children. The teachers at the Kindergarten noticed the change, too. Both of the parents arrived at the front door arm in arm to deliver Micha, and they came together to pick him up. The teachers shook their heads. It couldn't last.

It didn't. Frau Schneider again began seeing other men. And this time, it was worse. She wasn't just going out with them. She was bringing them home. Then one day she left and moved in with another man. Herr Schneider was devastated. He turned to the social workers for help. They took pity on him but told him they wished he would stand up to his wife. He was only making things worse by taking her back whenever she decided to return, only to watch things crumble again. Herr Schneider responded with laments: about how much harder things had gotten since the Wall had come down, that his world in the GDR, however precarious it was, had at least had some stability. In the old East Germany, he knew what to expect; in the new, he had no idea what to expect or what was expected of him. His prospects, he said, looked entirely bleak

Katrin and Micha reacted to their father's confusion and anxiety. Katrin not only wet her pants, but she began defecating in them as well. She was attending a school for children with learning disabilities and even there she was having trouble keeping up. The social workers suggested that Katrin go to the hospital for tests to determine whether there was something physiological causing her incontinence. After a short stay it was determined that there was nothing physical about it, that she was an emotionally troubled child.

By early 1991 the social workers decided that Katrin should be put in a full-time orphanage. She still wasn't going to school regularly, and she was falling further behind her classmates. When her father visited the orphanage, she cried and told him that the other children made fun of her because of the bed-wetting. She pleaded with him to take her home. But he was in too much despair. Unable to care for himself and Micha, he went to live for a while with another sister, who lived a few miles away, and made several visits to the social workers. They told him to stop hoping that his wife would return, and to file for divorce. But he couldn't bring himself to do it.

His wife did return. In May, she went to the Youth Agency and, teary-eyed, explained that she wanted to stay home with her family. She said again that she would mend her ways, that she could maintain some order in her life. The social workers wanted to believe her, and Katrin was allowed to return home.

That October, the pendulum swung back. The social workers heard that the Schneider family had gone three months without paying rent. Katrin's school called to report her spotty attendance. Then Frau Schneider started bringing men home again. So the social workers decided to pay an unannounced visit to the Schneider apartment early one afternoon in December of 1991. A groggy Frau Schneider answered the door, and on the living room couch sat a man in his underwear whom the social workers had never seen before. Frau Schneider explained coolly that she and her husband were not on speaking terms. There was no sign of Herr Schneider.

A week later, unable to tolerate the situation any longer, Herr Schneider took the two children to his sister's place in Babelsberg, on the other side of Potsdam. The social workers asked the sister if she would take Katrin in permanently. The sister said she liked Katrin, even though the child was occasionally cheeky. But with four children of her own, she said, she was already overburdened. A day later, Frau Schneider appeared at the youth office and demanded that her children be returned to her. She wanted Micha to be taken out of the Kindergarten and returned to her care. She identified the man who had been seated in the living room as her "life partner."

"How long have you known him?" asked the social worker.

"Fourteen days," she replied.

By this time, the social workers had noticed a pattern in her appearances and disappearances at home. Since the reunification of the two Germanys, the Schneiders had been receiving about $75 a month from the state. Frau Schneider had a knack for returning to her family at the first of the month, when the welfare check arrived. She would turn up, talk her husband out of the money and buy alcohol with it. The two would get dead-drunk, and after a few days she would leave again.

To test her hunch, one of the social workers waited until the first of the month, then returned for another unannounced visit one weekday morning. Frau Schneider opened the door, looking as if the daylight were hurting her eyes. Both children were at home, running through the apartment. Micha had a terrible cough. Frau Schneider wasn't wearing a stitch of clothing but didn't seem to notice. She complained of a terrible headache. Herr Schneider appeared behind her. She called him "sweetheart" and asked him to help her find her eyeglasses. While the two looked for the glasses the social worker looked inside the refrigerator. It appeared to be broken, and a rank odor escaped. Inside was a jar of marmalade and a can of bean soup. There was no bread in the house.

The following day, while walking through the center of town, the social worker saw Frau Schneider seated on a bench, on the lap of the same man who had been on the living room couch several months earlier.

Finally, in the spring of 1992, Herr Schneider seemed to crack. He arrived early one morning in March at the youth office, his face bright red. It was extremely cold outside, but Sabine Reisenweber suspected that his crimson cheeks were caused by heavy drinking. He was on the verge of tears.

"My wife has left again," he exclaimed. "She just ran out of the house. Without a jacket."

This time, Herr Schneider went to the neighbors' to look for her. They said they had seen her the previous day, and had told her to stop buying so much alcohol. They told him to stop encouraging her, to be tougher on her. "You're too good-natured," they said.

In May one of the social workers went to visit Frau Neumann at the Kindergarten. She could see that the big house at the bridge was a cheerful place. The children's pictures and paintings were all over the walls. Micha liked it there. He had friends and a lot to do. There was a structure to his day. He ate well.

The social worker asked Frau Neumann if she could take Katrin, who was now living at home, during the week as well. At nine, Katrin was technically two years past the age for Kindergarten and

Herr Schneider, as usual, hadn't paid his bills for several months. But Frau Neumann agreed to it. The more weekly children she had, the better her chances of keeping her Kindergarten open. But when the social worker suggested to Herr Schneider that he place Katrin in the Kindergarten with Micha, he refused.

Two months later, a neighbor in the Schneiders' building paid a visit to the social work office to report that there had been a terrible scene the previous night. Frau Schneider had broken into her own apartment and stolen things. The neighbor reported that she and her husband had had to hold Herr Schneider back from hitting Frau Schneider. The office took no immediate action, but a few days later, Herr Schneider showed up at the social work office and said he had no money and nothing to eat. Now he was ready to have Katrin go to the Kindergarten. The social workers gave him some money for the children for the weekend, and by the following Monday Katrin and Micha were together for the week in the Kindergarten. Both children seemed happy with the arrangement. Katrin liked it there. She knew the other children. It didn't bother her that she was older than the others.

To the social workers, the teachers at the Kindergarten expressed great compassion for Herr Schneider's plight. But among themselves they were extremely judgmental. They considered his alcoholism an indulgence, and his inability to keep a job scandalous. The children's clothing was in tatters and the teachers were fed up with asking other parents for castoffs for the Schneider children. When Micha arrived one Monday with a shiny new bicycle, the teachers immediately suspected that his father had stolen it. When Micha had first arrived at the Kindergarten, they thought there might be hope for him. But after two years, and no improvement in the Schneider household, they felt there was little they could do for him. He was beginning to show his aggressive side more frequently. And his high-pitched screams seemed to be on the increase.

Ulrike was the only teacher whose sympathy for Herr Schneider was genuine. When she heard her colleagues' verbal sniping, she did her best to ignore it. She and Ingo lived around the corner from the Schneiders' apartment, and on weekends she occasionally ran into Herr Schneider and the children. She tried to be friendly, but he seemed increasingly distracted and withdrawn. Ulrike never saw Frau Schneider any longer, and she assumed she had disappeared from the picture entirely.

By September of 1992, Herr Schneider's despair reached new depths. He hadn't seen his wife in months. His half-sister and her boyfriend had just moved into the apartment. Herr Schneider had run into them at the welfare office and when they told him that neither of them had an apartment, he had offered to have them stay with him until they found a place. The boyfriend, a tough character from West Berlin, was wanted by the police, although Herr Schneider wasn't quite sure what for.

Then the real trouble began. They, too, were heavy drinkers, and Herr Schneider let himself be coaxed into more drinking than he could handle. He reported to the social worker that the half-sister was taking all his money. She, her boyfriend and their large dog had taken over the apartment. They started selling Herr Schneider's things. The boyfriend was violent. He had thrown an axe out the front window. And for the past few days, they wouldn't let him in the apartment.

The social worker went to have a look for herself. She was surprised when Micha greeted her at the door. It was a Monday afternoon. He should have been at the Kindergarten. He told her no one had gotten up in time to take him that morning. She had only met Micha a few times, and each time she was surprised by his composure. Katrin, with all her problems, was far more what the social workers were accustomed to. Micha told her matter-of-factly that no one was at home, and they agreed to wait together for someone to return. He sat down in the kitchen with her. She was impressed by what appeared to be a brand-new kitchen table set.

Two people arrived: a woman and man the social worker had not seen before. The woman was cordial and said she was Herr Schneider's sister. She told the social worker that she hadn't seen her brother for several days.

She claimed that Herr Schneider had fallen prey to door-to-door solicitors. Hordes of itinerant salesmen had appeared in eastern Germany shortly after the currency union of July 1990, and consumers there discovered the darker side of capitalism when businesses from western Germany descended on their new compatriots by the hundreds, dispatching door-to-door sales agents and sending out junk mail and catalogues. Unwary consumers were ensnared by sales pitches offering a multiplicity of goods in exchange for easy monthly payments. Even the small lessons in free enterprise were difficult for some easterners to fathom. Not long after reunification, one man reported to the Berlin Consumer Center that he had seen a can of asparagus selling for $2 in one store and the same brand in a second store priced at $4. He wanted to know if this was legal.

Herr Schneider had ordered dozens of things from catalogues. Aside from the kitchen table set, he had bought a color television, a circular saw, a new refrigerator, bicycles for both children and countless smaller things. He was heavily in debt. The sister said she was forced to sell his things in order to whittle the debt down. Her story about the axe differed markedly from that of Herr Schneider. She said her half-brother appeared to be losing his mind. One morning he had thrown an axe out one of the front windows.

When Herr Schneider next appeared at Sabine Reisenweber's office, the social worker told him that as long as things remained unsettled at home, the children would not be allowed to go home at all. And since the Kindergarten closed for weekends, they would have to go to an orphanage. Losing her usual patience, she began to lecture him. He was thirty-eight years old, old enough to understand what was happening, even if he couldn't control it. The children, in their innocence, were in danger of being scarred for life.

At the Kindergarten, Micha and Katrin, ignorant of these events and the logic dictating their removal to an orphanage, were completely confused. Micha couldn't understand why he couldn't go home the following weekend. On Friday afternoon, his father arrived at the Kindergarten not to take him home but to bring some of his things. "Why can't I go home with you?" Micha demanded to know. Herr Schneider, flustered and red in the face, was speechless. He left quickly.

One of the teachers drove the children to a nearby orphanage able to take them for the weekend on short notice. On Monday morning they returned to the Kindergarten. Micha seemed shaken. When one of the teachers asked him whether the orphanage had been nice, he shook his head. "When I wake up in the middle of the night there I don't know where I am," he told her. "When I wake up in the middle of the night here I know where I am." The children were sent to the orphanage the following weekend as well. By the third week, the social workers decided they should move to a different orphanage and remain there until further notice. For days after arriving at the new orphanage Micha clutched a small plastic bag with drawings of dinosaurs on it that he had gotten at another child's birthday party earlier that day, one of the few he had ever been to. He refused to let the bag out of his hands, even to bathe.

Frau Neumann had been on vacation and did not hear about the Schneider children until she returned. She came to call at once on the social workers. She flitted around the room like a bird that had flown in from the outdoors by mistake. She was clearly upset, but she seemed less concerned about Micha and Katrin than about the fact that each weekly child she lost threatened her facility. This shouldn't be allowed to happen, she said. Sabine Reisenweber tried to explain the situation. If none of the teachers could stay for the weekend, or take the children with them, the children would have to stay in the orphanage. Frau Neumann threw up her hands. Several of the parents who were unemployed now had the time to take care of their children. Children were steadily being withdrawn from the overnight portion of the Kindergarten and now, with the loss of the Schneider children the number of weekly children was down to six. She expected a notice of closure to come any day.

The Claims Wars

After the Wall fell, when reunification appeared imminent, one of the first questions to arise was whether people who had owned property in East Germany were entitled to reclaim it. Certainly they had a legitimate claim, for as far as the West German government was concerned they had been stripped of their ownership unlawfully.

The most significant debate among German politicians centered on whether property should be returned or compensation paid to the previous owners. It was, in many ways, a question of what was more unjust. Was it more unjust to the former owner if the property wasn't returned, or more unjust to the current occupant if it was? Those who lobbied for the return of property argued that this was one of the few ways of making good on past wrongs committed first by the Nazis and then by the Communists. Communist leaders routinely seized the property of anyone who left to settle in the West. In addition, they confiscated land, houses and businesses from many thought to be unfriendly to the Communist cause. Proponents of returning property argued that if someone had been caught trying to flee over the Wall, and his house taken away while he sat in jail, it wasn't enough for the government now just to issue an apology or pay him a small restitution.

But Germany's liberal Social Democrats, who opposed the return of property, argued for financial restitution instead, claiming that the return of land would create a bureaucratic tangle so dense that it could take decades to sort it through, all the while stalling much needed investment in East Germany. They also believed that it was wrong to displace people who had spent so many years making a place their own. In a display of loyalty to this position, several prominent Social Democrats declined to pursue claims to their own family property in eastern Germany.

In the months before reunification in 1990, the Bonn government bowed to heavy public pressure and ruled that all properties would be restored to those who suffered losses on grounds of "race, politics, religion or philosophical outlook" between January 30, 1933, when Hitler seized power, and the German capitulation of May 8, 1945.

Immediately after the decision, lawyers who had even the most fleeting knowledge of the property claims law were flooded with inquiries from people seeking to reclaim a house or business long since written off. Claims started arriving by the tens of thousands at hastily erected claims offices throughout East Germany. Letters came from Israel and New York and Mozambique. Many were accompanied by documents—a deed, a page from a will, a yellowed snapshot—supporting the claim. Some were documented thoroughly while others were hopelessly vague, like the scrawled postcard one Berlin lawyer received from a Florida retiree whose Uncle Max was said to have owned a shoe factory somewhere near Dresden.

Greed set in immediately. Most of the people filing claims did not actually want to live in the houses, but rather to make money by selling them or renovating them and charging high rents to new tenants. In many cases, those claiming the houses had never actually lived in them. They were children or grandchildren of former residents, heirs to property that was suddenly quite valuable. Before the Wall fell, it wasn't unusual for an East German to sell a house for a few thousand dollars, in order to buy a Trabant, or a television set. Now those same houses, depending on their location, were valued at as much as $500,000.

In June of 1991, the German Parliament voted to reinstate Berlin as the nation's capital. Almost immediately, property values in Berlin soared, especially in eastern Berlin. After years of neglect, real estate in eastern Berlin boomed as it had in New York and Tokyo in the 1980s. Millions of dollars could be made in the course of a few weeks.

Administering the claims wasn't easy. Once the German government had opened property claims offices throughout the former East Germany, legal experts had to be recruited. But because of the unprecedented nature of the situation, there were no experts on the subject. So in a move dictated as much by economy as convenience, the government installed young graduates fresh out of western German law schools at the new claims offices. For lawyers on the claimants' side, property restitution became a lucrative business. Berlin's most prestigious law firms on Kurfürstendamm, catching a whiff of the money to be made, took on thousands of cases. Some of the most profitable cases were those where one family—often a Jewish family—had owned large tracts of land in the center of the former East Berlin. One large Berlin law firm went so far as to seek out the heirs to expensive, unclaimed property and offer representation.

A few months into the claims process, it became clear that in the main this would be far more than a simple matter of filling out a few forms. The question of what belonged to whom was now of central importance.

For many West Germans, finding that the property which they had all but erased from their assets portfolio was suddenly theirs to reclaim was like winning a lottery.

After a while, it seemed that everyone in western Germany had a claim to something large and valuable that had gone to ruin at the hands of the Communists. The running joke among western Germans was, "Oh yes, my family lost a castle, too." Some towns were besieged with claims. In the small exclusive town of Kleinmachnow, where Ulrike grew up, nine of every ten houses was being reclaimed by the spring of 1991.

By the summer of 1992, more than two million claims had been filed throughout the former East Germany. About half of them were for private houses. Nearly 200,000 claims were in Berlin alone. It was estimated that it could take from twenty to forty years to sort through the entire mess.

Those who had opposed the return of property seemed to be vindicated. The historic city of Leipzig, for example, home to Johann Sebastian Bach, showed particular promise after the Wall fell. The city was already renowned for conventions, book publishing, banks, services and industry. But one development project after another seemed to get stalled while property claims were disputed. Plans for a downtown hotel and for a business park on the city's outskirts got bogged down in the planning stages because of property rights disputes surrounding specific land tracts and buildings.

At first, the claims process had a unifying effect. Family members who hadn't seen one another for years were suddenly in close touch, negotiating as co-heirs. But just as swiftly as a common piece of property brought families together, it often divided them as well. Most typical were families that had been separated during the forty years of Communism. The family member who had stayed behind in the East and lived in the family house suddenly found that other members were returning to press their claims to the house. Families often disagreed over just who the rightful heirs were, or whether the property should be sold, or to whom.

If westerners reacted to the new law with jubilation, eastern Germans were outraged. The threat of a property claim on houses that eastern Germans had occupied for decades only added to the growing friction between east and west. It seemed to bring out the worst in everyone. Westerners who had long since written off their property or their parents' property began returning to Germany by the hundreds to survey their land. Western Germans arrived in run-down eastern German towns in their Mercedes and BMWs, parked in front of houses that had been occupied by others for four decades, got out and snapped a roll of photos, then drove away. Sometimes they even knocked on the door and, though strangers to the inhabitants, asked for a tour.

Fed up with such aggressive behavior, some eastern Germans put up signs telling western Germans to stay away. Eastern Germans were appalled at the western Germans' assumption that they could simply show up after nearly half a century and reclaim something they had neglected for decades. In some places, residents came together and occupied buildings in protest. Some threatened to burn their home down rather than let it go to a rich westerner.

The decision to return property was to have its tragic consequences as well. In early 1992, a young eastern German politician
living in a small town forty miles from Berlin whose house had a
claim on it hanged himself from his balcony. In his suicide note he
wrote that the prospect of losing his house left him "with no other
possibility than public death." A few months later, another resident
facing eviction from his house in the same town hanged himself as
well. One elderly resident of Kleinmachnow suffered a heart attack
after a claimant arrived at his home from western Germany, removed the door and took it with him.

For their part, the western Germans' nostalgic journeys back to
the town where they had been born became an emotional trauma
when they discovered that their single-family home had been divided into apartments for three and four families, or that the property had gone to ruin. Understandably, they may have been
oblivious to the fact that keeping a house in decent repair in East
Germany was nothing like doing the same thing in West Germany.
Building materials—everything from lumber to paint to nails and
screws—were difficult to come by in the East. And even when they
were available, there wasn't much incentive to maintain a dwelling.
Most East Germans had rented their homes for an average of $40 a
month, and as far as they were aware, their landlord was the state.

There were exceptions. Some eastern Germans had renovated
their homes at great expense and effort through the years, only to
see the property become the object of a western claim. Some eastern German families paid thousands of marks for the right to purchase a home that had been abandoned by a family that fled west,
or thousands to make repairs and improvements. When the western
owners returned to one such home in 1991, the eastern German
family threatened to hack to bits the renovations they had made,
tear the paneling from the walls and pave over the goldfish pond.
Another western German claimant lost patience waiting for his
claim and took a bulldozer to the property.

Proving one's rightful ownership wasn't always easy. The most reliable source of proof of ownership was the property registry. The
German word for it is *Grundbuch*. For centuries, Germany has kept
precise records of every piece of land, detailing a plot's location
and history of ownership. Each entry in the Grundbuch was made
by hand in meticulous script in large heavy books, which makes

tracing the lineage of a plot of land a simple matter of looking in the book. But as soon as East Germany became a Communist state in 1949, and land gradually went into the hands of the state, the land registries became nothing more than artifacts of the much vilified capitalist past.

In the 1950s, most of the books were collected and stored, appropriately enough, in an abandoned eighteenth-century Baroque castle in Barby, a town not far from Berlin. For decades, the two-hundred-room castle in Barby served as one of the state's central archives, containing some nine miles of files, dating back to the seventeenth century. Other official files of the state were left in the damp cellars of municipal offices around the country. At the decrepit, abandoned office building in East Berlin where some property registries were stored, pigeons roosted for years. But in spite of the state's compulsion to keep the archives—if not necessarily preserve them—there was little or no public access to them.

Not only did the Barby castle contain many of the property registries, but all the attendant records as well—sales contracts, credit contracts and inheritance certificates. Lists of expropriations by the Nazis and seizures during the land reform of the 1950s also resided in Barby. There they were stacked helter-skelter and left to decompose. Over the years, files that didn't corrode and fade from poor storage conditions were in danger of being destroyed by East German officials, who blackened out many of the pages for security reasons and ripped off file covers to reuse.

After the Wall fell, claimants and their lawyers began taking trips to the Barby castle to sift through the books in search of proof of ownership to a particular property. But a trip to the archive did not guarantee success. At the start just two dozen clerks worked there, and they couldn't begin to keep up with the number of inquiries. Gradually more were employed, but the requests for information multiplied so quickly that it took as much as a year to get a reply.

Particularly unsettling was the old store of emotions and prejudice that the return of Jewish families visited on the newly unified Germany. Just before the proposed property law was adopted it became retroactive to January 30, 1933, when Hitler came to power. During the Nazi period, in the process of Aryanization of all property in Germany, thousands of Jews had been forced to sell their homes and businesses to non-Jews for negligible sums in return for permission to leave the country. After 1938, Jewish property owners were simply stripped of their property, which was then sold, or given, to Gentiles.

After the Wall fell, some eastern Germans living in houses formerly owned by Jewish families hinted to neighbors that they hoped that all of the family members had died in a concentration camp somewhere, leaving no heirs to pursue a claim. The same was true of some western Germans whose claims competed with Jews who had owned the property first, then been forced into a sale with the claimants' forebears. Some western German claimants grumbled that Jews had it easier when it came to reclaiming their property. In one well-publicized case two western Germans with separate claims to a house near Berlin banded together to block the claim of an eighty-year-old Jew. He had owned the house before both of the western Germans prior to his fleeing to the United States in the 1930s.

Among the most scandalous claims was the one pressed by Marika Roekk, a Hungarian dancer and film star who had been a personal friend of Hitler's. The Nazi government had installed her in a two-story villa near Berlin that had been abandoned by a Jewish film producer who fled to London with his wife. In 1945, Roekk moved to West Germany. But after the Wall fell, she wanted the house back. Public outcry was so great that Roekk eventually withdrew her claim.

There were indeed cases where a Jewish family had been exterminated so thoroughly as to leave no heirs. But that didn't make the claim disappear. As soon as it became clear that property would be returned to its former owners, the Conference on Jewish Material Claims Against Germany, an organization based in Frankfurt and New York, set about the painstaking task of determining precisely which pieces of property had been left without any heirs to claim them. The Claims Conference had already spent years pressing compensation claims for relatives of Holocaust victims. Few who had fled Germany actually wanted to return to live there, so there weren't many efforts made to reclaim houses. But after the war and through the 1980s, an estimated $80 billion in compensation flowed to Israel, Jewish institutions and individual Jewish survivors around the world. Some 150,000 Holocaust survivors received pensions from West Germany. The unexpected turn of events in eastern Germany suddenly opened up thousands of additional claims. The group's only challenge was in proving that a particular piece of property had belonged to Jews, even if no heirs stepped forward with a claim.

A macabre help to Jews pursuing property claims was that the Nazis had kept meticulous deportation records of Jewish families and the camps they were sent to. The Third Reich also kept thick files detailing the "legal" process by which thousands upon thousands of homes or businesses were expropriated in accordance with the laws governing Jews' rights. The German Communists in turn kept equally careful lists of the property they seized. For a time, perhaps with compensation to victims of Nazism in mind, Communist bureaucrats also maintained a record called a C List, a detailed accounting of everything—from sewing needles to business empires—that the Nazis had confiscated. Compiling the C List apparently became too cumbersome and it was discontinued, but the partially completed record remained intact. In its pursuit of proof of previous ownership, the Claims Conference relied heavily on the C List. By the December 31, 1992, deadline for filing claims, the Claims Conference had filed more than forty thousand claims for Jewish property. Many of those claims, of course, would be duplicated by claims from living heirs of whom the Claims Conference wasn't aware. It would be years before they could all be sorted through.

Monika Enlists

Before the Wall fell, there were about five hundred lawyers in all of East Germany, and most of them were unversed in West German law. After the Wall fell most of the young recruits for legal work in eastern Germany came from the west. And because they had to be willing to work for nominal wages in working conditions unacceptable to most western Germans, the lawyers who were hired were, for the most part, fresh out of western German law school. Some of them did it because of the tight job market. Others did it for the challenge.

For Monika Hagen, it was a little bit of both.

Monika Hagen was twenty-nine years old when she received her law degree from the Free University of Berlin in 1990. It wasn't a particularly good time to go job hunting. Her law school classmates were waiting from six months to a year to find jobs, and she feared the same for herself. Then one day a few weeks into her job search she saw an article in the Berlin newspaper about the local government in Potsdam opening an administrative office for legal matters. They planned to hire four western lawyers and four eastern lawyers. The mail between eastern and western Germany, even when traveling a few miles, was still so unreliable that Monika drove from Berlin to the address mentioned in the article and placed her résumé directly in the letter box.

A few weeks later, to her surprise, she received a letter inviting her to a job interview. During the interview, the head of the office asked her if she was prepared to put up with terrible working conditions and a meager salary of 1,300 marks per month at the start. In return, he said, she would have some of the most interesting legal work in Germany. She said yes. He held out his hand, and before she knew it she had a job on the basis of a handshake. Such a swift, informal hiring would never have taken place in western Germany.

Monika started out working as a city attorney. She did everything from defending the city in its decision to fire employees who had worked for the Stasi to advising people on western divorce laws. But a few months after she was hired, as soon as an office for property claims opened in the building, it became clear that property claims would make up the bulk of her work. Although Monika was just out of law school, the job gave her tremendous power. She made the initial decisions on property claims, and unless they were appealed to the claims office for greater Brandenburg, her decisions were binding.

Some of the most haunting claims Monika dealt with were Jewish. Her job became a thorough and occasionally emotional lesson in contemporary German history. First, there was Otto Mendelssohn's villa. Otto, a banker, was the grandson of the composer Felix Mendelssohn, and great-great-grandson of Moses Mendelssohn, the eighteenth-century philosopher and literary figure. Otto had a house near Cecilienhof. Remarkably, Otto had managed to survive in Germany until the end of World War II by hiding in an apartment over the stables on his own property. After the war, the Russians had forced him into the tiny gardener's cottage, which he shared with two other people. Now Otto's heirs were claiming the house.

Monika's education about World War II, the Holocaust and its aftermath had consisted of a few scattered lessons at her Berlin high school. She had little acquaintance with the details of the more harrowing aspects of the Third Reich. It was in the course of her new job that she learned details of the Holocaust she had not imagined.

It upset her to see old sales contracts from the Nazi era revealing that Jewish women were required to adopt the middle name Sara, and Jewish men had to adopt Israel. She saw records filled with the bureaucratic nomenclature of the period: *Mischehe,* a marriage of Jew and Gentile; *Volljude,* for full Jew; and the ubiquitous "Heil Hitler." And once she began delving into the Nazis' meticulously kept records, she was horrified by what they revealed: a systematic whittling down of a Jew's right to own property in any form. Such files usually closed with a clerk's passing reference to the camp the owner had been shipped to. This was accompanied by a final stamp, indicating that now the file could be closed. The same was true for a piece of property seized by the East German government and transferred into *Volkseigentum,* or property of the people. Each such expropriation was accompanied by a stack of forms and letters. The Nazis and the Communists, good bureaucrats, had simplified Monika's job immensely.

Monika had grown up fascinated by East Germany. She was born in West Berlin and, like so many other Berlin families, hers was sundered by the division of Germany. But unlike most West Berliners, as Monika learned more about her family in the East she developed an urge to travel there. She took her first trip to East Berlin in 1972, just after West Berliners were allowed to visit East Berlin for the first time. By the time she was in her teens, she had been to East Germany dozens of times, visiting relatives in East Berlin and in small villages in the deepest countryside. Somehow she felt more at home there than in the West. Monika was a serious child, and there was something about the somber environment that suited her temperament, and something about the directness of her relatives that made her want to be with them. Later, when she learned to drive, she took her parents' car to East Berlin. Once, when she took a wrong turn and got lost in East Berlin's empty side streets, it was chilling. After a few seconds she was stopped by an East German police officer, who grilled her until she was able to convince him of her innocent mistake. By the time she was eighteen she was traveling to the East so much that she caught the attention of the Stasi, who, through an East German friend of Monika's, made an effort to recruit her—an effort she did her best to ignore. For several months after that, she did not go to East Berlin.

She counted among her closest friends the ones in East Germany. Her cousins and her cousins' friends were as much a curiosity to her as she was to them. She was impressed with their grasp of political theory, even if she didn't necessarily agree with their interpretations. When she was sixteen, her cousin invited her to a meeting of the Free German Youth. He belonged to the organization not so much because he wanted to but because it was required of him. Monika was amazed by the group's pious acceptance of Marxist-Leninist dogma, but she kept her opinions to herself. The only slightly awkward moment she had with her East German relatives followed her mention of travel. Monika once made the mistake of telling her cousins how much she wanted to take a trip to Spain. As soon as the words left her mouth she wished she could snatch them back. After all, they could only hope. Monika could really go. Oddly, once the Wall fell, the closeness between Monika and her eastern German relatives disappeared. They could visit her anytime they pleased but they seldom did. It was as if overcoming a concrete fortification had kept them close.

Though some of Monika's friends looked at her askance when she did it, taking a job in the east made perfect sense to her. The working conditions in Potsdam were indeed less than ideal. The building itself, like most other official buildings in eastern Germany, had been done over in linoleum the color of bread mold, and faux wood paneling. There was no air conditioning in the summer and unreliable coal heat in the winter. The overburdened electrical circuits made Monika's computer unpredictable and prone to crash.

When she started work at the claims office, it seemed to Monika that everything in Potsdam had a claim on it. In the downtown area, some eight out of ten buildings were the object of a claim. Some of the cases were exceedingly complex. Say, for example, a house had first been "Aryanized" in a forced sale at a price well below market value, inhabited by the new owners for some years, then seized by the Communists. In the morning Monika would be visited by the heirs to the Jewish owners, then in the afternoon the offspring of the non-Jewish owners would appear to stake their claim.

After a while, Monika was juggling hundreds of claims at once. Files began to pile up on her desk. But her mind for details enabled her to memorize dozens of particulars concerning each case.

Monika was one small if pivotal part of the restitution process. She couldn't simply decide a case based on what the claimants gave her by way of proof. First, title searches had to be conducted, which often meant spending weeks looking for the proper title registry.

Then she had to gather any other records relevant to the claim. But claimants easily grew impatient. Many of them held Monika personally responsible for the sluggish tempo of the entire process.

When still fresh to the job, Monika thought that the decision to return property was a good one, that it provided a just solution to this unexpected twist in history. But gradually disappointment set in. The impatience on the part of the claimants was equalled in intensity only by the eastern Germans' sense of entitlement. She wasn't necessarily convinced that eastern Germans had a right to a house simply because they had lived in it for several decades. But whenever she heard stories of eastern Germans who had spent all their free time and savings to keep their house in good repair she was put in mind of her own uncle in the GDR, who had once spent six months searching high and low for a simple bathtub. Still, she tried to remain impartial.

Nor was she pleased to see the total lack of regard many of the western Germans displayed for those who were likely to be displaced as a result of a claim. She was uneasy about seeing so many westerners file claims with the intention of selling the property again. And she was especially irked when claimants came in and told her of their great emotional attachment to a piece of property they had never even seen before the opening of the Wall, or of grand plans they had to improve the property, or invest in it, when in fact they planned to sell it for as much as they could get. Monika tried to divorce herself entirely from the sad tales she heard. She had to base her decisions on the letter of the law. Often this was painful. For example, she had to decide against one compelling Jewish claim because she saw that the Jewish owners had sold the property before January 30, 1933.

She couldn't help but be moved by some of the cases that came to her. One case stood out for reasons she couldn't quite explain. In 1940, the claimant had sold her house to two people who signed an affidavit confirming they were "Aryans." In order to avoid any doubt about the legality of the sale, shortly after the transaction the seller was required to sign the papers again with the name "Sara," since under Nazi law Sara was part of her legal name. When such cases cropped up, when the facts were transparent enough to expose history, Monika recalled, "it made my skin crawl." Such cases inevitably became the subject of conversation between Monika and her colleagues. There was something about knowing the details of these sales, both during the Nazi period and during the GDR period, that made their imaginations take flight. And where did the dispossessed go after losing their homes? When a former owner's heirs returned to file a claim, Monika would learn the entire story, not necessarily because she asked to hear it but because the claimants told her.

The process was indeed slow. By the summer of 1991, out of thousands of claims only a dozen or so properties had been returned.

By then, Monika was falling further and further behind in her work. She was expected to resolve three cases a day. But it was impossible. She considered it a good pace if she managed to do three a week. For the first year or so of her job, she had recurring dreams about various pieces of property. One early dream was about the Truman Villa, known as such because it was the mansion that Harry Truman stayed in during the Potsdam Conference. Now Monika was handling the claim on the villa. Since most of the properties she dealt with were nothing more than a point on a map to her, the dreams were always the same: she saw the plat diagram of a single piece of property, usually one that she was behind on, or where the claimants were particularly bothersome, and applying all the pressure they could to get her to speed up their case.

When the office got reliable telephone lines it only made things worse. Now claimants could call, instead of having to make inquiries in person. The secretaries began ignoring the phone when it rang. The office was just too short-handed to bother with a ringing telephone.

Before long, Monika's office floor was covered with case files. She had put in a request for new file cabinets but they hadn't arrived. She developed a scheme for keeping track of where on the floor she could locate each file. To make things worse, the summer of 1992 in Berlin was one of the hottest on record. In a city that seldom got hotter than eighty degrees in the summer, temperatures rose into the low nineties. Monika's office was stifling. Of course there was no air conditioning. How could an office that could barely afford pencil sharpeners request air conditioners? Her only relief from the heat came at the end of the day, when she went swimming in the Heiliger See, a lake in the Berliner Vorstadt.

Monika was also fearful of fire. Not from the dry heat but from arson. Early in the summer an arsonist had set fire to one of the buildings in Potsdam containing property records—but these were government records that had nothing to do with private property. Monika and her colleagues guessed that the fire had actually been meant for their building, where all the case files for private property in Potsdam resided. Every morning when she arrived at work and saw that the building was still standing, she was relieved.

The lawyers in the office were mostly from the west, and the administrative staff was from the east. Monika had established a good rapport with her colleagues from the east, though she seldom socialized with them, and she was occasionally surprised to see how lackadaisical they could be about their work. And sometimes there was an undercurrent of tension because of the salary disparities: even though they all had the same employers, the Ossies were paid 60 percent of what Monika and all the other Wessies made. This disparity was based on the fact that the cost of living was lower for easterners.

Monika never shied away from getting into political discussions with them. Particularly because of the nature of what the office was dealing with every day, idle conversations often turned political. Monika was often surprised to hear the prejudices that surfaced with little provocation.

"You know, just as many Germans died at the hands of the Nazis as Jews," one of the assistants in the office proclaimed one day. Monika was stunned to hear things like this, but she wrote it off to the distorted education in the GDR, which taught that German antifascists were the Nazis' true victims. And there was an undercurrent of bitterness among some of the staff in the claims office. Many of the Ossies who worked there had been in positions of far greater importance before the two Germanys melded. The man in charge of sorting files and fetching them for the lawyers, for instance, had been a historian at one of East Germany's most prominent universities. He was generally friendly, but whenever he got to talking about the dismantling of the eastern German universities he grew visibly bitter, and whoever he was speaking with sought a route to a different topic.

Each Tuesday Monika held open office hours, when members of the public were invited to visit the claims office and have the ear of the lawyers who made the decisions, and it was always the most harrowing day of the week. Elderly claimants, many of whom had driven for hours from points all over western Germany, sat for hours on rickety chairs for the chance to speak with Frau Hagen. Occasionally they were indignant to see someone so young in the position of deciding their fate. But more often they were impressed and delighted to encounter someone within the German bureaucracy who was so sympathetic.

Monika anticipated Tuesdays with a kind of welcoming dread. On the one hand, she was glad to get a day of distraction from the bog of paperwork. But Tuesday was a day of uninterrupted stress as well: claims ceased being mere file numbers, or street addresses, and took the human form of elderly couples from the west, or desperate Potsdamers trying to stop a claim, or slick Berlin lawyers representing overseas clients. Regardless of their wealth or status, they all sat and stood together in the building's dark, inhospitable hallways and waited for their time with Frau Hagen. Some had driven six hours from western Germany just for twenty minutes with her. In one odd coincidence, one elderly claimant looked familiar but Monika couldn't place her. The woman turned out to have been one of Monika's teachers from her high school in West Berlin.

Monika honed to a fine craft her ability to conduct her office hours. By the time she arrived at 7:15 A.M. there were already people waiting. She took some time to gather herself and take care of pressing matters, and starting at precisely 9 A.M., she called them in one by one. During the excruciatingly hot days of summer she and her visitors did their best to ignore the heat. If the claimants were particularly old she worried that they might succumb to heat stroke. Even on the hottest days, Monika kept her door shut during the individual conferences. The doors were padded GDR-style (for sound insulation), with Naugahyde and batting nailed down with large chrome tacks, which only made the office hotter. Flies zipped in through the open window and Monika swiped at them periodically as she spoke.

Monika's office was still GDR-furnished, with uncomfortable standard-issue office furniture and the ubiquitous orange-brown linoleum, and a fluorescent light hanging from a single cable. She had tried to brighten her office up a bit with a poster of Franz Marc's famous blue horses.

The claimants entered her office nervously, dressed in their best clothes, aware that this was the person who would be deciding the fate of their property. Monika's first request of each was that they present their identification card, which every German is required to carry. They came with colorful plastic shopping bags from the Her-tie and Karstadt department stores, filled with tattered, fifty-year-old papers, or with thick folders stuffed into large handbags, all hoping that if they presented her with more proof of their rightful owner- ship their case would move more quickly. Sometimes Monika re- ceived photographs of property in the mail.

Claimants needed only to mention the address and Monika recog- nized the claim. Monika had hundreds of cases stored in her head, but she reacted to each as if it were the only one to occupy her thoughts. She displayed such a remarkable command of the random particulars surrounding each case that any skepticism they may have had toward her due to her youth quickly dissolved. And she had a knack for putting everyone at ease. On the few occasions when she was completely perplexed by a case, she didn't let on.

The oddest thing about Monika's work was how the vestiges of a defunct legal system came into play, and some of the GDR-specific language she used. If, for instance, the Communists had seized a piece of property because the owner had left the country "ille- gally"—what the East Germans called *Republikflucht*—the offender was convicted in absentia and the crime recorded. In a peculiar recognition of a body of law that no longer existed, the western German government required that claimants go through a battery of bureaucratic procedures to have judgments for such crimes against the former East German state formally annulled before their prop- erty could be returned.

Her understanding of the East German laws governing property seizure was complete. She invoked their legal concepts as if the East German justice system still applied. For lack of any other way of putting things, Monika adopted the same terminology. "Your mother committed Republikflucht in 1965," she told one middle-aged claimant. But rather than reply with statements like, "No, she turned her back on a system she didn't believe in and was punished for it," the claimants had a peculiarly docile way of nodding their heads in agreement.

Monika spent a good portion of each session asking the claimants for patience. She pointed to the hundred or so files on her floor. It could take another six months or a year before she would get to theirs. She couldn't expect them to appreciate the laboriousness of the process. How could they understand the many hours it took first to gather all there was to gather, then assess all that she had gathered, then write a lengthy decision that included a description of the property's long and often convoluted history? But she could ask for their patience. Some said they would be patient. But others gave a compelling reason as to why she should give their claim preference: The place was going to ruin and needed immediate attention. Or they were old and frail and didn't have much time left for enjoying their once and future villa. Or their parents were old and frail and didn't have much time left. Occasionally, moved by the faces behind the claims, in an effort to reassure her visitors while they sat before her, she placed their file on top of a stack of files behind her and promised to try to give their case prompt attention. She had heard stories of briberies, and attempted bribery, and was a bit surprised that no one had tried it with her.

Once in a while Monika had to tell a visitor that the chances of getting a piece of property back were small. One citizen of the former East Germany had had the bad luck to sell her house—then worth about $3,500—in exchange for a color television—worth about $6,000—and leave just before the Wall fell in 1989. Another unfortunate claimant had bought his property during the interregnum of Hans Modrow, who served as prime minister for barely five months between late 1989 and early 1990 and during his tenure declared that East Germans would be permitted to buy their residences.

Monika's job, she found out, was an exercise in coping with personalities of all kinds. One man from the west, a physician, simply appeared at the claims office one day as it was closing at 5:30 and demanded to speak to someone. His seventy-five-year-old mother had fled East Germany on August 12, 1961, the day before the Wall went up, with nothing but a suitcase. He flew into a rage when Monika pointed out that his mother's claim was not as black and white as he might want to believe. Another exercise of Monika's patience was exacted by an elderly woman who simply couldn't grasp what Monika was trying to explain to her. She, like everyone who came to Monika's office, saw herself as entitled to her property. And like the others, the idea that she may not get the house back hadn't occurred to her. Monika was unable to get her to see that there were complexities to the case that could lessen her chances of getting it back.

Monika couldn't seem to get away from her job. At social gatherings, as soon as she told people what she did for a living, they asked her something about their own claim, or a relative's claim, or a friend's claim.

The Wallich Claim

Monika hadn't been in the job long when she was assigned the Wallich case. At first glance it seemed straightforward enough, a claim like many another—a family of Jewish origins had abandoned the house shortly before the war.

Whenever she was describing the location of the house to someone within earshot of one of her eastern colleagues, they quickly corrected her Wessi way of viewing the world. "It's not the first house on the right after crossing the bridge into Potsdam," they would say. "It's the last house on the left before leaving Potsdam."

The Wallich claim, however, was different from many others in one important aspect. She knew the house itself well, at least from the outside, because she drove by it every morning on her way to work. It, too, haunted her dreams.

And like most claims, this one turned out to have unexpected wrinkles. There were several parcels of land, all of which had been purchased by the Wallichs at different times. And although this looked like a Jewish claim, it was not. Monika had seen in the old records she examined that Paul Wallich had transferred the property to his wife, Hildegard, a non-Jew, in 1932, the year before Hitler came to power. Perhaps Paul Wallich had been prescient about what was to come and transferred the property in order to save it. But more likely than not the transfer had been strictly business, an internal transaction that had nothing to do with Jewish ownership. In any case, since Hildegard held title to the property at the time the family left, the claim couldn't be decided under the law's provision for Jewish-owned property.

There was one fact that altered the handling of the claim in one important way. If a piece of property was being put to a public use that benefited the community at large, then the city could contest the claim and, if the objection was upheld, the former owners would receive monetary compensation, which promised to be far less in value than the property was actually worth. Monika Hagen knew that the Wallich property was a Kindergarten, and she expected the local education authorities to dispute the claim, as they had with other claims to child-care facilities. She wrote to the education department to alert them to the claim and asked for a response within thirty days. A month passed, and she received no response.

Over the four decades of Communist rule, private property was confiscated piecemeal. In some cases it was seized outright. In others, citizens who fled for the West and abandoned their homes and businesses left knowing that they were giving up control over their property's fate. After they had left, their house in Berlin, or their laundry business in Leipzig, or their bakery in Weimar, became the de facto property of the state. Businesses were turned into state-run enterprises and houses divided into multifamily dwellings for citizens of East Germany, who paid nominal rents. Citizens of East Germany, too, were often stripped of their shops, factories and farms until, by the time the Wall opened, much of the property in East Germany was *Volkseigentum,* or people's property, which meant that it belonged to the state.

The majority of the property in East Germany, however, was administered by the state for the absentee owners. Such arrangements often meant nothing but frustration for Western owners, who could do little about ensuring the property's upkeep. In the 1970s, the city of Potsdam imposed charges against all of the property still nominally owned by Westerners, purportedly for capital improvements. Such was the case with the Wallich property. For years the house remained in Hildegard Wallich's name and for years the East German government continued to accrue debt on the property. Finally, citing an accumulated debt burden, on May 13, 1983, the East German government formally seized the house and turned it into Volkseigentum.

Property in both categories—seized property and state-managed property—came to serve a wide range of functions. In the case of larger estates, public institutions often took over: medical clinics, schools, homes for the elderly. Monika saw some of everything.

The Wallich case was well known around the office, partly for the sheer bulk of the file and partly because it was one of those cases that Monika just couldn't seem to wrap up. She had thought she would be finished with it, or at least with a preliminary decision, by the fall of 1991. But the fall of 1991 came and went and she was still laboring on other cases. The file sat for months on the floor behind her desk. Finally, she handed it over to another colleague, thinking he might be able to do it more quickly. But he, too, dragged his feet on the case.

In late 1991, when she went to the wedding of a former law school classmate, Monika bumped into Frank Walter-von Gierke, the Berlin lawyer representing the Wallich descendants. She knew him from law school. He wanted to know what the status of the claim was. Monika started to tell him, then stopped herself. She couldn't believe it was 1:30 A.M. and she was talking about a property claim. She smiled, said something about not mixing business and pleasure, and steered the conversation elsewhere. When Monika looked at the affluent young lawyer she wondered whether she should have gone for a high-paying job with a firm like the high-profile one he worked for, with a comfortable office. He was her age and making at least three times her salary. That night she had a dream about the Wallich house that was so intense it woke her up. But when she tried, she couldn't remember any of the details.

8: THE WALLICHS

In Search of Old Records

Christine Wallich had been emboldened by her visit to the villa with her brother, Paul, to do her best to see the house return to the family fold. She believed there was something to be said for the old belief that if a house is lost, the family follows. The Potsdam house had very nearly been lost, and here was a chance to keep it from slipping away entirely.

After leaving the house they had driven into central Potsdam to find the office where the property records were kept. When they found it, it was already four o'clock, and the office appeared to be closing for the day, as someone was busy mopping the floor. But Christine managed to convince one of the clerks to look in the property registry for them. The clerk told the siblings that the property at Berliner Strasse 86, formerly Stalinallee 86, and before that Neue Königstrasse 62, was listed as Volkseigentum, property of the people. Its last private owner was listed as Hildegard Wallich, but that was all she could tell them. She told them to go to another office around the corner and inquire there. This one was called the Finanzamt, or tax office. It was an old building with long corridors, floors covered with linoleum that looked exactly like the linoleum they had seen in the house, and a long row of quilted leather doors for blocking out sound.

It was here that Paul began to feel uncomfortable. The Wall hadn't been down for very long, and although reunification of the two Germanys was imminent, East Germany was still very much its own entity. Paul and Christine reflected that they were the first Americans that many of these people had ever met. They had anticipated far more hostility. At the Finanzamt they were regarded kindly by a middle-aged woman who told them they would need a certificate decreeing them the legal heirs to Hildegard Wallich's estate. "One of the surprising things," Paul Wallich recalled, "was how people were acting fairly friendly and did exert themselves when they could have said, 'Look, it's four P.M., were leaving, we've had a long day.' "

In the fall of 1990, six months later, Christine flew back to Berlin, intent on pursuing the family's claim to the house by the bridge. She was accompanied this time by her mother, Mable.

They made directly for the office of Frank Walter-von Gierke, the young lawyer Christine and Paul had been to see. By this time, they had gotten word that the property was even larger than Paul's rough estimate had concluded. A student working on a paper about the house had called Mable from Berlin to tell her this.

As Walter-von Gierke later recalled, when Mable and Christine arrived at his office late in the day on a Friday, they were very excited, and told him of the latest estimate of the property's size.

It was shortly before the October 13 deadline for filing claims and everyone was anxious to see the claim filed. It was agreed that they would do it right away. While the two women sat in his office, the lawyer picked up his telephone and ordered a courier to take the paperwork to the Potsdam claims office. A short time later, the claim was official.

Christine Mounts a Campaign

Christine's task throughout the next months was going to be to convince her siblings and her cousins that it would be imprudent simply to turn around and sell the property as soon as the title had been transferred back to the family. Her hope was to keep the house in the family. This derived in part from a belief that this was what Henry would have wanted, and partly from her belief that this was a chance to right the wrong committed against her grandfather. But other members of the family were wary. Some of them ascribed deeper, perhaps even subconscious motives to Christine. They suspected she was trying to please her father even in death, that this was one more way in which she was trying to prove herself to him.

Perhaps they were right. Christine had spent years in pursuit of her father's approval. In high school, she had been interested in German literature and the classics. At Cambridge, she began to explore the field of economics ("the family business," as she described it years later), developed a concentration in it and returned to the United States for graduate school. Yale was her school of choice, although her father had already left Yale for Washington to serve on the Federal Reserve Board of Governors by the time Christine entered. Like her father, Christine was interested in development economics, which took her to Chile for a year to work at the U.N.'s Economic Commission for Latin America. And she wanted to follow her father into the public service sector of economics. In 1977 she started to work at the World Bank.

So it wasn't surprising that when the opportunity to save her father's house arose, Christine seized it. She knew she was facing a great deal of resistance from siblings and cousins. In considering Christine's attachment to the house, Hans Frank, the family lawyer, once alluded to writer Heinrich von Kleist's Michael Kohlhaas, the horse trader with a hyperdeveloped sense of justice who insisted on righting a wrong.

But Christine believed that if she could get the rest of the family to view the house as she did—as a slice of the Wallich destiny—then they would come around. Her greatest hope—an idealistic one, she readily conceded—was that the others would agree to keep the house and restore it for their own use. At the very least, they should consider, as a condition of a sale, retaining an apartment on the third floor of the house. She hadn't seen it yet, but she imagined that it must be a wonderful atelier, far cozier than the rest of the house.

The other Wallich heirs were mixed in their attitudes toward the house. The British cousins wanted nothing to do with it, largely because they wanted a complete break with the German side of their heritage. Walter's wife, Muji, had had nothing but trouble from Hildegard, who treated her as if she were invisible. Muji passed her animosity on to her children. In his determination to melt into British culture, Walter spoke no German with his children. Only one of the five British children, Robert, had chosen to study German, and he was also the only one who had spent any part of his youth in Germany.

The Argentines, on the other hand, grew up speaking German, and Fritz Körte, the second son of Christel and her husband, had an attachment of sorts to Germany. German traditions were upheld in the Körte home. In some ways, Fritz's upbringing was more German than if he had stayed in Germany. He was taught to sing German *Volkslieder*, the folk songs so discredited for their association with the Nazis. The Körte children listened to Wagner operas and the works of other German composers, and at bedtime they were read the German classics.

Fritz also grew up hearing stories from his mother about a youth spent under the supervision of nannies, and of being presented to the grown-ups after supper every night to say good night. Christel referred to the villa as "the Potsdam house," so as to distinguish it from the estate in Jerchel and the apartment in Berlin.

Fritz and the other Argentines knew from an early age how and why their grandfather had died. They also knew that their parents had emigrated in 1937 because they could not get married in Germany due to the Nazi prohibition against mixed marriages, and had married secretly in Buenos Aires. Fritz heard his father tell of times he had to do business at the German embassy in Buenos Aires and was reminded in no uncertain terms that he had done something "very bad" in furtively marrying a woman with Jewish blood. Fritz also heard the story of the *Lahn* and the Goebbels Prize. But Fritz and his siblings did not see these as reasons necessarily to hold on to the house in Potsdam.

Mable was not an heir to Hildegard's estate. And, as her son, Paul, put it, she was probably just as glad that the Potsdam house was "somebody else's problem." On the other hand, she let her children know that she certainly was not opposed to a sale.

To make Christine's job still harder, in the spring of 1991 her cousins began to hear about the skyrocketing property values in Berlin. After years as a political and geographic island, Berlin was suddenly in the midst of a real estate boom. And the Potsdam house stood in one of the city's most attractive locations: property in the Berliner Vorstadt, where the house stood, was selling for 500 marks per square meter and it continued to rise. Despite its unresolved property claim, and although it was not advertised for sale, the house was already attracting attention. Every few months another prospective buyer surfaced. And each successive offer rose significantly.

By early 1992, Christine was beginning to feel worn down by her effort to save the house for her family. Her job at the World Bank was increasingly demanding, as her reputation as a specialist in Eastern Europe grew and her career at the bank spiraled upward. She was making frequent trips to Russia and each time she traveled there, she made a point of stopping in Berlin to visit relatives and see the house, for reasons that she conceded were more emotional than practical. As the plane descended into Berlin, it sometimes flew directly over Potsdam and gave her a clear and stunning view of the bridge and the house. While there, she had appointments with officials who might have some influence over how the property could be developed, but it was suggested that she refrain from visiting the office of Monika Hagen, the administrator deciding the case, so as not to seem too pushy.

On one of Christine's trips, in March of 1992, her husband, Leo, accompanied her on a visit to Berlin. Leo, a Chilean whose family was partly Jewish, had resisted going to visit Berlin with Christine until then. The two of them arrived at the house at a busy point in the day for the Kindergarten. There were children everywhere. Video camera in hand, they toured the house with Frau Neumann. With Leo as cameraman, they went from room to room, then outside, where a young pretty teacher was on duty. When they saw the camera, the children rushed over and demanded to know what it was. Christine was struck by how unrefined and coarse these children seemed, compared with other small children she knew. Afterward, Leo told Christine that he now understood her attachment to the house much better.

At around the same time, vandals struck the house. Herr Brunke went outside early one morning to discover that the large lion statue of copper alloy that resided in a niche in the garden wall had disappeared, pried from its perch sometime during the night. Herr Brunke reported it to Frau Neumann, who reported it to the police.

The Potsdam landmark preservationists estimated the lion's value at 30,000 marks. Such a thing would not have happened while the Wall was still up.

News of the theft landed in the Potsdam newspaper's police blotter, which printed a description of the large-maned victim in case readers should spot it: "Distinguishing marks include a hole two centimeters in diameter on the upper left shank, and a wasp's nest inside."

Christine panicked when she heard about the theft of the lion. If vandals had no qualms about lifting the lion, then certainly they might come back for the still more valuable statue of Athena, which stood inside an arch carved into the front of the house.

Christine made a point of letting her cousins and the Potsdam authorities know that until the future of the house was settled she did not want the Kindergarten to move out, as the house remained much more secure with the children and the teachers in it.

During several of her business trips Christine stopped in London as well, to see her British cousins and try to convince them to consider keeping the house. Each time she went, she had to prepare herself for their resistance.

Frustrated and weary of her campaign, Christine gradually arrived at a decision. If the others would not agree to hold on to the house, perhaps she could find a purchaser who would preserve the house in a spirit that was somehow connected to the family. She would write to the German Bundesbank. For months she had been in correspondence with directors of the Bundesbank about purchasing the house and reserving the top-floor apartment for the family. It would be fitting, at least, that a bank should take over the house, and particularly fitting that Germany's counterpart to the Federal Reserve should do it.

It was during conversations with officers at the Bundesbank, one Günter Storch in particular, that Christine was reminded of how Germans tended to view her family. More than once the Bundesbank official made reference to an "obligation" to the Wallich family and its Jewish roots, an obligation to pay for a past wrong. Such remarks made Christine uneasy, for she did not see this as a Jewish case. When a German television producer called her to tell her he'd like to do a documentary about the Jewish family that returned to Germany to reclaim a historic villa, she didn't bother to tell him that her family had not observed Judaism, or even considered itself Jewish, for several generations. She did tell him that if he planned to emphasize the Jewish angle she would have nothing to do with the project. And when she met with one Potsdam official to discuss future plans for the villa, he asked somewhat brusquely whether she was planning to turn the house into an office for the city's Jewish community, as if that would be the villa's only suitable function.

By now the family had hired an architect to draw up a proposed building plan for the site and present it to Potsdam city planners and landmark preservationists for their approval. Since the house was a historical landmark, it was likely that the city would limit the degree to which the property could be developed. As the reasoning went, a sale would be easier if prospective purchasers knew how much they would be allowed to develop the property.

Herr Storch of the Bundesbank did go so far as to fly to Berlin from Frankfurt to visit the house one day in early July of 1992. He was a bit baffled by the whole thing, mostly because he didn't see that the Bundesbank really needed any property in Berlin. The bank already held two substantial pieces of property around Berlin. But his boss, Helmut Schlesinger, had known Henry Wallich and apparently the bank considered such a purchase a strong symbolic gesture, clean penance. If the family hadn't been Jewish, the Bundesbank wouldn't have considered it. And then there was the banking angle. Henry had been a central banker of world renown. And Hermann Wallich had played a prominent role in German banking history. The combination held a certain emotional appeal.

But then Herr Storch saw the house. Not only was it a ruin, but it stood too close to the street for his liking. He thought it would require several million dollars to renovate. And when he drove up to the house in a rented Mercedes, Herr Storch encountered the mayhem of a child-care center in full swing—dozens of children were in the backyard, and the teachers were in the midst of preparations for a party. One of the children called out to him, "Want to play a game with us?" "No thank you," the banker replied. He introduced himself to Frau Neumann, but didn't tell her of his actual mission, and she didn't ask. She explained that they were busy preparing for a big party for the children and parents. "Allow me to make a contribution," Storch said. With the flourish of a man most comfortable when reaching for his billfold, he produced a 50 mark note and held it out to Frau Neumann. She accepted the money readily, thanked him without looking at him and said it would help a great deal.

When Storch reported back to Schlesinger, he was pessimistic. The Wallich family had let him know that one of Berlin's large developers indicated the property could be purchased for some $13.5 million. But the most that the bank should consider offering, he advised, was $11 million. Even that was a lot of money to spend on something that was more or less a gesture aimed at doing one's part in lightening the burden of the Holocaust. Perhaps the house had been nice to live in at the turn of the century, when that corner was quiet and sedate. But this was now a major thoroughfare, with cars speeding by, a taxi stand directly under one of the windows and tourists parking their cars every which way in front of the house. Perhaps this would be a nice spot for a hotel, or a restaurant, but not necessarily for what the bank had in mind. After all, this could not be just a good-works project for the bank. The house would have to serve a function, and the best use that Storch could think of was a training center for new employees. But even the rooms themselves—there were too few of them for lodging trainees—fell short of ideal for what Storch had in mind. That meant that the bank would need to be allowed to build a sizable building on the neighboring plots. Since the villa was a historical landmark the bank would be at the mercy of Potsdam's landmark preservationists. Storch had no desire to deal with those people, known to be unyielding and exacting.

Christine's hopes in the meantime were growing dimmer. Should her attempts fail completely, at the least Christine wanted the chance to spend a night in the house before it went to new owners.

9: ULRIKE

A Threat of Dispossession

When Ulrike arrived for work at the Kindergarten one afternoon in the spring of 1990, less than six months after the Wall fell, a flustered Frau Krabbes told her that two Americans had been by that morning and they were going to reclaim the house. They would have to move out, she claimed. They were all going to lose their jobs. Ulrike didn't believe it but Frau Neumann confirmed it. She too was beside herself. Grim-faced, she told Ulrike that a pair of siblings by the name of Wallich who said they were the grandchildren of the original owners had been by and toured the house. They were polite and spoke excellent German, Frau Neumann told her. But they had refused to say when or whether they would be moving back to Germany.

Ulrike had heard the stories of westerners returning after four decades to reclaim their houses. By deciding that Germans who had lost property after 1933 could take it back, the German government had aggravated the tension between eastern and western Germans. Ulrike had heard from her friends about Wessies showing up at the doorsteps of East Germans to inform them that they were the rightful owners and the residents would have to leave. And those Wessies not busy making a claim, it seemed, were busy buying up real estate. But Ulrike hadn't thought something like this would happen in her small world. The fleeting appearance of these two strangers cast a new pall over the Kindergarten. The teachers had a new reason to resent the west. Ulrike was the only one who thought that this was something that could be fought. The others seemed resigned to it.

She wasn't sure where to turn, but decided to go to the city's education authorities. She wrote a letter to the new director of education, an austere, sour-miened woman in her fifties named Frau Knoblich. Frau Knoblich had been a high school history teacher before being elected to her new post. She was fond of her authority, and her superior air frightened many of the people who worked for her. She and her husband, the president of the local parliament, were Potsdam's new power couple. But Ulrike wasn't intimidated by the formidable Frau Knoblich. She wrote her a letter, and in it she explained the importance of preserving the house at the bridge as a place for children. Then she and Frau Neumann made an appointment to see her.

When they arrived, they were summoned into Frau Knoblich's office. The education director immediately produced Ulrike's letter. "Are you the author of this letter?" she asked, waving Ulrike's correspondence in the air. Ulrike nodded. Frau Knoblich's brow lowered. "I am disgusted by such a display," she said. It was not Ulrike's place to tell the education department how its facilities should be used. And with that she dismissed Ulrike from the meeting.

The threat of a property claim on the house was the last thing the women at the Kindergarten needed, and they took their anxiety out on one another. The teachers began to snub the "downstairs workers"—the cooks and the seamstress and the cleaning woman. For years everyone had taken their coffee breaks together upstairs in the loggia while the children napped. But now a tension, aggravated by a new sensitivity to class, developed between the teachers and the kitchen staff. The women who worked in the kitchen accused the teachers of being petty snobs, and the teachers in turn regarded the kitchen staff as simple and divisive. The kitchen staff began drinking their coffee downstairs. Ulrike didn't know how much the foul relations had to do with the threat of being shut down. Going to work became something she dreaded. She began to think about ways she might quit Kindergartens altogether and start a new career.

She wished everyone in the east who was now so frustrated over reunification could be returned to that day after the Wall fell, so they could see how happy and optimistic they had been at the time. She wished that her co-workers in the Kindergarten would stop and listen to themselves complain. They were actually well off. They still had work, they all had apartments, a western car, and a patch of garden in the communal garden colonies scattered around Potsdam. Frau Zierke was running a wine business on the side, which was doing well.

It frustrated Ulrike that so many artifacts of the Communist regime were simply being cleared away like so much rubble: the removal of the house-sized Lenin bust in East Berlin; the renaming of all the streets. In Ulrike's mind, these things should have been preserved as reminders of a collective guilt. Not guilt for having taken part in socialism, but guilt for having remained quiet about all the injustices that took place in Honecker's state. She called it the "*Verstricktsein im System,*" being so entangled in the system, saying yes for so long that it became impossible to do anything else.

One of the most upsetting incidents was a party that Ulrike and Frau Neumann attended on the grounds of the Glienicke Castle in the summer of 1991. They had been invited to the gathering by Dirk Heydemann, a student who had written his thesis about the history of the garden behind the house. Dirk was one of the first westerners Ulrike had gotten to know, and at twenty-nine, he was close to her age. She hadn't been sure at first whether the continuous smile he wore was an assumed cheerfulness she had noticed in other westerners, or whether it was his own strange quirk. He was so ingratiating that Ulrike and the other teachers had invited him in for coffee, and told him rich stories of the house's past. Ulrike then felt betrayed to hear that he was recommending to the city that the house be turned into a museum. Implied, of course, was that the three dozen children and eight teachers be turned out.

But she and Frau Neumann accepted the invitation to Dirk's afternoon party, which he held across the river on the grounds of the Glienicke Castle. What she saw there enraged her. All of the guests—chic Wessies—were toasting Dirk's work and toasting the house, as if it had lived one life for 150 years, as if it had served one function, as if its forty years as a place for children could be paved over along with the rest of East Germany. And all those references to the Wallich family, as if they still owned the house! After all, they had abandoned the house decades ago, hadn't they? She and Frau Neumann left the party as quickly as they could.

A few weeks later, she bumped into Dirk on a street near her apartment. He greeted her as cheerfully as ever. But Ulrike was not about to exchange pleasantries. She told him exactly what was on her mind. How could he have such a proprietary attitude about the house? Didn't he understand what it meant to the children? Couldn't he appreciate the function it was serving, which was far more socially redeeming than a museum and a parking lot? Dirk looked a bit taken aback, but he didn't respond. And the smile didn't leave his face as he wished her well and went on his way.

Ulrike realized later that she had taken out all her "Wende frustration," as she put it, on Dirk, when it wasn't necessarily justified. She knew enough to accept others' perceptions of the house, whether or not it fit with her own. The frustration she was feeling, and that she shared with her friends, was more than the "Wall-in-the-Head" the press kept writing about, the psychological Wall that stood in stead of the physical one. It was a feeling of halfway assimilation. They had yet to shed the vestiges of their GDR past and they hadn't yet integrated themselves into the western life, or a western frame of mind.

Caught Between Two Worlds

Both Ulrike and Ingo were now willing to admit that they had made an error: they had thought they could improve the system, and create a better socialism. They had agreed with the nation's writers and intellectuals, who even after the Wall fell implored their fellow citizens to stay in the east and help build a democratic socialism, a Third Way. But Ulrike and Ingo now saw how futile that was. The little community they had formed in Langerwisch had been more escape than solution.

She missed small things. She missed her close circle of friends, which was splitting apart because everyone was too busy to get to-

gether. It had become nearly impossible to do anything sponta-
neously. Everything had to be planned in advance.

The children at the Kindergarten were clearly happy about their
new freedom. They could take walks across the bridge and play
hide-and-seek in the woods around the Glienicke Castle. Ulrike noticed that the new freedom brought out differences between the day
children and the weekly children, who were eager for attention.
During walks, the ones who stayed there during the week were
quick to go up to strangers and talk to them, while the day children
were far more reserved.

Explaining the change to the children wasn't easy. What reason
was there to offer for the new freedom to wander anywhere now,
when it used to be forbidden to walk more than a few feet from the
front door? Or to explain the fact that parents could come to the
front door to pick up their children instead of waiting behind the
barrier gate down the street? Or to explain the disappearance from
the walls of the pictures of the stern-faced men who were yester-
day's heroes and today's villains?

Ulrike was even disappointed by what had happened to the Stube
since the Wall fell. It no longer possessed any of its thrown-together
charm. Instead, it seemed a parody of itself. It was usually so full
that everyone was pressed against one another and now the music
was strangely off-putting. One group, calling itself Leningrad 44,
sang rock 'n' roll versions of the old songs she knew from her
school days: Soviet marching songs, and Russian folk songs.

Now she was seeing all the positive things that she had taken for
granted in the GDR. Even though Ulrike hadn't necessarily agreed
with the system, or with the notion of a closed society, its effects on
her everyday life had permeated her thinking. She believed that the
GDR had kept her much more closely tuned with seasonal rhythms.
Oranges and bananas were expensive and came to the stores only
around Christmas and only for a few days, but if you were willing to
queue up you could buy them. She was able to calculate to the day,
taking the weather into consideration, when the strawberries would
come to the markets. Her two children understood that apples grew
in East Germany in apple orchards, and that there was a season for
them. Now perfectly good eastern apples were left to rot on the
ground because eastern Germans wanted the shinier ones from the
west, and fruits were available at any time of year from all over the
world.

Ulrike and Ingo missed other things, too, things they hadn't expected to miss, such as the freshly baked, dense, flavorful rolls that had been a staple of East Germany. The rolls at the bakeries now were mass-produced and, to Ulrike's palate, tasteless.

And then there were the flowers, which Ulrike was also willing to stand in line for. As she understood the cycle of nature, tulips came in the spring and asters in autumn. Buying tulips that had been grown in some greenhouse somewhere in the middle of winter seemed entirely inappropriate.

Even Wolfgang's retreat at Langerwisch was no longer what it had been before the Wall fell. He still had big parties in the summer, but they were different. The people from Potsdam still brought their tents, sausages to grill and beer. But now lots of chic Wessies came, in Mercedes and BMWs. No one was sure where Wolfgang had met them or why he invited them. They stood around in their own circle, eating pasta salads and exotic cheeses they had brought with them, and drinking dry white burgundies. The scene at Langerwisch, once a self-contained idyll, now seemed comically distorted, with the poor Ossies roasting their wursts over pitiful little fires while the *schicki-micki* (a bit too chic for comfort) Wessies gathered in a tight circle of self-satisfaction.

The village itself had changed as well. Nearly all the villagers now worked in Potsdam, and more and more people were moving there. Two of the largest farmhouses had been bought by Wessies, who were busy renovating them in a most conspicuous way. Wolfgang was now an accepted fixture in town, regarded as a nexus to the more interesting worlds in Potsdam and Berlin.

One of the first things Ulrike wanted after the Wall fell was a car. But first she needed a driver's license, which meant enrolling in driving school, the only way to get a license in Germany. With the demise of the Wall eastern Germany had become a breeding ground for driving schools. Every third car, it seemed, was a VW Golf with a sign, "Driving School," in the window. It would be expensive to get her license—about $600 to go through the course—but her father offered to pay her tuition as a "reunification" gift. Once she had completed the twenty lessons and gotten her license, she used her own savings to buy a green 1978 Golf. Compared to the underpowered, uncomfortable and awkward little Trabant, the western car was luxurious.

Ulrike surprised herself by how much she liked the liberation that came with her new car. It made everything accessible, on her timetable, not that of a bus or streetcar. She liked being insulated from strangers while she traveled, and she enjoyed the high-speed Autobahn. She could be in central Berlin in twenty minutes. She was eager to explore west Berlin—the pubs in Kreuzberg, west Berlin's hip and grungy quarter, and the tony bistros and cafés closer to the Kurfürstendamm.

Ulrike took to going out at night with friends, leaving Ingo at home with Philipp and Benni. Ingo was just as happy to stay away from the scene in west Berlin. He took a dimmer view of the possibilities created by the automobile, just as he took a dimmer view of the effects of reunification in general.

Ingo was still teaching at the school for aspiring Kindergarten teachers, but his job was in jeopardy. As if to tempt fate, he stuck to a syllabus that seemed hopelessly outdated now. He still had the young women read traditional political theory, but he had little success in holding their attention. Now, when they did read, they turned to the trashy romance novels that had been outlawed before the Wall fell. Ingo felt at times that he was lecturing to an empty classroom.

Ulrike began to sense that she and Ingo were occasionally living at cross purposes. When they got together with friends now, Ingo spent most of the time grousing about reunification, about the colonization of the east at the hands of the Wessies. He complained that the best jobs in the east, particularly those in education, were going to mediocre Wessies who couldn't get jobs in the west. Though Ulrike agreed with much of what he said, she tired of his diatribes.

The more she wanted to go out, the more he wanted to stay home. For New Year's that year, Ingo did consent to join Ulrike and their friends to drive in a caravan to a big party in Dresden. It was during that trip that Ulrike's relationship with Ingo's best friend, Lutz, changed. She had known Lutz for ten years. He had always played a role in her life with Ingo. For a long time, however, she had guarded her time with Ingo, and she didn't get along well with friends of his who claimed too much of his attention.

Lutz was different from Ingo. Where Ingo was intense and stubborn, Lutz was relaxed. His smile came easily, while Ingo's was often strained. Lutz's prospects for work were worse than Ingo's, but he showed no sign of letting it bother him. He seemed content to let reunification wash over him, and when Ulrike was with him, she did the same. Lutz loved some of the small things that came with re-unification, such as the many varieties of beer. In East Germany there had been two kinds of beer to choose from—dark and pilsner. Reunification brought dozens of different beers to choose from. When Ulrike danced with Lutz at New Year's, it was like dancing with an old friend; at the same time it was like meeting someone for the first time.

The group drove back to Potsdam early on the morning of January 2. Ulrike had to work the night shift at the house. She was a bit distressed when she arrived at work and learned that Frau Neumann had taken in another weekly child, Marianne. This little girl, age three, didn't speak yet. She had been hospitalized in the past for what appeared to be epileptic seizures, and now her mother, too drunk most of the time to care for her children and with nowhere else to put Marianne, had brought her to the Kindergarten. The little girl didn't sleep for more than two hours at a time and had to be comforted through the night. Ulrike was put out with Frau Neumann for taking the child, who would demand more time than three other children put together. Ulrike suspected she had done it not simply out of goodwill but to keep up the number of weekly children as well.

By the time Ulrike had put the children to bed she was in a strange mood. Rather than calm her, the house only vexed her. She found the place unspeakably ugly, cold and uncomfortable. It put her in mind of the rigidity that persisted there in spite of the radical changes in Germany. She spent a long time that night looking at the furnishings in the loggia. Everything reeked of the discarded GDR: the plastic table of faux oak covered with a pitiful plastic tablecloth; the anemic GDR plants—the clivia that never bloomed, the sullen agave; and the sappy pictures on the wall that had been there for as long as Ulrike could remember. One in particular—a picture of a little boy with an oversized head and blank eyes, holding a kitten—was all at once more than she could bear. The child reminded her of the speechless Marianne, who cried out every hour or two, and needed to be picked up and walked around until she drifted back to sleep. Ulrike ripped the poster from the wall and took it downstairs to the trash. She was tempted to deliver the same fate to the plants, or even toss them straight out the window. But she restrained herself. She wondered if anyone would notice the missing poster.

Ulrike was growing increasingly fed up not just with the house, but with her colleagues. Every time she went to work she felt like someone who had long since cast off a troubled relationship but kept finding unwelcome reminders of it on old slips of paper pulled from her pockets.

Ulrike was moving on, but every day at work was littered with evidence that many of her colleagues had no such intention. When the Wall fell, Ulrike had looked forward to jettisoning all the rigidities of education under the old system. She pushed for more experimentation at the Kindergarten, or at least for an approach that encouraged more creativity. But women like Helga Neumann and Hannah Krabbes, who had stuck to the education plan for thirty years, were not about to change their ways overnight. Instead, in what Ulrike considered a ridiculous attempt to hold on to the house, they renamed the house the "Kindervilla," and hung a hand-painted sign bearing the new name beneath the front doorbell. With a claim now hovering, renaming the house to Kindervilla seemed particularly naive.

The number of Kinderwochenheims in East Germany had peaked at 126 in the mid-1970s. By the time the Wall fell in 1989 the number of Kinderwochenheims had dropped to 65. And by 1992, the Kinderwochenheim in Potsdam was the only one still operating in eastern Germany. Like everything else that had differed in the east, the child-care system of eastern Germany had been subsumed into the child-care system of western Germany. Since there were no weekly Kindergartens in the west, those in the east were gradually shut down, or converted to strictly day-care facilities. As more women in the former East Germany became unemployed, and as industry in eastern Germany ground to a halt, the need for a place to put children for the week diminished. In fact, the laws governing child care in the Federal Republic made no provisions for such a facility, which made their very legality open to scrutiny. Still, for reasons that no one completely understood, Frau Knoblich, the peremptory head of the education department, was able to keep the Potsdam Kinderwochenheim open.

The Kindergarten at the Glienicke Bridge had been a subject of irritation to Frau Knoblich for some time. A few months earlier she had received word from the Potsdam claims office that there was a claim on the house and that if the education department objected to the claim it should make it known within thirty days. Frau Knoblich had routinely—and successfully—been disputing claims on buildings that were being put to community use. But she had heard rumors that this was a Jewish claim and, knowing that Jewish claims were given special dispensation, had not filed an objection. She did not know that the Wallich claim was not technically a Jewish claim. Had she objected to the claim, her objection might have been upheld and the family would then have received monetary compensation instead of the property.

The house itself was slowly deteriorating, and because of the claim pending, all repairs had stopped. Edgar Brunke, the maintenance man, continued to live on the third floor but had been reassigned to a different school. If the teachers wanted any work done they had to do it themselves. It wasn't until a second-story cornice came crashing to the ground one day, narrowly missing one of the children, that city workers responded and came to haul off the broken pieces.

Ulrike's romance with Lutz, begun in Dresden at New Year's, continued through the winter. Their biggest problem was finding a suitable rendezvous spot, as Lutz, too, was living with someone. When Ulrike was on the night shift at the Kindergarten, they were able to meet there. But that happened only once a week. So they carried on much of their affair in Ulrike's car, parking it on dark, quiet streets in Potsdam. Rather than hide the affair from Ingo, she decided to defuse the issue by telling him. He was devastated. When he confronted Lutz about it, Lutz replied with a casual, "Well, she wanted it. What was I supposed to do? Turn her down?"

Ulrike's involvement with Lutz came to be the breaking point for Ingo. He railed more than ever against the reunification and its insidious effects. On the nights that Ulrike stayed out, he sometimes stayed up and drank, occasionally at a bar, but more often at home. He managed to rouse himself enough in the morning to teach his classes, but on occasion he arrived at work smelling of drink from the night before. One night he took a black pen to the walls of the apartment and wrote "I love you" in large letters. Seven-year-old Philipp responded with his own grafitto underneath: "You're stupid."

Ulrike herself didn't know if the affair with Lutz was simply a wild interlude, if she would then settle back into life with Ingo. She knew she wasn't in love with Lutz, but she also sensed there was something irretrievable about what she was doing. She moved into a separate room in the apartment. She and Ingo barely spoke. He cooked for himself and the children but excluded her.

In the early spring she found out she was pregnant. As strongly as she had felt about wanting her first two children, she knew she did not want a third. At least not at the moment. In western Germany, strict rules governed a woman's ability to terminate a pregnancy. In order for a woman to have a first-trimester abortion in the west, two doctors had to certify that the pregnancy resulted from rape or caused great physical or emotional distress to the mother. In eastern Germany, where about one pregnancy in four was terminated, not only was a first-trimester abortion an option for every woman, but the national health system provided abortions free of charge. Abortion, in fact, became one of the most divisive issues between East and West Germany leading toward reunification.

Ulrike saw no reason to hide the abortion from the other women at the Kindergarten. Why not give them something to talk about? Besides, she would have to explain her absence somehow. In eastern Germany, an abortion was no outpatient procedure. Even a first-trimester abortion required general anesthesia and a hospital stay of several days. For some reason that Ulrike didn't understand, she feared the abortion more than childbirth. She talked with friends who had been through it and took comfort in their reassurances. Perhaps relieved that Ulrike didn't want to have a child with Lutz, Ingo accompanied Ulrike to the hospital, visited her there and took her home.

After the abortion, Ulrike all but ended the romance with Lutz. But her choice of an abortion didn't mean she wanted to continue life as it had been with Ingo. She was more remote than ever. By now, Ingo's sadness had turned to anger. He resorted to verbal attacks in front of the children. Ulrike did her best to avoid him. Since he showed no willingness to move out, Ulrike began looking for a new apartment for herself and the children. She had little luck. Since reunification, Potsdam's population had exploded, and housing was now difficult to find. Thousands of people were looking for apartments, and even though Ulrike knew a lot of people in Potsdam she had no connections among the Potsdam housing authorities. So she and Ingo continued to live separate lives under one roof.

In the spring of 1992, Ulrike decided she needed a drastic change, one that had nothing to do with men. She would quit the Kindergarten and change careers altogether. She wasn't sure of her future but it seemed that anything was possible now. She gave notice for April 1.

Frau Neumann was beside herself. She knew that the city, nearly bankrupt and looking for every opportunity to cut back, wouldn't fill Ulrike's position, which would increase the workload on everyone else. She didn't say anything to Ulrike directly, but as Frau Neumann saw it, Ulrike would be able to collect unemployment and laze about at home while everyone else worked harder than ever.

One day during her last weeks at work a couple appeared at the door of the Kindergarten. Frau Neumann greeted the woman familiarly. The woman, dressed in a business suit, spoke German with a noticeable accent. The man, dark and stout, appeared to speak no German at all. From what she could gather, these were the Americans with the claim on the Kindergarten. The man was carrying a video camera, and as they walked through the house with Frau Neumann the camera remained stuck to his right eye. When they came out to the garden where Ulrike was watching a group of children, the children rushed up to investigate the strangers and the black gadget the man was holding. They asked the man what it was but he couldn't answer, and they were mystified by his inability to communicate with them. Ulrike went up and introduced herself. Figuring she had little left to lose, she decided to speak her mind to these people.

"It would be nice if the house could be used for social purposes, and not as a private residence," Ulrike said. Oddly, the man kept filming her as she spoke.

For several awkward seconds, the camera caught Ulrike and the woman facing each other uncomfortably. Then the woman turned to the man and said in English, "Should we go?" His face emerged from behind the camera and as he turned it off, they both said good-bye to Ulrike and went back inside.

For her last day, Ulrike decided to cook a big Chinese meal for the teachers. It was something she and Ingo had done together dozens of times, and something she had already done for the teachers once or twice. She wasn't really sure why she wanted to do the meal, since her colleagues had been anything but civil to her over the past few weeks. But she didn't want to descend to their level. Earlier that day, she had reminded the others of her impending freedom when, during the weekly staff meeting, she announced that she didn't care how much she drank that evening, and she joked that she would simply have to drive home drunk. Frau Neumann began to scold her. Ulrike cut her off abruptly, wagged a finger at

her and said, "*You* don't have anything more to say to me." Frau
Neumann recoiled and looked completely taken aback. Her reaction
was more of sadness than anger. Ulrike suppressed an urge to apol-
ogize.

She shopped that afternoon for the food, and decanted the wine
well in advance so that no one would notice that the wine was so
cheap. When it came time to cook the meal, she enlisted the help of
a young college student who was working at the Kindergarten as an
intern. Ulrike put her in charge of deep-frying the shrimp chips in a
pot of hot oil. She was so accustomed to the cramped kitchen at her
apartment that working in the villa's oversized kitchen was a happy
luxury. She sipped at wine and chatted with the other teachers
while she cooked. The six-year-olds came in to present her with a
handmade farewell book. The teachers gave her two small plants.

They ate in Frau Neumann's office, which, by putting some tables
together, they had transformed into a dining room. Frau Neumann
started off the meal with a prepared speech. She now started every
gathering and meeting with a short speech, something she had
learned at a post-Wende seminar. "We'll miss Ulrike," she said. "She
has made very important contributions to the Kinderwochenheim,
and always brought new ideas." Ulrike had to smile. It was those
new ideas that had gotten her into trouble, and made her want to
leave.

During the soup course, Kerstin, one of the regular staff cooks,
tapped Ulrike lightly on the shoulder and said she needed to show
her something. Ulrike followed her into the kitchen. To her horror,
the pot on the stove frying the shrimp chips was enveloped in black
smoke, and before anything could be done flames were climbing up
the side of the pot. Kerstin tore a small pail and shovel from the
wall and, remembering that one shouldn't pour water on an oil fire,
ran outside to the children's sandbox. But when she poured a buck-
etful of moist sand on the pot, the fire only grew. By now the flames
were reaching up to lick the window curtains. Just as Ulrike was
watching the house burn down in her mind's eye, the flames died
down, then went out completely. She looked at Kerstin, and Kerstin
gave her a big smile of relief. They returned to the unsuspecting
diners and Kerstin helped Ulrike serve the rest of the meal.

1 0 : D I R K

On the evening of November 9, 1989, Günter Schabowski, East Germany's chief of the media, gave a press conference. At the very end, in what he presented as a most casual postscript, Schabowski announced that East Germany's borders were to be opened. Even before the news made it onto television, hundreds of East Germans were gathering at border crossings throughout the city, persuading skeptical guards that the border was now open.

That night, Dirk Heydemann was in bed in his dormitory room with his girlfriend, Tessa. Sometime after midnight his best friend called and scolded him roundly.

"What are you doing lying in bed when all of Berlin is in the streets!" He told Dirk to get dressed and come pick him up. His friend instructed him to bring along a sledgehammer. Dirk didn't have one but he did find a pickaxe. He and Tessa dressed and made for the door.

When they arrived at the Brandenburg Gate it was a mob scene.

Germans from both sides were crying, laughing, embracing and dancing on top of the Wall. When others saw the pickaxe they cheered. "Super idea!" "Wonderful!" "Great!" The trio began by turns chipping away at the concrete with the axe. The delicate tool wasn't intended for such a sturdy surface, and every blow sent painful vibrations through their hands. Chunks of concrete were flying in all directions. And because of all the steel rebar inside the Wall each blow brought a spray of sparks. People who were watching shaded their eyes with their hands. Before long a television camera crew discovered them. Then another one did. Before long, they were awash in klieg lights.

Dirk then passed the axe to others on top of the Wall. One of the first to take it was a man in a suit. He accompanied each blow with a loud, "For all the years!"

The opening of the Wall was to have a direct and lasting effect on Dirk's life. A student of landscape architecture and planning in Berlin, he was searching for a topic for his final thesis when his advisor came up with several suggestions. Two of the suggestions involved a close look at remote corners of the vast gardens at Sanssouci in Potsdam. A third involved a small villa at the foot of the Glienicke Bridge. Dirk's advisor knew the house had been built by Ludwig Persius and, although he had no evidence to support his hunch, he thought there might be something interesting about the garden. He suggested that Dirk look into it. A few months earlier, when East Germany was still sealed tight, such an assignment in the heavily guarded border zone would have been impossible to undertake. But now much of East Germany was ripe for academic investigation.

The villa at the bridge was the most uncertain of the suggested assignments, as there was always the chance that after hours of research, the garden would prove merely ordinary, lacking in any historical distinction. But, like his advisor, Dirk was intrigued by the possibility of being the first to take a close look at it. And an investigation of the villa was more suited to his professional preferences. According to his advisor, this garden consisted mainly of large trees, and not the panoply of bushes in the Sanssouci gardens. Dirk was indifferent to bushes but he had a passion for trees. He had grown up in a small town near Cologne, and spent much of his youth hiking in the dense woods. There was something about trees that had always been a source of fascination for him. The planting of a tree was the planting of a legacy. Trees were often the focal point of a landscape architect's design—the living room around which the rest of a garden was planted. A landscaper used trees to shade an entire house, or to frame it. In their root systems, their self-sufficiency, their hardiness and quirky vulnerabilities, trees had always intrigued Dirk. Besides, Sanssouci was already a much trampled subject for academic investigations. Studies of the Sanssouci gardens were so common they bordered on cliché. The relative obscurity of the villa at the bridge appealed to Dirk.

Dirk had yet to see the garden, but he had seen the house before, at least from the front. He and Tessa had often taken her dog walking on the grounds of the Glienicke Castle on late summer evenings. Included in their walk was a stroll to the bank of the river on the West German side to look at the Berlin Wall on the opposite side. The upper story and cupola of what looked to be an old Italianate villa was one of the few objects visible behind the Wall, and at night the lights along the Wall's periphery conspired to cast a yellowish glow onto the house. Occasionally they could see lights on in the villa. It made them wonder who would choose to live so close to the Wall, amid such unnerving desolation, where guard dogs ran in the death strip and guards were posted twenty-four hours a day.

Shortly after the Wall fell, Dirk set out from West Berlin one day and bicycled over the bridge to visit Potsdam. The Communists had spared no expense maintaining the magnificent Sanssouci Palace and its grounds. But the rest of the city wore the face of a gnarled old man. Everywhere Dirk looked, building facades were crumbling. Many of the streets were still paved in cobblestone, but not to quaint effect. The city would require huge sums to rebuild. One of Potsdam's most famous neighborhoods, the Dutch Quarter, was in such a state of disrepair that it was difficult to imagine rebuilding it at all. What impressed him most, however, was that although the city had been badly neglected, it still had an air of aristocracy to it. Dirk supposed it wouldn't take long for developers and speculators—the German word was *Haie,* for sharks—to descend on the city that had once been Prussia's most prized jewel. The villas he had heard so much about in the Berliner Vorstadt were, for the most part, still standing. It was nothing like East Berlin, where grand old homes had been destroyed and replaced with rows of high-rise apartment buildings packed together in a thicket. But this part of

Potsdam, too, looked like it needed to be shaken from a long deep sleep.

In the spring of 1990, soon after he decided to focus on the house at the Glienicke Bridge, Dirk set off for a visit to the house. East German soldiers at the bridge, genial and accommodating since the opening of the Wall, asked to see his passport, then waved him through. From afar, the house still maintained a certain stateliness. But when he got close to it he saw its broken condition. First he walked around the house, just to figure out what was there. Like so many other buildings in East Germany, this one contained clues to a former life. One of the first things he saw was a wrought-iron gate with a "W" fashioned into the iron work. Sitting inside the wall that ran alongside Schwanenallee was a majestic statue of a lion. He wondered about its significance. Then he saw signs of children— playground equipment in the back, and a few miniature bicycles standing near the gate. It looked like a child-care facility of some kind. From over the garden wall, he saw the trees his advisor had been referring to—a mammoth oak and two red beeches in early leaf.

Dirk mounted the three steps at the front door and rang the bell at "KWH." He stepped back from the door a bit so as not to seem too intrusive. He could imagine what the occupants might think when they saw a young man in Western clothes carrying a briefcase. The door was opened by a short, round, middle-aged woman with unkempt hair and wide eyes. She looked extremely distrustful. He introduced himself, said he was a student from West Berlin inter- ested in the garden in back and asked if he might speak with the di- rector. A second woman then came to the door. She looked similarly skeptical. He tried to make it clear that he wasn't in the least bit in- terested in the house, just the garden. After a moment's awkward- ness, they led him through the house to the back door.

From the little Dirk could see on his way to the back, it wasn't hard to imagine that there was once something special about this place. Traces of an understated elegance were everywhere. He could tell that over the years the house had been stripped of much of its original hardware. In a country where one solid brass window pull had a bartering value roughly equivalent to a pack of Camels from the West, it was a miracle that any of the original fixtures re- mained. It would have been fun to take a closer look around inside, but he resisted the urge to ask for a tour.

For the most part, the garden in the back was a helter-skelter collection of rusted climbing equipment and discarded tires that had been turned into playground toys. By now there were children everywhere, laughing and screaming and running. Dirk was immediately fascinated by the immense old trees. One beech tree was at least 150 years old. Its roots spread for yards across the garden. It was rare to see powerful trees like that. Then he noticed something different about the two beech trees. For one thing, they weren't ordinary beeches. They had been cultivated—trained in a certain way, a sign to him that the garden had been carefully planned, probably by a professional landscaper. And there was something about the juxtaposition of the red leaves of one of the beeches and the green leaves of the oak next to it that made him think of the famous landscape architect Peter Joseph Lenné. Lenné had been Prussia's preeminent landscape architect; he had designed some of Germany's most famous gardens. In fact, Lenné was a consummate tree man. He used them to create art, to build perspectives and texture into a garden. He especially liked playing with colors and sunlight. One of his favorite tricks was to plant green next to red for contrast. Lenné also made a point of planting red beeches on a garden's western edge in order to catch the light of a setting sun. Lenné had played with colors this way across the river at the Glienicke Castle, achieving a highly dramatic effect.

Dirk decided that if the garden hadn't been designed by Lenné, then it must have been designed by someone who worked closely with Lenné. If this hunch turned out to be correct it would be a significant academic coup. For years, students of the landscape along the Havel had been churning out papers and dissertations and books about the uniqueness of the area. But their explorations stopped at the Berlin Wall. As far as Dirk knew, no one had looked into what was just beyond the bridge. It made sense that this old villa, modest though it was, had once been part of the entire constellation of castles built by the royal Hohenzollerns.

Dirk threw himself into the project. For the next six months he went to the house nearly every day to survey the garden and measure each of its trees and plants. The first obstacle to overcome was the skepticism of the women at the Kindergarten. They let him in each time he came but he sensed they were reluctant to do so. Gradually, using his relentless good cheer, he chipped away at their aloofness. Within a few weeks the women were inviting him to take coffee with them. The coffee breaks were invaluable for gathering information about the house, all of which had some bearing on the garden. One of the teachers, Frau Krabbes, who had opened the door that first day, had been there for thirty years. The seamstress, Lydia, had worked at the house for nearly twenty years. Both women liked to talk, and they told Dirk many stories. They told him about what it was like to live within a hat's toss of the Berlin Wall. They told him about the former director, a volatile, passionate woman named Helga Kempa who lived in the third-floor apartment for three decades. They told him about the spy exchanges, and the transport of corpses across the bridge. But they didn't seem to have any idea who owned the house before the war.

The more time he spent there, the more convinced Dirk became that this was a historic garden. When he wasn't at the house taking measurements, he was poring through various archives in and around Berlin and Potsdam for the original plan to the garden. He also found out some things about the history of the house. He found letters that Prince Carl had exchanged in the 1840s with his courtier, the Hofmarschall von Schöning, letters discussing the purchase of the land and the construction of the Villa Schöningen.

But the question of who owned the house most recently remained a mystery. It wasn't until he talked to a garden director at Sanssouci that Dirk learned that the house had once belonged to a family called Wallich, and that one of the Wallichs had been one of the original directors of the Deutsche Bank. It was the first time Dirk had heard the name. Thus began his search for descendants of the Wallich family, who he hoped would be in possession of the original plans to the garden.

Dirk discovered the name of an old school friend of Paul Wallich's. But he was long since deceased. However, he did find the name of the school friend's daughter, old and frail and living in Berlin. She was distrustful of the young stranger at first, but eventually warmed to the student's open, ingenuous manner. She gave him the address and telephone number of a Mable Wallich in McLean, Virginia, with the warning that she hadn't spoken with Mrs. Wallich for years.

At around the same time, in one of the archives Dirk found old site plans for the property, listing each plot and its ownership. From what he could tell, the Wallichs had owned a considerable tract of land. He wondered if the descendants were planning to press a claim to the property and, if they were, whether they knew how much land had been in their name. He sent several letters to the address in Virginia, asking for old photographs of the garden, or anything else Mable Wallich might be able to provide. When he heard nothing in reply, he called the telephone number he had been given. Mable Wallich answered the telephone and he introduced himself. He told her that his precise measurements of the property concluded that the entire square footage was larger than the plat diagrams suggested. In excellent German, Mable Wallich thanked him and said she might have some useful photographs for him and she would send them. But after several months of waiting, he received nothing.

Short of finding a Wallich who was willing to cooperate, Dirk had to make do with various family memoirs, of which there was no shortage. He found Hildegard's volume most useful, although in her many pages of description of the house, she did not mention who had designed the garden.

Dirk was growing increasingly ill-disposed toward the Wallichs. He may have been disappointed at Mable's lack of response, but he was incensed by what the family had done to the house in the 1920s. The addition that Paul and Hildegard Wallich had built was, he felt, an aesthetic outrage, the architectural equivalent of tone deafness. They had taken a masterfully proportioned building and tacked on two massive blocks to the back, just to make room for themselves. Such a thing should never have been allowed to happen.

Dirk then turned to a diary of the architect Persius himself, poring over its pages in search of some mention of the villa and its garden. He found nothing. He looked through every biography of Lenné that he could find, but none mentioned the Villa Schöningen.

Having encountered these dead ends he was at a loss as to how he might find the original garden plan. Without it, he might as well give up on the project, as there was no other way to trace the history of the garden. But he couldn't bring himself to give up. He kept searching. He combed through state archives in Berlin and Potsdam, and as far away as Leipzig. He interviewed every landscape architecture historian he could find, and although some were familiar with the Villa Schöningen, none could tell Dirk the origins of the garden.

He sought out the various site plan archives scattered around Berlin and Potsdam. These contained city maps and blueprints for each plot of land dating back to 1683. But they were arranged chronologically, not geographically, which meant he had to sort through each one. He found nothing.

Time was running out. Although he had gathered a great deal of fascinating information about the construction of the villa, the courtier von Schöning and the Wallich family, it was not enough for a degree in landscape planning. As a final resort, Dirk turned to a photo archive in the city development office for Berlin. There he went one by one through thousands of photographs of old site plans. Then, on one gray-and-white photograph the size of a standard index card, he spotted first the Glienicke Bridge, then, beyond the bridge, the villa. Behind the villa, in tiny fading lines, was a sketch of the plan for a formal garden. Trees, more than two dozen of them, were lined up like so many soldiers in two straight rows. The plan was simply marked "Schoeningen." Dirk was ecstatic. Of the dozens of scholars who had devoted their careers to studying the formal gardens in the Havel surround, none had bothered, when examining old plans, to do the obvious: look across the bridge.

The signature on the plan was that of Gustav Meyer, a landscape architect who worked closely with Lenné. If Dirk could show that the measurements on this plan corresponded to the spacing of the trees behind the villa, then he would have solid proof that those trees had been planted by Lenné and Meyer, and that the garden behind the Villa Schöningen was a crucial piece of the overall landscape. There were four large trees left in the garden. Once he had measured their precise location, he would know whether they corresponded to the original plantings proposed in the sketch. As he suspected, four of the trees in the original diagram matched exactly the placement of the trees that still stood.

For such a discovery to be made under the noses of the rest of the academic community was one thing. But for such a discovery to be made by a young graduate student who had yet to finish his studies was nearly unheard of.

In the spring of 1991, Dirk published a 150 page paper, exacting in its detail, which proved beyond a doubt that a small, long-ignored aesthetic treasure lay just beyond the Glienicke Bridge. In his conclusion, the preservation-minded student proposed that the house and garden be restored to their original condition and turned into a museum. He even included watercolors by Tessa of the villa as it should appear after the restoration. Dirk's discovery became the talk of Berlin's small circle of landscape architecture historians. Dozens of people asked for copies of his thesis. A few months after its appearance, the paper was awarded a coveted national prize for outstanding work in the field of landscape planning.

The experience gave Dirk a special affinity for Potsdam, and for eastern Germans in particular. He continued to visit the Kindergarten, the teachers there and the caretakers who lived on the third floor. One day soon after completing his paper he showed up at the Kindergarten with a bottle of champagne under one arm and a copy of his thesis under the other. He invited the teachers to join him in the garden for a celebratory toast and a brief presentation of his thesis. A group gathered around as Dirk carefully turned each page and told the history of the property, the significance of the bridge through the years and the story of the Wallich family.

When it came time to state his conclusion, Dirk bent his head with a slightly embarrassed smile and said, "Well, you probably won't like this, but this is what I think should happen to the house now." And he turned with pride to the watercolors. Gone were the rusted swing set, sandbox and rickety jungle gym. In their place stood a formal garden of stately trees and hedges along a regal pathway scattered with concrete benches. The teachers were suddenly silent.

Not long after finishing his thesis, in the summer of 1991, Dirk finally met Christine Wallich. She had heard about Dirk's work from the family lawyer, and during one of her stops in Berlin she called Dirk and asked to meet him for breakfast. He brought along a copy of his thesis and gave Christine the same tour of his work that he had given the teachers. When it came time to announce his conclusion—that the house be restored (and the abominable addition ripped away) and turned into a museum—he was glad to see that she did not flinch. Although she didn't say precisely what the family had in mind for the house, she did not appear to disapprove of his idea. She asked how she might obtain extra copies of the thesis; she was on her way to England and wanted to show it to her cousins there. He gave her the copy he had brought along.

A few months later, in July, Dirk's advisor insisted on throwing a party on the lawn of the Glienicke Castle, across the river from the Villa Schöningen. The party was to be a celebration of Dirk's achievement. He told Dirk to invite anyone he pleased. Dirk sent invitations to local historians, to landscape planners and landmark preservationists. He sent one to Christine and Mable Wallich as well. He went to the Kindergarten and invited all the teachers. Given their reaction to his thesis, he rather doubted they would come. Neither Christine nor Mable attended the party. But Frank Walter-von Gierke, the Berlin lawyer representing the Wallich family on its claim, not only showed up at the party but presented Dirk with a bottle of Moët & Chandon champagne.

Two of the teachers, Ulrike Weichelt and Frau Neumann, did come, but Dirk was dismayed to see them keeping a distance from the festivities. When he saw Ulrike a few weeks afterward and asked her whether she had enjoyed the party, she responded in venomous tones about his Wessi way of looking at the world and his lack of compassion for the children in the Kindergarten. Dirk didn't want to let her see that her words had hurt him, and he extracted himself from the awkward encounter as quickly as he could.

A few months after receiving his degree in 1991, Dirk started a job in the Potsdam Department of Landscape Planning. It was his dream job. As a city official, Dirk was charged with recommending whether or not a piece of land should be developed. Since reunification, Potsdam had become one of the most attractive spots in all of Germany for new building. Dirk became now something of a lone crusader against many of these projects. As far as he was concerned, if a proposed project meant the destruction of trees, it should be blocked.

Not surprisingly, many of the proposals before him were for gas stations. When Dirk started his job there were just two gas stations for Potsdam's 150,000 residents. To meet the city's goal of making one available for every 10,000 Potsdamers meant building twelve more. Dirk had many meetings with executives from British Petroleum, who spent hours trying to convince him of the worthiness of their projects. Ultimately, the decision lay in the hands of the city council. But if a patch of open space was to be sacrificed for something as aesthetically unredeeming as a gas station, Dirk wanted something for the city in return. After all, Dirk knew that any development allowed in the 1990s would alter the look of the city for decades to come. Occasionally, he succeeded in getting petroleum companies to agree to build gas stations with green roofs. In another case he told a group of corporate executives hoping to build a large office building that if their plans meant displacing a certain amount of open space, they would have to make it up by creating an equal amount of park space somewhere else in the city. They had little choice but to agree.

Not surprisingly, one piece of Potsdam property in which Dirk took a special interest in his new capacity as a landscape planning official was the Villa Schöningen. In early 1992, Dirk heard that the Wallichs had hired a Berlin architect to come up with a plan for an additional structure next to the house. This would mean the destruction of a small orchard planted by Hermann Wallich, which contained varieties of apple trees that had all but disappeared in western Germany. Though Dirk was opposed in principle to any building on the site, he was willing to think about a compromise. But when the Wallichs' architect arrived at Dirk's office one day and unveiled his plan for the property, Dirk objected at once. For the new structure, the architect had sketched out a long low building in the style of an orangery. The idea was to turn the house into a conference center of some kind and use the new building for offices and housing. Dirk thought the proposal completely out of step with the spirit of the villa. He suggested to Christine that they return to the drawing board.

Of all the Wallich descendants, Christine was Dirk's favorite. She wore a businesslike patina, and Dirk delighted in trying to break through to her humorous side. He respected her determination to keep the house in the family, or at the least to keep the house away from sharks. It seemed to Dirk that Christine was the one who was the most concerned about the use to which the house would be put, while some members of the family were only interested in selling it at the highest possible price. Dirk heard that one of Berlin's largest development firms had indicated the property could be sold for approximately $13.5 million, even before the Potsdam property claims office had issued a decision. If that was the case, then his chances for seeing the property restored to its original condition were growing slimmer by the day.

11: THE FAMILY SUMMIT

*I*n 1992, the Wallich heirs decided they had to resolve the question of what to do with the Potsdam house—the last vestige of Hermann Wallich's millions—once and for all. It was agreed that they would convene a family meeting in London that summer.

Even before the meeting took place, the outcome was fairly clear. Of Hildegard's twelve heirs, Christine was the only one who had openly lobbied to keep the house in the family. The previous Christmas she had sent her siblings and her cousins reproductions of the watercolor of the house that hung in McLean. Her principal sales tool, however, was Dirk Heydemann's thesis. In making clear the historical significance of both the house and the garden, she hoped she could convince them of the worthiness of keeping the property in the family. She encouraged Dirk to have extra copies printed and talked her cousins into donating the money for the cost of the extra printing. But as impressed as they were by the document, they were not so easily persuaded. Christel's son Fritz Körte, now an executive for Mercedes-Benz living in Cape Town, South Africa, told her that he would like to hold on to the house but he was put off by the high cost of restoring it. And his siblings, still living in Argentina, appeared to be happy to let Fritz speak for them.

Some of the Wallich heirs were already spending their share of the profits in their heads—on large houses in the country, or additions to existing homes. One of the British cousins was thinking of using the money to buy himself the freedom to quit his corporate job and do volunteer social work. Of Christine's two siblings, Paul had little or nothing to say on the matter, and Anna remarked to Christine that she thought the house would make a good restaurant. When Christine expressed horror at the suggestion, Anna quickly repeated, "A *good* restaurant, Christine."

Family members were beginning to get nervous about the bills that were already piling up. The Berlin architect had charged several thousand dollars for his plans. And then there were the lawyers.

At the same time, the potential property prices the family was hearing were ever more tempting, depending on how much property was included. Letters from Hans Frank to the Wallichs indicated that during the spring of 1992, an investor apparently affiliated with Brandel was prepared to purchase portions of the property for approxiamtely $10 million. By summer, Hans Frank repeated that Brandel would offer some $13.5 million for the property which Frank calculated would be approximately 115,000 square feet (which is nearly two and a half acres). And now some of the family members believed they might be able to sell the house for even more: the Kampffmeyer Villa across the street had just sold for $20 million, and the Los Angeles architect Charles Moore was designing a housing development on the property.

Now resigned to a sale, Christine was still awaiting word from Herr Storch of the Bundesbank, who had paid a recent visit to the house to consider a purchase. But by the time of the family gathering she had still heard nothing.

Moreover, the preliminary decision from the Potsdam claims office had not yet been issued. The delay was mystifying. Monika Hagen had had all the documents she needed for more than a year. Without the house reentered in the property registry in the family's name, or even official word that they were to get the house back, a sale was still premature. Nevertheless, the lawyers in New York and Berlin kept reassuring them that the decision would be coming any day.

The family summit was scheduled for July 8, 1992. On that day eight of the Wallich heirs gathered in northern London in the cramped living room of Robert Wallich, the second eldest of the British cousins. Christine flew there on her way to Russia. Anna, who lived in New Hampshire, sent her husband in her stead. Fritz came from South Africa to represent the Argentine cousins.

When the vote was taken, all but Christine voted to sell. She asked that her opposition to a sale be put on the record. The others voted to sell not only the house, but the adjoining lot as well, as subdividing the property would reduce the value of the whole.

Most family members were inclined to sell to the Berlin developer. The heirs voted to secure a firm offer directly from Brandel in order to minimize risk and ensure a maximum payment up front.

Christine raised the possibility of taking out an advertisement to reach more potential buyers, but the others objected to her idea on the grounds that it would cost too much. She did manage to convince her cousins to agree, as a condition of any sale, that an apartment in the villa be retained for the family, which was a condition Brandel appeared to be willing to meet.

The cousins also agreed that Fritz would be the family contact point in Berlin, and that he should fly to Berlin to get a firm offer from Brandel.

A house sitter would be needed in the interim, and it was decided to give that job to the Brunkes, the caretakers living on the third floor.

If any mention was made of the children in the Kindergarten, it was done so only in passing.

12: THE MOVE OUT

*B*y early November of 1992, it was clear that things could not continue as they were. Fewer and fewer new children were coming to the Kindergarten, and the Kindergarten at the bridge was now stigmatized as a *Heim,* or orphanage. Ironically, of the children that were now there, just a handful were weekly children. Helga Neumann's nervousness had turned to desperation. When Michael and Katrin Schneider were taken away, she saw in their removal a direct threat to the future of the Kindergarten. And to her own future.

So when the call finally did come in early November, it wasn't exactly a surprise. Helga Neumann got the phone call from Frau Knoblich's office on a Monday, summoning her for a meeting the following morning. When she arrived, a half dozen other Kindergarten directors were also present. In her official, unsmiling way, Frau Knoblich announced that she had called together all directors whose facilities would either be closed or cut back by the end of the year. She turned to Frau Neumann and said that the Kinderwochenheim would have to move out of the building it was in and join another Kindergarten on Menzelstrasse, the neighboring street. Although that Kindergarten was not a live-in facility, Frau Neumann could continue to board children for the week. The move should take place by the end of the year and Frau Neumann should determine the precise date on her own.

"Anything but Christmastime!" Frau Neumann exclaimed. Frau Knoblich ignored the remark. Frau Knoblich said nothing about why the facility would be closed, but Frau Neumann guessed that the reasons were financial.

Before leaving Frau Knoblich's office, Frau Neumann asked if she might ask her a question or two. Tight-lipped, Frau Knoblich nodded.

"What should we do with the curtains?" Frau Neumann asked.

"The curtains?" Frau Knoblich looked puzzled.

"Should we take them with us?"

The education director's expression changed from puzzlement to incredulousness. She couldn't believe that Frau Neumann was asking about such minutiae when the education director had much larger problems to worry about.

Frau Knoblich certainly had a lot of other matters on her mind. Burdened by the costs associated with reunification, the city was nearly bankrupt. Moreover, the birth rate throughout eastern Germany had declined as dramatically since reunification as it had in the 1960s after the introduction of the Pill. In 1989, 200,000 children were born in East Germany. By 1992 the number of new births had dropped to less than 100,000. As a result, the demand for child care was declining as well. Frau Knoblich had no choice but to close day-care facilities throughout Potsdam. Given that there was a claim pending on the Kinderwochenheim, and that she had chosen not to protest the claim, the place would have to close down sooner or later anyway.

"Frau Neumann," she replied. "I do not care what you do with the curtains. That is your decision."

Most of the staff would keep their jobs, but some, the two cooks in particular, might have to be let go, as there was no proper kitchen in the house on Menzelstrasse.

Mealtime at the Kindergarten had always been something far more than institutional. One of the cooks usually did the shopping, and all morning the children could smell the food being prepared. Several months earlier, perhaps in anticipation of closure, the education department had ordered that the cooking stop, and the midday meals were delivered in large containers, having been prepared hours earlier at a central kitchen that supplied precooked meals to Potsdam Kindergartens. Once the daily ritual of planning and shopping and cooking, and of inviting visitors to share a warm meal, disappeared, so did much of the soul of the house.

Still worse was the prospect of the garden at the Menzelstrasse Kindergarten. The garden at the new Kindergarten was a fraction of the one everyone was accustomed to. There were no old trees to climb around on and a dearth of good equipment. The soil was very dusty, and when the wind picked up it whipped the dust into everyone's face.

The initial reaction to the news was one of resignation. The younger women saw it as an opportunity to switch careers. Ulrike was already gone and Liane, a teacher who was close to Ulrike in age, decided to begin training as a dental technician. The older women were relieved to be keeping their jobs at all.

The move would affect the children most, particularly those who stayed the week. It was difficult enough for them to adjust to the house every Monday, but an adjustment to brand-new surroundings would be especially hard for them.

After the meeting, Frau Neumann panicked. She went straight back to the house and announced the grim edict. The move, she said, would take place in two weeks, starting on Friday and continuing through the weekend. They were to start packing immediately.

They removed the curtains from the windows, and boxed some toys and books. They transported rugs, children's closets, dishes, gym equipment and small kitchen appliances over to the new place. The women were upset, and they took it out on Frau Neumann, accusing her of letting her panic affect everyone else.

And there was an eerie silence among the teachers. They volunteered no information to the caretaker. Finally, Frau Brunke, the caretaker's wife, worried that the telephone line was tapped, went to a phone booth and called the one person whom she thought might be able to help: Dirk Heydemann, the friendly student who had written about the house. She asked him what she and her husband should do. Their incomes were meager and, given the housing shortage in Potsdam, they had no idea where they would go. Their rent for the upstairs apartment had already soared from its pre-Wende level of $20 per month to $225. And that was still considered relatively low. He told her not to worry, that it would be a while before they would have to leave.

It already promised to be a bleak winter. For weeks the temperature hovered near freezing and the dark skies that characterized Berlin winters had descended on the city in October. The day before the move was to take place, the weather turned particularly miserable, with hurricane-strength winds and rain. But by the following morning, the threat of a storm had disappeared and, though cold, moving day was pleasant.

Although she was under no obligation to do so, Ulrike volunteered to help with the move. When she arrived that morning, she saw two large moving trucks parked in front of the house. Seven men, most of them participating in an "employment creation program" for unemployed eastern Germans, were there to do the heavy lifting. The house was spitting out furniture: children's closets; tiny tables and chairs; a checkered sofa. And men were busy lifting it into the moving vans.

On this tumultuous day, tinged with finality, life went on in other ways, lending the day an odd air of normalcy. As if oblivious to the move, the postal carrier arrived as usual, parked her bicycle against a post, navigated her way through the clutter and mounted the steps to deposit for a final time the mail in the box marked "KWH." On the other side of the street workers from the Bundespost continued to dig a trench for laying telephone cable. On the windows were paintings of trees and snowflakes.

It was immediately clear to Ulrike that her former colleagues planned to take all they could with them, rather than seize the opportunity to toss out the trappings of the GDR past. One might think that by relieving themselves of the material weight from previous decades, they could come closer to starting anew. She was surprised to see them taking things they wouldn't need in the new place, and hadn't necessarily needed in the old one: ruined chairs, broken lamps, torn tarpaulins. But they were obviously finding comfort in these things. Curiously, they hadn't packed carefully. They tossed everything, fragile or not, haphazardly into cartons.

When Ulrike stepped into the house she encountered chaos. It looked as if everything was still there, but pushed to the front of the house, into the foyer. Immediately upon seeing her, one of the cooks pressed a basketful of bread and rolls into her hand and told her to drive "over there" with them. She used the word *drüben,* the word for "over there" that East Germans had always used to refer to West Germany; it had come to signify another world. The new Kindergarten couldn't have been more than a hundred yards away, but the cook made it seem as if Ulrike was to drive to Africa.

In the new Kindergarten, Ulrike noticed that the teachers were busy re-creating precisely the furniture arrangement of the old Kindergarten. Even the wallpaper was the same! Ulrike thought she must be deluded, but it turned out that the teachers had already re-hung leftover bits of wallpaper from the old house.

When she returned to the old Kindergarten she saw to her relief that some objects were in fact being discarded. They were piling up outside for a garbage pickup: an old television; blankets laced with holes; an old broomstick with a burlap bag tied on the end for erad-icating spider webs; an old ballot box from GDR times; a GDR flag; and a sun lamp, which had been used regularly on East German children to cast a healthier glow on their pale complexions.

Frau Zierke told Ulrike that she had worked the final night shift. She described it as a "nightmare." She noticed for the first time how filthy the house was, as if the preamble to the move had stirred up the dust of forty years. She told Ulrike that when she dozed off in the loggia that night, she dreamed of dark castles and terrible rooms with no end in sight. She said she would never forget that dream or that night in the house. Lydia the seamstress joked to Ulrike that she would end up as a leftover in the garbage pile outside. Then she turned somber and told Ulrike she had no desire to get accustomed to another place. Her working days were numbered anyway.

Ulrike went inside, squeezed past the accumulated objects in the foyer and, determined to have a last look around, climbed the large staircase. At the head of the stairs hung a paper cut-out of a clown's face. The first room she entered was the loggia, the room where everyone had gathered through the years for their coffee breaks. It was the one room in the house where the teachers' emotions, both good and bad, were loosed. The loggia was the only room that had contained a hint of collective spirit.

She went to the window and looked out. Directly below her, pedestrians were walking on the former death strip at river's edge because the moving trucks were blocking the entire street. A small tugboat was floating under the Glienicke Bridge. The noise of the cars going over the bridge jogged her memory of the quieter days there, living with the Wall, and for some reason that she didn't understand, the sight of all those vehicles suddenly struck her as absurd. She thought of all the hours she had spent looking out that window early on, gazing over the Wall and across the water. And she was reminded once again of how strange it was to have a view uninterrupted by a border, or guards, or patrol boats.

The room itself was dirty and empty and cold. In the corners lay old pens encased in dust, bits of cookies, erasers and dozens of lost little plastic pieces that the kids used to place on a board to fill in a pattern or picture. The pieces inevitably fell off the table and into corners and stuck to the floor. Ulrike hoped that some of the little pieces would escape the final brooms and remain as a reminder of the children.

In one of the children's sleeping rooms Ulrike saw that a Franz Marc poster, *The Sleeping Cat,* was still hanging. A few closets—with doors that wouldn't close and drawers that wouldn't open—were still in the rooms, their legs tapered at the bottom in the style of the 1960s. The light brown floor rugs looked particularly ugly against the parquet floors.

Ulrike noticed that in the spots where the heads of the beds had been, bits of wallpaper were torn away, scratched away, really. When the children were unhappy, or frightened, or bored, they often scratched at the wallpaper with their fingernails. The little works of art—for that's how Ulrike had always viewed them—were enlarged night after night, centimeter by centimeter. Frau Neumann had always grown upset when she discovered the exposed bits of wall ("How is that going to look if someone comes?") and scolded those she caught. The wallpaper that was scratched away was then covered with new wallpaper, sometimes two or three times, but the children inevitably scratched it again. But seeing the scarred wall now reminded Ulrike not of art but of animals in a cage trying to get out. Their handiwork was most conspicuous in the corners, where the difficult children had been made to sleep.

Within a few hours, the bulk of the contents of the house were moved out. By this time it seemed to Ulrike that Frau Neumann was a nervous wreck. It was freezing outside but she was perspiring visibly. Ulrike had never seen her so frantic; she looked literally as if she were about to boil over.

Ulrike returned the following morning, more out of curiosity than a compulsion to help. This time she went to the new place. Lydia the seamstress was crying. She had just had a fight with Frau Neumann, who had told her to share space for her personal belongings with one of the cooks. She was indignant. "Every common construction worker has a certain place for his things," she told Ulrike. The ceiling in Frau Neumann's new office was in terrible condition and looked ready to cave in any minute. One of the cooks laughed and said, "Look, Helga, now the ceiling will come down on your head, too." Frau Neumann responded in a grave tone. "Let's hope it comes down soon. Then everything will be over."

Later that morning a group of them returned to the old Kindergarten for one last sweep of the place. They fanned out through the house like harvester ants, going after small things they had forgotten, taking pictures and calendars and mirrors from the walls.

Frau Neumann wanted to leave as quickly as possible, but Ulrike wouldn't allow it. She convinced her and the rest of them to remain for a while and talk. They stood in the upstairs hallway and agreed on the evils inherent in an "elbow society," where everyone pushed, like the one that had been thrust upon them by the west. "There's nothing more to strive for anyway, so why even bother?" the cook remarked. The events of the past few days seemed to heighten their nostalgic view of the GDR, with its employment security and social safety net. In fact, the GDR had never looked better.

Only the caretakers stayed behind in the empty house. Frau Brunke, furious that Frau Neumann planned to take the telephone, became obsessed with the need for one. "Who knows? Maybe asylum-seekers will come and squat here," she remarked to Ulrike. "And the Wessies are constantly streaming past here on the weekends. Who knows what they're going to do."

Christine Visits

The preliminary decision to return the house to the Wallich family was issued by the Potsdam claims office on November 20, 1992. By sheer coincidence, Christine happened to be on her way to Russia that week for the World Bank. She decided to stop in Berlin to visit the house and, finally, to obtain a key. A few days before her departure she received a fax from Dirk Heydemann informing her that the Kindergarten was in the process of moving out. She dreaded seeing the condition of the house once it had been stripped of all signs of habitation. She had not requested the removal of the Kindergarten. As she understood it, the decision to close the Kindergarten had been made by the education department for financial reasons.

For the first time in all the years she had been traveling to Germany Christine had the sense that she was not welcome. Since the Wallich family had filed its claim, violence against foreigners in Germany had risen tenfold. A wave of anti-Semitic and xenophobic violence had claimed several lives. By the end of 1992, the German government estimated there were more than eighty right-wing extremist organizations. Several dozen Jewish cemeteries throughout Germany had been desecrated. Some of the other Wallich heirs had pointed to violence as another reason to sell the house. Eastern Germany, in particular, where frustration over reunification was running high, appeared to be a breeding ground for anti-foreigner sentiment. Eastern Germans were blaming foreigners for taking jobs that should be given to Germans and aggravating the unemployment situation. Although there wasn't necessarily a correlation between claims on formerly Jewish property and the rise in anti-Semitic outbursts, some people argued that Jewish claims were arousing the anti-Semitic sentiment. Frau Neumann's husband had gone so far as to suggest that right-wing extremists might burn the Kindergarten down because of the Wallich family's Jewish origins.

But when Christine arrived at the house Frau Brunke greeted her as if she were a holy savior. Christine was not prepared for what she encountered inside. The house was in a worse state than she had imagined. It looked as if it had been hastily abandoned by an occupying army. The beautiful tiled foyer had become the depository for an array of objects: discarded art projects by the children, various bits of broken office furniture.

Christine took out a notebook and busily recorded the wreckage while Frau Brunke showed her around. There were large holes all over the walls. Frau Brunke explained that the old brick walls had been too hard for regular nails, and shelves and pictures had been fastened with dowels, then ripped out. Several door handles were missing. As the tour continued, she took fewer and fewer notes, then stopped altogether. She had a camera with her but didn't use it.

Frau Brunke asked if she and her husband would be allowed to stay. Christine replied that of course the Wallich family wanted them to stay and watch over the house. Visibly relieved, Frau Brunke said that they were concerned about trespassers and vandals, especially because of the growing "asocial" element in Potsdam and the possibility of some ne'er-do-wells squatting at the house.

Upstairs, when they opened the bathroom door, a fierce stench escaped. Christine was shocked to see that all the toilets and sinks had been torn from the wall—apparently without the aid of tools—leaving the plumbing open and exposed. Frau Brunke stood next to her and wrung her hands. She told Christine that she worried about water rats entering through the pipes.

"Where did all the bathroom fixtures go?" Christine asked Frau Brunke. The caretaker's wife heaved her large shoulders, shook her head, and said she believed they had been taken to the new Kindergarten.

In spite of all the disarray the stars on the ceiling over the stairway remained intact. The fire bell at the top of the stairs had disappeared, but a sign was still posted, with instructions for what to do in the event of a fire, a nuclear explosion, an air attack or a chemical alarm.

Many of the children's drawings still hung in the empty rooms, as well as a few Christmas decorations. Scattered in lonely isolation around the main room upstairs were a doll cradle, a play kitchen and some old mattresses. Christine went straight to the telephone in the adjacent room to call Dirk Heydemann. She considered Dirk an ally of sorts, and wanted him to come over and see the destruction for himself. When she failed to reach him, she went into the loggia and looked across the water.

Seeing that Christine had used the telephone, Frau Brunke scuttled over to her and told her that Frau Neumann planned to take the telephone. The caretaker's wife did little to veil her dislike for the Kindergarten director. While under the same roof, the two women had done their best to avoid each other. Frau Brunke had disparaged Frau Neumann at every opportunity. "She can recite the birthday of Stalin, and tell you when Honecker gave every speech, but she can't operate a dead bolt," she once sniped. She asked Christine what she should do about replacing the telephone. Christine had no answer.

In the kitchen, the unswept floor was strewn with old seeds that had fallen from rolls, and scraps of paper with numbers on them, apparently reflecting meal payments.

When Christine requested a key from Frau Brunke, the caretaker's wife replied that she wasn't certain whether her husband had an extra one, but she knew that Frau Neumann still had two or three in her possession.

"Frau Neumann has nothing further to do with this house," Christine fairly snapped.

By this time, Christine had had enough. She thanked Frau Brunke, told her she would be in touch and left. As she drove back to Berlin the image of the empty house stayed with her. She felt as if she had just attended a funeral.

EPILOGUE

The Family

A few days after the July 1992 family meeting, Fritz Körte traveled to Berlin as the Wallich family representative to secure in writing what they hoped would be a $13.5 million offer from Brandel & Co. But when Fritz met with Lothar Collberg, Brandel's owner, Collberg told him that although he was still interested in purchasing the villa, he needed more time before committing his offer to paper. He was still waiting to hear from the Potsdam city planners about how much of the land could be developed. But the offer from Brandel & Co never materialized.

By the winter of 1992, the real estate boom in Berlin had tapered considerably. Accordingly, the new offers the family received were far below what they had anticipated. By late 1993 the new offers hovered around $3.5 million. As of this writing, the family still had not sold the house.

By the middle of 1994, Christine had not yet spent a night in the villa.

The Villa

The house continued its descent into disrepair. A splotch of blue grafitto appeared on the front. The facade continued to crumble. One night in the summer of 1993, someone threw a bottle of beer against one of the windows, shattering the pane. Edgar Brunke closed off the bottom two floors of the house as best he could and continued to live on the third floor with his wife, who was afraid to stay in the house alone, even during the day. To ease her fears, Herr Brunke installed heavy locks on the front door. He also hung some curtains around the house to make it look inhabited.

When Frau Neumann returned once to retrieve something she had left behind, the Brunkes refused to let her in.

Monika Hagen

After a six-month maternity leave, Monika Hagen returned in April 1994 to the Potsdam claims office as its director.

Ulrike Weichelt

Although Ulrike had ended her relationship with Ingo, the housing shortage in Potsdam and Berlin forced them to continue to share the same apartment. They seldom spoke to each other. He finally moved out in late 1993, taking little with him. Ulrike rented a Dumpster and did a thorough sweep of the apartment. She threw out dozens of books, kitchen equipment, old cupboards and broken chairs.

In 1992, Ulrike began studying social work at a local college. She took to the subject immediately and applied to the city of Potsdam to work with a family. She requested that she be assigned to the Schneider family.

The Schneiders

The situation for Herr Schneider and his two children, Michael and Katrin, grew steadily worse. Herr Schneider arrived home one evening in 1993 to be greeted by an acquaintance brandishing a gun. The man claimed that Herr Schneider owed him money. He shot Herr Schneider once in the leg and ordered his dog, a large German shepherd, to attack him. The dog bit Herr Schneider repeatedly in the arm. Neighbors found him the next morning and called an ambulance. He spent several weeks in the hospital, and the children were not allowed to see him. As he recovered, Ulrike visited him regularly and worked hard at convincing the Potsdam social work offices to grant him more time with the children, who were still in the orphanage. She arranged outings for him and the children. In 1994, the children's mother resurfaced and demanded her children back. Her request was denied.

Just before his eighth birthday, Michael entered school. According to reports from the orphanage, he had no problems adjusting.

Dirk Heydemann

In 1991 and 1992 Dirk Heydemann underwent a kind of "Ossification." That is, he became a "Wossi," an easternized Wessi. In the summer of 1992, he moved into a small apartment in Ulrike's neighborhood in West Potsdam near the Sanssouci Palace. He was entranced by the area—the dappled light, cobblestoned streets and historic lime trees. But in spite of steady promotions at his job in the Potsdam Department of Landscape Planning, Dirk began to encounter some resentment from his eastern colleagues for his Wessi ways and his general air of confidence, which the easterners interpreted as arrogance. They said nothing to Dirk directly, but he heard about their discontent from others.

To celebrate his thirtieth birthday in September 1992, Dirk invited a mix of friends from both west and east to his newly renovated apartment. When the discussion turned to the asylum seekers in Germany (a topic that had been in the press a great deal following outbreaks of violence against foreigners), a verbal brawl ensued. One of his guests, an easterner, took the position that all foreigners should be returned to their native countries. Another guest, from western Berlin, was enraged by the remark. When she suggested in turn that he exercise some tolerance, he replied, "Well then why don't you take them in?" Disgusted, she left.

During one of Christine Wallich's trips to Berlin, Dirk accompanied her to the house. The Brunkes were now the sole occupants. Frau Brunke was beside herself with worry over possible intruders, and she asked Christine if the Wallich family would provide her and her husband with a watchdog. According to Dirk, Christine suggested they get a tape recording of a barking dog instead.

When Dirk returned a few months later as the Brunkes' dinner guest, he asked for a tour of the house. The rooms were dark and cold. The stench in the bathroom was overwhelming. In the basement there were empty milk bottles and canning jars scattered on shelves and on the floor. Shelves were still piled high with yellowed copies of *Neues Deutschland,* the official newspaper of the Communist Party. Other shelves contained old accounting ledgers. In one corner stood a large rotary iron for pressing sheets. The enormous apparatus, which apparently no one through the years had considered worth trying to move, dated back to the turn of the century. It was perhaps the sole remaining household object from the Wallichs' years in the house.

The Teachers

The teachers and the children settled quickly into the new Kindergarten. It, too, was an old villa. Its rooms weren't as grand, but they suited the teachers well. The children grew accustomed to the smaller garden. Six children stayed on as weekly children and, to protect the Kinderwochenheim from the vagaries of the Potsdam education department's financial situation, Frau Neumann began seeking funding from private sponsors.

Soon after moving in, however, they learned that two elderly women, sisters from western Germany, had filed a claim on the building. As of this writing no decision on the claim had been made.

After the Berlin Wall fell, Erich Honecker was charged with ordering guards at the Berlin Wall to shoot anyone attempting to escape and with stealing millions in state funds. A German court eventually halted the trial against him on the grounds that prosecutors had violated the civil rights of a gravely ill man. He flew to Chile in January 1993 and died there sixteen months later, at age eighty-one.

Nostalgia for the former Communist system continued to wax in eastern Germany. The Trabi, once reviled, became a beloved reminder of the GDR. In late 1993, a member of the Democratic Socialists, the revamped Communist Party, ran for mayor of Potsdam. Running as a champion of the forgotten easterner, he lost by a narrow margin.

NOTES

INTRODUCTION

PAGE

15 *"People here saved"*: Anne McElvoy, *The Saddled Cow* (London: Faber & Faber, 1992), 219.

2: THE WALLICHS

The section of this chapter that discusses Hermann Wallich's career, courtship of and marriage to Anna Jacoby, and relationship to his religion is based primarily on his memoir, "Aus meinem Leben," from Hermann Wallich and Paul Wallich, *Zwei Generationen im deutschen Bankwesen* (Frankfurt am Main: Fritz Knapp Verlag, 1978). The section of this chapter that discusses Paul Wallich's early life is based on his memoir, "Lehr- und Wanderjahre eines Bankiers," in the same volume.

The discussion of Paul's attempts at assimilation and search for a non-Jewish wife is based on the case study by Werner E. Mosse, "Prob-

lems and Limits of Assimilation: Hermann and Paul Wallich, 1833–1938,"
in the *Leo Baeck Institute Year Book,* No. 33, 1988, 43.

PAGE

24   *By 1911:* Werner E. Mosse, *The German-Jewish Economic Elite,
      1820–1935: A Socio-cultural Profile* (Oxford: Oxford University
      Press, 1989), 192.

26   *Hildegard Rehrmann came from a middle-class:* Hildegard Wal-
      lich, *Erinnerungen aus meinem Leben* (Westerwald: Wilhelm
      Dieckmann, 1970).

28   *Although Potsdam first received mention:* Dirk Heydemann,
      "Die Villa Schöningen und die Potsdamer Kulturlandschaft,"
      Diplomarbeit, Technische Fachhochschule Berlin (Berlin, 1991),
      13.

30   *The prince's solution:* Walter Wallich, unpublished memoir, n.d.

30   *For all its opulent history:* Hildegard Wallich, *Erinnerungen aus
      meinem Leben.*

31   *As in all upper-class households:* Walter Wallich, unpublished
      memoir.

38   *When he began attending an elite:* Henry C. Wallich, "Some
      Uses of Economics," *Banca Nazionale del Lavoro Quarterly Re-
      view,* June 1982, 119.

39   *For her schooling:* Walter Wallich, unpublished memoir.

41   *While Henry was at Oxford:* Henry C. Wallich, "Some Uses of
      Economics," 120.

42   *In 1936 Henry left Chemical Bank:* Ibid., 121.

42   *Later lodged in family lore:* Robert Wallich, interview with the
      author, June 1992, London.

42   *Undeterred, they emigrated:* Fritz Körte, interview with the au-
      thor.

42   *For years afterward:* Hildegard Wallich to Walter Wallich, 24
      July 1947.

44   *By 1937, it was clear:* Hermann Wallich and Paul Wallich, *Zwei
      Generationen im deutschen Bankwesen,* 25.

45   *In a memoir:* Johannes Schultze, *Meine Erinnerungen* (Berlin,
      1976), 60.

45   *Shortly after Paul's return:* "Reichskristallnacht in Hannover:
      Eine Ausstellung zur 40. Wiederkehr des 9. November 1938,"
      Historisches Museum am Hohen Ufer, Hannover, 1978.

45   *On the day following Kristallnacht:* Police report, November
      1938.

48 *The only possession:* Hildegard Wallich to Walter Wallich, 21 May 1946.

49 *So mindful was she:* Hildegard Wallich to Walter Wallich, 5 January 1948.

49 *"I somehow kept the idea":* Hildegard Wallich to Walter Wallich.

50 *The Berlin Walter returned to:* This and subsequent passages in which Walter Wallich describes postwar Berlin are taken from a letter he wrote to Hildegard Wallich, 4 November 1945.

50 *One third of the city's buildings: Berlin, Berlin: Die Ausstellung zur Geschichte der Stadt* (Berlin: Nicolai, 1987), 565.

54 *The soldier yelled:* Walter Wallich to Hildegard Wallich, 1 September 1945.

55 *When Mamsell walked across:* Walter Wallich to Hildegard Wallich, no date.

56 *From her remote California outpost:* Hildegard Wallich in letters to Walter Wallich, 1946–1948.

56 *To offset the expense:* Walter Wallich to Hildegard Wallich, 19 April and 10 June 1946.

57 *"Do people in Germany hold rabbits":* Hildegard Wallich to Walter Wallich, 5 May 1946.

57 *It was her son Henry:* Henry Wallich to Herr Guenther. Hollywood, California.

58 *At first they believed:* Hildegard Wallich in letters to Walter Wallich, 1946–1948.

58 *Another topic of obsessive discussion:* Hildegard Wallich in a letter to Walter Wallich, 7 September 1947.

59 *Finally, in 1946:* Walter Wallich to Hildegard Wallich.

59 *"It seems strange that":* Hildegard Wallich to Walter Wallich, 5 May 1946.

59 *The same year:* Walter Wallich to Hildegard Wallich, 26 May 1946.

60 *"I cannot imagine myself"* Hildegard Wallich to Walter Wallich.

61 *"It seems to be the only solution":* Hildegard Wallich to Walter Wallich.

61 *"They're the last valuables":* Hildegard Wallich to Walter Wallich, 7 October 1947.

61 *Although she continued to doubt:* Hildegard Wallich to Walter Wallich, Hollywood, California.

61 *She rejected Germany:* Hildegard Wallich to Walter Wallich.

3: MAMA KEMPA

The details of Helga Kempa's experiences at the Kinderwochenheim are based on an interview conducted with Helga Kempa by the author in Rendsburg, Germany, on January 7 and 8, 1992.

PAGE

63 *An alternative to traditional Kindergartens:* In Germany, Kindergartens are not connected with the public schools as they are in the United States. German children start Kindergarten at age three and continue to age six, when they enter public school.

67 *Josef Stalin, or rather his likeness: Strictly Propaganda,* a film written and directed by Wolfgang Kissel, 1992.

68 *In the Hitler Era:* Laura Kaye Reneau, "A Contextual Study of the Grimms' Fairytales" (Master's thesis, University of Texas at Austin, 1983), 21.

70 *The construction began:* Norman Gelb, *The Berlin Wall: Kennedy, Khrushchev, and a Showdown in the Heart of Europe* (New York: Times Books, 1986), 163–72.

70 *In the months leading:* Anne McElvoy, *The Saddled Cow,* 119.

73 *Little was left to chance:* M. Honecker, *Programm für die Bildungs- und Erziehungsarbeit im Kindergarten* (Berlin: Volk und Wissen, 1985).

73 *The woman who did not work: Statistisches Jahrbuch der DDR, 1978–1989* (Berlin: Staatsverlag der DDR, 1987).

75 *The obligation of every educator:* M. Honecker, *Programm für die Bildungs- und Erziehungsarbeit im Kindergarten.*

75 *So important was this message: Strictly Propaganda.*

76 *In films aimed at children:* Ibid.

4: ULRIKE

The details describing Ulrike Weichelt's life in East Germany are based on interviews conducted with Ulrike Weichelt by the author from June 1991 to May 1993.

PAGE

91 *In one East German border village:* This detail is based on research conducted by Daphne Berdahl of the University of Chicago in the course of field work for her Ph.D. dissertation in anthropology, 1990 to 1992.

100 *Several went on maternity leave:* Sabine Berghahn and Andrea

Fritzsche, *Frauenrecht in Ost und Westdeutschland* (Berlin: Basisdruck Verlag, 1991).

106 *The Glienicke Bridge had first gone up:* Fritz Schmidt-Clausing, "Sie ist ebenso köstlich wie wohlgeraten," *Der Kurier,* March 16, 1963.

107 *Fifty years later:* "Geburtstagskind Glienicker Brücke," *Potsdamer Lokal Anzeiger,* November 21, 1936.

107 *The answer lay in a speech:* Peter Jochen Winters, "Die DDR sperrt vorübergehend die Glienicker Brücke in Berlin," *Frankfurter Allgemeine Zeitung,* November 16, 1984.

107 *In 1977, the East Germans:* Ekkehard Schwerk, "Nun unter gemeinsamem Schutz," *Tagesspiegel,* December 6, 1991.

108 *The first famous spy exchange:* Craig R. Whitney, *Spy Trader* (New York: Times Books, 1993), 27.

109 *Anatoly Shcharansky, a Soviet Jew:* Ibid., 187.

119 *As it turned out, the Leipzig demonstration:* In his book *Berlin Journal* (New York: W. W. Norton, 1991), Robert Darnton offers a rich insight into the fact that the Leipzig demonstration avoided a violent end: "In retrospect, the decision to call off the police appears as the most important turning point of the East German revolution, the moment when the people stood up to the authorities and forced them to back down" (p. 98).

5: THE WALLICHS

The details surrounding Christine Wallich's childhood, upbringing and attitude toward the Potsdam house are based on interviews with Christine Wallich conducted by the author in 1991 and 1992.

PAGE

129 *Hildegard's enterprising eldest son:* Henry C. Wallich, "Some Uses of Economics," 122.

132 *"The present political":* Henry C. Wallich, *Mainsprings of the German Revival* (New Haven: Yale University Press, 1955), 21.

139 *Finally, in 1979:* The description of Henry and Mable Wallich's 1979 trip to East Germany is based on an unpublished memoir written by Henry Wallich in June 1979.

140 *Henry never would enter the Potsdam house:* The descriptions of Henry Wallich's illness and Mable Wallich's choice of a tombstone inscription are based on an interview with Gail Veenstra, Henry's longtime secretary, conducted by the author on March 9, 1992.

141   *Shortly before the Berlin Wall fell:* The description of Hans Frank's attitude toward the Wallichs is based on two interviews with Hans Frank conducted by the author. The first took place in Berlin in April 1991, the second in New York City in May 1992.

141   *It was with a mix of apprehension:* The description of Christine and Paul Wallich's trip to Berlin in 1990 is based on interviews with Christine and Paul Wallich conducted by the author between April 1991 and January 1994.

143   *In early 1990, Hans Frank:* Hans Frank to Mable Wallich, London, April 17, 1990.

144   *Brandel's proprietor was a man in his middle years:* The characterization of Lothar Collberg and his offices was drawn following a visit to Brandel & Co. made by the author on February 18, 1994.

6: MICHAEL

The description of the Potsdam social workers and their involvement with the Schneider family is derived from interviews conducted with Sabine Reisenweber by the author and by Regine Wosnitza in Potsdam from August 1992 to May 1993.

PAGE

153   *Alcoholism was a well-hidden problem:* Paul Brieler, "Der Suff im Osten," *Psychologie Heute,* December 1992.

7: MONIKA

The descriptions of Monika Hagen's childhood and her job as a claims official are based on interviews conducted with Monika Hagen by the author and by Regine Wosnitza from May 1991 to February 1994.

PAGE

165   *By the summer of 1992:* Stephen Kinzer, "Anguish of East Germans Grows with Property Claims by Former Owners," *New York Times,* June 5, 1992.

167   *The decision to return property:* Ibid.

8: THE WALLICHS

The description of the October 1990 trip that Mable and Christine Wallich took to Berlin is based on interviews with Christine Wallich conducted by the author from June 1991 to May 1992.

PAGE

184 *In the fall of 1990:* Once the German authorities realized that the October 13, 1990, deadline for filing claims was too soon for many potential claimants, they extended the final deadline to December 31, 1992.

188 *News of the theft:* "Löwenfigur gestohlen," *Märkische Allgemeine,* April 16, 1992.

9: ULRIKE

PAGE

192 *When they arrived:* The description of this meeting was derived from an interview with Ulrike Weichelt conducted by the author.

199 *By now, the Kinderwochenheim:* Hannelore Knoblich, interview with the author.

201 *Abortion, in fact:* Like most everything else about eastern German society, the laws governing abortions in reunified Germany eventually came to conform more closely to those of the west. A woman in the first trimester of pregnancy whose health is not endangered by the pregnancy, carrying a healthy fetus, may have an abortion only after a formal consultation with a counselor, who is required to try to convince the woman not to terminate the pregnancy. If, after the consultation, a woman decides to have an abortion, she is free to do so. Strangely, such an abortion is illegal but not punishable.

10: DIRK

PAGE

204 *On the evening of November 9, 1989:* There have been many and sundry accounts of the night the Berlin Wall opened. I have relied on the excellent, insightful reporting of Anne McElvoy, Berlin correspondent for *The Times* of London, who attended the Schabowski news conference and describes the events that followed the press conference in her book *The Saddled Cow,* 206.

11: THE FAMILY SUMMIT

Details surrounding the meeting that the Wallich family convened in July 1992 are taken from minutes of that meeting, written by Robert

Wallich, and from an interview with Robert Wallich following the meeting.

12: THE MOVE OUT

PAGE

218   *When she arrived:* Details surrounding the meeting that the Wallich family convened in July 1992 are taken from minutes of that meeting, written by Robert Wallich, and from conversations with Robert Wallich.

221   *Although she was under no obligation:* The description of the move out of the Kinderwochenheim is taken from an interview with Ulrike Weichelt by the author in November 1992.

225   *But when Christine arrived at the house:* Christine Wallich was accompanied by Regine Wosnitza, who supplied the author with a description of the visit.

EPILOGUE

PAGE

228   *By the winter of 1992:* Jens Friedemann, "Auf dem ostdeutschen Grundstücksmarkt drohen Gefahren," *Frankfurter Allgemeine Zeitung,* July 3, 1992.

BIBLIOGRAPHY

BOOKS

Agee, Joel. *Twelve Years: An American Boyhood in East Germany.* New York: Farrar, Straus & Giroux, 1981.

Borneman, John. *After the Wall: East Meets West in the New Berlin.* New York: Basic Books, 1991.

Bornstein, Jerry. *The Wall Came Tumbling Down.* New York: Outlet, 1990.

Chandler, Marilyn R. *Dwelling in the Text: Houses in American Fiction.* Berkeley: University of California Press, 1991.

Chernow, Ron. *The Warburgs.* New York: Random House, 1993.

Darnton, Robert. *Berlin Journal: 1989–1990.* New York: W. W. Norton, 1991.

Dennis, Michael. *The German Democratic Republic: Politics, Economics and Society.* New York: Columbia University Press, 1988.

Gilbert, Felix. *A European Past: Memoirs, 1905–1945.* New York: W. W. Norton, 1988.

Just, Ward. *The Translator.* Boston: Houghton, Mifflin, 1991.

Kupferberg, Herbert. *The Mendelssohns: Three Generations of Genius.* New York: Charles Scribner's Sons, 1972.

McElvoy, Anne. *The Saddled Cow: East Germany's Life and Legacy.* London: Faber & Faber, 1992.

Schneider, Peter. *The German Comedy: Scenes of Life After the Wall.* New York: Farrar, Straus & Giroux, 1991.

Shapiro, Michael Steven. *Child's Garden: The Kindergarten Movement from Froebel to Dewey.* University Park, Penn., and London: Pennsylvania State University Press, 1983.

Smith, Martin Cruz. *Red Square.* New York: Random House, 1992.

Viergutz, Rudolf F. *Von der Weisheit unserer Märchen.* Berlin: Widukind Verlag, 1942.

Wallich, Hermann, and Paul Wallich. *Zwei Generationen im deutschen Bankwesen.* Frankfurt am Main: Fritz Knapp Verlag, 1978.

Wallich, Hildegard. *Erinnerungen aus meinem Leben.* Westerwald: Wilhelm Dieckmann, 1970.

Wander, Maxie. *Guten Morgen, du Schöne: Protokolle nach Tonband.* Berlin und Weimar: 1980.

Whitney, Craig R. *Spy Trader: Germany's Devil's Advocate and the Darkest Secrets of the Cold War.* New York: Times Books, 1993.

Wyden, Peter. *Wall: The Inside Story of Divided Berlin.* New York: Simon & Schuster, 1989.

ARTICLES

"Baby-Baisse in Ost-Deutschland." *Die Welt,* December 11, 1993.

"Eine Schatzkammer für Alteigentümer." *Süddeutsche Zeitung,* April 28, 1993.

"Erst vereint, nun entzweit." *Der Spiegel,* January 18, 1993.

"Germany in Transition." *Daedalus,* Winter 1994, vol. 123, no. 1.

Hafner, Katie. "The House We Lived In: Reclaiming Family Property in Eastern Europe." *New York Times Magazine,* November 10, 1991.

Jackson, James O. "Unity's Shadow." *Time,* July 1, 1991.

Kempe, Frederick. "After the Euphoria: Specter of Capitalism Haunts East Germans Used to Certainties." *The Wall Street Journal,* June 14, 1990.

Kinzer, Stephen. "Where Is Optimism in Germany? Among the Bedraggled Easterners." *New York Times,* December 27, 1993.

Kramer, Jane. "Letter from Europe." *The New Yorker,* May 25, 1992.

Lebert, Stephan. " 'Bleibt, wo ihr seid.' " *Der Spiegel,* December 3, 1990.

Marshall, Tyler. "New Wall Goes Up in Germany." *Los Angeles Times,* August 20, 1992.

Stern, Fritz. "Freedom and Its Discontents." *Foreign Affairs,* Sept./Oct. 1993, vol. 72, no. 4.

Tagliabue, John. "Bonn Will Return Property in East." *New York Times,* March 2, 1991.

INDEX